The Language of Liturgy

The Language of Liturgy

A Ritual Poetics

David Jasper

scm press

© David Jasper 2018

Published in 2018 by SCM Press
Editorial office
3rd Floor, Invicta House,
108–114 Golden Lane,
London EC1Y 0TG, UK
www.scmpress.co.uk

SCM Press is an imprint of Hymns Ancient & Modern Ltd (a registered charity)

HYMNS Ancient & Modern

Hymns Ancient & Modern® is a registered trademark of
Hymns Ancient & Modern Ltd
13A Hellesdon Park Road, Norwich,
Norfolk NR6 5DR, UK

All rights reserved. No part of this publication may be reproduced, stored in a retrieval system, or transmitted, in any form or by any means, electronic, mechanical, photocopying or otherwise, without the prior permission of the publisher, SCM Press.

The Author has asserted his right under the Copyright, Designs and Patents Act 1988 to be identified as the Author of this Work

Unless otherwise indicated Scripture quotations are from the New Revised Standard Version of the Bible, Anglicized Edition, copyright © 1989, 1995 by the Division of Christian Education of the National Council of the Churches of Christ in the USA. Used by permission. All rights reserved.

The author and publisher acknowledge with thanks permission to reprint material from the following sources: David Scott, 'The Book of Common Prayer 1549', in *Selected Poems*, Bloodaxe Books, 1998. R. S. Thomas, 'The Prayer', in *Laboratories of the Spirit*, Palgrave Macmillan, 1977. Permission sought. Seamus Heaney, 'Exposure', in *New Selected Poems, 1966–1987*, Faber & Faber, 1990. Philip Larkin, 'Church Going', *The Less Deceived*, The Marvell Press, 1966. Permission sought. T. S. Eliot, 'Journey of the Magi' and 'Burnt Norton II', in *The Poems of T. S. Eliot: The Annotated Text*, Christopher Ricks and Jim McCue, eds, Faber & Faber, 2015. Permission sought.

British Library Cataloguing in Publication data

A catalogue record for this book is available
from the British Library

978 0 334 05571 6

Typeset by Regent Typesetting
Printed and bound by
CPI Group (UK) Ltd

Contents

Preface

Books never turn out in quite the way expected. Sooner or later every author discovers that books have a life of their own and however hard one tries some things demand to be said while others, on which great store might have been set, choose to pass quietly by unwilling to attract much attention. I could never have written this book without my father, Ronald Jasper, who died on Maundy Thursday, 1990. With a learning that I can never match he spent his life in the service of the Church and its worship, and I am sorry that some of what I will say in this book might seem critical of some of his work. I think, however, that he would have been tolerant of such criticism and would have enjoyed serious discussion about it. I regret that that has never been possible, though I feel his nurture inasmuch as the essential reading of this book has been provided for in his magnificent liturgical library that I still possess. I offer these chapters without making any claim to be a liturgical scholar. My professional interest has been in the relationship between literature and theology and this will become very quickly clear in the early pages of Chapter 1. I hope that I have managed to transcend much of the debates in the Church of England between the traditionalists and revisionists in liturgical matters, as I seek to discover what I have rather hesitantly called a poetics of liturgy, or a ritual poetics.

Books, in my experience at least, have a habit of beginning to write themselves, but this in no way absolves the authors from shouldering the burden of responsibility for their faults and shortcomings. There is a shadow of a theological principle here. I certainly do not wish to make any excuses – the faults and weaknesses of this book are entirely my own. Many people, however, have contributed to it both wittingly and unwittingly. In particular I would wish to thank Heather Barcroft, John Davies, Jeremy Smith, Nicholas Taylor, Ramona Fotiade, Bishop Gregor Duncan, and my students and colleagues in Theology and Religious Studies at the University of Glasgow as well as on the Liturgy Committee of the Scottish Episcopal Church. More indirectly, but no less significantly, I thank my brother-in-law Bishop Nicholas Reade and my teacher at Oxford, the late Bishop Geoffrey Rowell. I would not expect them by any means to agree with everything I have said here! My thanks also are due to Lambeth Palace Library and to Sue Moore, Administrative Secretary of the Church of England Liturgical Commission. Finally, and as always, I thank my wife Alison for putting up with all of this. I keep promising her that this is the last book and that evenings in the future will be spent in a more companionable manner – but she has learnt never to trust such promises.

Liturgy and the worship of the Church is, of course, not finally about us, our academic disputes and our likes and dislikes. It begins and ends in giving glory and thanks to God and if, in the midst of all my words, the reader can find something here that makes that a little more possible, then I shall be content and this work will not have been entirely in vain.

Passiontide, 2017

Introduction

The Language of Liturgy, as a study in the nature of liturgical language, will focus primarily, though not exclusively, on the liturgical traditions of the Church of England from the late Middle Ages until the early twenty-first century. This is the tradition with which I am most familiar, having been an Anglican priest since 1977, in England and more recently Scotland, ordained three years before the publication of the *Alternative Service Book*. For most of that time I have been teaching in universities with a principal concern for the relationship between literature and theology. I am not trained as a liturgist but primarily as a student of literature. But I cannot deny a strong element of personal interest and experience in liturgy and liturgical reform in the later twentieth century as I am also the son of Dean Ronald Jasper, who was Chairman of the Church of England Liturgical Commission through the years of preparation up to the *Alternative Service Book* (1980), a role which, among other things, earned him such traditionalist sneers as in the proposed additional clause to the Litany: 'From the Dean of York, and all his detestable enormities: *God Lord, deliver us*.' Another member of the Liturgical Commission, Professor David L. Frost, happened also to have been one of my tutors when I was a student of English Literature at Cambridge between 1969 and 1972, and he would try out on his students (or on me, at least) proposals for new prayers or new translations of psalms as exercises in what was then called in literary studies 'practical criticism'.

In some ways this book continues the work of a collection of essays edited by myself and my father, and published shortly before his death, entitled *Language and the Worship of the Church* (Macmillan, 1990). But that is now almost thirty years ago, and many things have changed. Yet neither the earlier work nor the present book makes any claims to be comprehensive. It is certainly far from the case that the liturgy of the Church of England remained static and unchanged between 1662 and 1980. I grew up knowing my father's first book, *Prayer Book Revision in England, 1800–1900* (1954), and I am well aware that historically much has been left unsaid in the pages that follow. But I hope that there is enough to make my primary point, and that is a literary one concerning the nature of liturgical *language* – which is odd and upon which heavy demands are made.

And so, my primary concern in this book will be with the nature and form of liturgical language. This is not entirely a new venture, and one might find well-established precedents in such works as Stella Brook's old but still useful *The Language of the Book of Common Prayer* (1965). Although my main focus will be on the liturgies of the Church of England, I do not in any way intend to replicate, even if I were qualified to do so, the historical work of W. H. Frere (and before him Francis Proctor) in their *New History of the Book of Common Prayer* (1901), or more recently G. J. Cuming in *A History of Anglican Liturgy* (second edition, 1982). The latter, especially, has been crucial in my thinking, not least in its background to English liturgy at the end of the Middle Ages and Reformation liturgies in Europe prior to 1549. Geoffrey Cuming is careful to describe how theological shifts of emphasis and understanding affect the nature of prayer and its language. In addition he makes it clear that the use of the vernacular in the English medieval liturgy was by no means uncommon (much of the marriage service was in English[1]), while at the same time the power of liturgical language was greater than any capacity to understand it so that, in the words of Brother Gararde, a Minorite friar from the Low Countries whose work was translated into English in 1532, 'it is sufficient if the man be present at the Mass, whether he hear and understand the words or no'.[2] This is a point to which I shall return in due course. In the same year, a young Thomas Cranmer travelled to Nuremberg as part of the embassy of Sir Thomas Elyot, the English Ambassador to the emperor Charles V, finding there not only a wife, but also a ferment of liturgical experiment under Johann Brenz and Andreas Osiander that was widely influential in Germany. The Reformation liturgical influences on Cranmer are well documented by Cuming.

Cuming, however, like most liturgists of his time, was trained as a historian. My approach is different and is a plea that liturgical study give serious attention to other disciplines, above all what I have termed 'poetics', and that its pastoral responsibilities suffer where this is not the case. (One could, of course, go much further, and suggest that such works as Michel Foucault's *On the Government of the Living* (2012), with its provocative discussions of baptism and the theology of Tertullian, among many others, should be required reading for all concerned with liturgy and liturgical theology.) At the same time I have limited myself in modern times to the Church of England, merely noting that almost nothing is said about language in a standard study of liturgical reform in the world-wide Anglican Communion after the Lambeth Conference of 1958, Colin Buchanan's *Modern Anglican Liturgies, 1958–1968*, or, indeed, in its predecessor B. J. Wigan's *The Liturgy in English* (1962).

Having acknowledged the work of Stella Brook, now more than fifty years old, I would wish to claim that this book will be the first systematic and multi-disciplinary return to the rather bad-tempered and, indeed, often extremely ill-informed debates about liturgical language that accompanied the processes of liturgical revision in England in the second half of the twentieth century after the watershed of the Second Vatican Council and seen in its ecumenical perspective. The alternatives in those later years of the last century appeared to be either unyielding devotion to the glorious language of the *Book of Common Prayer* as a seemingly immovable pillar of Anglican identity, or a more shallow adherence to what many people saw as the crass linguistic modernizing of the new liturgies, which found their most recent form in England in *Common Worship* (2000) and the books that followed it. This debate now needs to be revisited and unpicked with the benefit of hindsight and clearer reflection from a more literary perspective.

The book is divided into four major sections. The first three chapters will develop a poetics of liturgy, seeking to distinguish this as a particular 'ritual poetics' that is set apart from a more specifically 'literary' poetic tradition. It has not been unusual for those concerned with liturgical revision to turn to poets of the day for assistance and the result has rarely been particularly productive. I will suggest why this is almost inevitably the case. At the same time I want to be quite clear from the outset why the pursuit of simplicity and comprehensibility in liturgical language, especially in a time when, unlike the England of Archbishop Cranmer and the later Elizabethan Prayer Book of 1559, relatively few people are familiar with liturgical worship, is a mistake. Brother Gararde did not even think it was necessary to *hear* the words spoken, let alone understand them, though perhaps we should not wish to go that far!

In the second section I will return to the liturgies of the early Church, and above all to the crucial text of Hippolytus' *Apostolic Tradition* – specifically received through the critical editions of Burton Scott Easton (1934) and, more importantly, Dom Gregory Dix (1937, revised by Henry Chadwick, 1968), prior to the publication of Dix's great work *The Shape of the Liturgy* (1945). Attention will also be paid to the controversial teaching of Amalarius, Bishop of Metz (*c.* 780–850) on the Mass as performance. Section three will move on to the development of vernacular devotional and liturgical language in the later Middle Ages in England up to the *First*

Prayer Book of King Edward VI in 1549, emphasizing not the discontinuity but the continuity between the English of medieval lay devotion and the language of Cranmer, and unpicking that which has been called Cranmer's monopoly on liturgical English. This then will establish the second great hinge of the book. For if I am concerned to identify and defend a clear 'ritual poetics' within liturgical language, I would also wish to establish a vernacular continuity in the Anglican tradition that goes back much further than Cranmer's reforms of the earlier sixteenth century. 'Common prayer' must be in the language of the 'common man' (or woman), but this does not consign it to banal simplicity – indeed quite the contrary. This return to the late Middle Ages and their transition into Reformation England is a broad field of study that has attracted some attention in recent literary studies by, among others, Katherine Zieman and Annie Sutherland.[3] A further chapter on the Reformation liturgies themselves, extending into the devotional writings of Bishop Lancelot Andrewes and others in the seventeenth century, will further open out the discussion on the nature of liturgical language and the language of prayer from an interdisciplinary, and more particularly literary, perspective. Granted that there has been recent fine work in this field by such scholars as Timothy Rosendale, Ramie Targoff and Daniel Swift,[4] still there remains a clear division between the work of theologians, liturgists and literary scholars as they address these questions. The present study as the work of a scholar of literature *and* theology, together with the practical experience and concerns of a parish priest, seeks to bridge gaps that have hitherto been left open.

A final section will focus on the liturgical debates of the later twentieth and early twenty-first centuries in the Church of England, particularly after 1974, when Parliament relinquished legislative responsibility for the doctrine and worship of the Church of England, up to 1981 when a Prayer Book Protection Bill was proposed in the House of Commons, that is over the period of the publication of the *ASB* in 1980. This will lead to a final chapter (10) on the nature and possibilities for liturgical language today in the light of the provisions of *Common Worship*. This will necessarily include some attention to philosophical issues in language and the crisis of language in the twentieth century, and to the ecumenical aspect of liturgical reform after the Second Vatican Council in the work of such groups as the International Consultation on English Texts (ICET) and the Joint Liturgical Group (JLG).

The last chapter will be rather different from those preceding it, being a theological meditation on the eucharistic body, spreading beyond the confines of the Church of England and reflecting upon the implications of the book's proposals.

And finally, given that I am practising Anglican priest with the pastoral charge of a church (albeit in the Scottish Episcopal Church), the Conclusion will venture upon some of the similarities and differences between the two great periods of liturgical activity and revision in the English Church, that of the sixteenth century and that of the later part of the twentieth century, seeking to draw together various practical, literary, historical, theological and liturgical threads. I will offer no significant suggestions or advice on the way forward in the form, or forms, of language appropriate for public worship in the contemporary and future Church, but more modestly propose a few hints as to language of worship that might be appropriate in an age when the tiniest minority of the population have any experience of public liturgy beyond the very occasional wedding or funeral, and quite probably not even of this. Yet the praise of God will continue to be sounded and the words must be found for this in the Church today as in the ages past.

PART I

The Poetics of Liturgy

I

Poetry and the Language of Prayer and Worship[1]

In 1851 Archbishop R. C. Trench published a now forgotten but in its day oft-reprinted work, *On the Study of Words*. It was first delivered as lectures at the Diocesan Training School in Winchester, and it established Trench's reputation as a philologist. As late as 1927 the literary scholar George Sampson wrote in an introduction to yet another reprint of Trench's book 'that words have a genuine life of their own', but that now a lively interest in words has been 'almost swamped by indifference. Purley has other diversions.'[2] His final allusion to Purley will, I suspect, escape most people today. But at the end of the eighteenth and the beginning of the nineteenth century any reasonably well-read person with an interest in language would have known John Horne Tooke's *Epea Pteroenta, or, The Diversions of Purley* (1786–1805). Far and away the leading philologist of his day and a friend of the poet Samuel Taylor Coleridge, Tooke deserves greater attention in respect of his thinking on linguistics and philology than he has lately received. In the first part of his work Tooke – known as a radical politician who was once tried for high treason – sets out to establish language within the context of the empiricism of John Locke. Thus Tooke denies for the mind any creative role in the formation of language.[3] Rather he seeks to show that all speech can be reduced to the noun and the verb, nouns being (following Aristotle in *De Interpretatione*) both historically and logically prior to verbs.

The noun/verb discussion actually goes as far back as Plato's *Sophist* and *Cratylus*, and has more recently been revisited by Catherine Pickstock in her argument, in *After Writing: On the Liturgical Consummation of Philosophy* (1998), that it is actually in Platonic philosophy that we encounter a primacy not of metaphysical presence but of liturgical theory and practice.[4] To Pickstock's thesis we will return later in more detail. But to begin with it is Coleridge's development of Horne Tooke's linguistic theory that is of most significance for us. In September 1800, Coleridge wrote to William Godwin encouraging him to '*philosophize* Horn [sic]

Tooke's System' for, Coleridge goes on, 'I would endeavour to destroy the old antithesis of *Words* and *Things*, elevating, as it were, words in Things & living Things too.'[5] This is a brief summation of what John Coulson once described as the *fiduciary* understanding of language,[6] perceiving words as living organisms that resist any reduction into what Coleridge graphically called 'a Chaos grinding itself into compatibility'.[7] In these discussions, as Coulson knew very well, we are not far from the later Wittgenstein of the *Philosophical Investigations* and other more recent debates on the theory of language, but more significantly for us, language that is understood as fiduciary suggests a form of *liturgical language* that has rarely been discussed in the energetic debates on the language of worship in both Roman Catholic and Protestant churches following the Second Vatican Council in the later part of the twentieth century.

Anglicans today, however devoted to the *Book of Common Prayer* they may be, are not citizens of the sixteenth century, but this does not mean that the language of the liturgy should be simple, straightforward or necessarily easily understood. But it is not the vocabulary and particular words used in public worship that I am concerned with here so much as the *form* of liturgical language. Most of my examples will be from the liturgies of the Church of England, though no doubt they will illuminate similar issues in other traditions as well.

Prior to the publication of *Common Worship* in 2000, Michael Perham, who was later to become Bishop of Gloucester, wrote that 'the main texts of any future service book will be in modern English, not unlike the style of the present book'.[8] A few years earlier the Preface to the *Alternative Service Book* (1980) had suggested that 'words, even agreed words, are only the beginning of worship'.[9] Both of these statements, I suggest, are incorrect. Liturgical language, like all theological language, but perhaps especially so, is odd and strange. It is not like the language used in a textbook even when its vocabulary is relatively simple. Nor are words the *beginning* of worship: they are at the very heart of worship, even when that is almost silent, living things that, in Coleridge's description, reflecting upon Ezekiel's chariot 'when the hand of the Lord was upon him, and he saw visions of God', 'move in conjunction and form the living chariot that bears up (for *us*) the throne of the Divine Humanity'.[10]

Words are gestures, becoming physical in their utterance, and the words of our liturgy are suspended between the oral and the textual, with a clear bias towards the former. Such words have a shaping power, reaching out and resisting that privatization of religion that has crept upon Christianity in the Western churches of our time. The words that are uttered in the liturgy are never quite what is said in everyday speech for, like poetry, the language of worship defamiliarizes and makes strange, thereby shifting and disturbing the very categories of time and place that bind us to our place in history. To repeat the direct theology of Lancelot Andrewes (1555–1626), Bishop of Winchester, on the incarnation, taken up again by T. S. Eliot in his poem *Gerontion*, we hear and behold 'the Word within a word, unable to speak a word'.[11] At the heart of all the words of worship is, finally, silence.

But I must not get ahead of myself. Underlying these preliminary reflections on the language of worship is a broad thesis that has been proposed most clearly by Catherine Pickstock in her book *After Writing: On the Liturgical Consummation of Philosophy*. I have many reservations about this book, and I have never been persuaded, I must admit, by that broad school of theological thought known as Radical Orthodoxy and its final rejection of Enlightenment thought. Nevertheless, Pickstock's proposal is persuasive, not least in its careful examination of the 'space of doxology' in the medieval Mass of the Roman Rite. Beginning with the orality and suspicion of writing in Plato's *Phaedrus*, Pickstock seeks to show

> how philosophy itself, in its Platonic guise, did not assume, as has been thought, a primacy of metaphysical presence, but rather a primacy of liturgical theory and practice. This same primacy ... was developed, and more consistently realized, in medieval Christendom. However, it will also be described how it was during this period that the destruction from within of a liturgical city and a doxologic, took place, culminating eventually in the restoration, during the early modern period and beyond, of those very Greek sophistic positions which the Platonic liturgical philosophy had initially refused.[12]

It is precisely this liturgical and doxological loss in early modernism that characterizes the difficulties of articulation in twentieth-century liturgical reform, and I will suggest that a radical review of the deep structures of the language of worship is necessary, rather than an adaptation of languages and vocabulary, too often simply textual rather than oral, to the conventions of the contemporary world. As the American scholar Philip Pfatteicher has succinctly expressed it, 'Changing language is generally not the place to begin. It is too easy, and it is too deceptive.'[13] Furthermore, it should be noted that liturgical language does not come naturally to us; rather it is a language that must be practised and learnt, like music or poetry.[14]

Behind Pickstock lies the work of the French philosopher of phenomenology Jean-Luc Marion, the Catholic theologian Jean-Yves Lacoste and his Heideggerian sense of 'living liturgically'[15] and, perhaps above all, Henri Cardinal de Lubac in his magisterial work on the Eucharist and Church in the Middle Ages, *Corpus Mysticum* (1944). Important though this is, it will not be my purpose to engage directly with these thinkers. My concern with liturgical language is more immediate and perhaps more simple, though it is well to note its complex origins.

Although the processes of liturgical reform in the later twentieth century have seen somewhat anxious, and finally unsuccessful, exchanges with poets, it is strictly correct to affirm that 'liturgy is not poetry'.[16] I will expand upon this at some length in Chapter 3. Yet this is not to suggest at the outset that liturgical language is not, in a real sense, 'poetic', and it will be valuable to examine the form of such language through a reading of a poem of one of the most 'liturgical' of English poets – the seventeenth-century priest George Herbert. As an ordained Anglican (and erstwhile Cambridge academic), Herbert was saturated in the languages and rhythms of the Bible and, perhaps even more, the Elizabethan *Book of Common Prayer* of 1559, which among other things might be described as a handbook of Protestant humanism, the prayer book of a queen of England who, in the words of John Booty, 'read Isocrates and Cicero, Saint Cyprian and Philip Melanchthon, and was well acquainted with the works of Desiderius Erasmus'.[17] Herbert wrote two poems entitled 'Prayer', and it is the less well known of these to which I shall give some attention.

Of what an easie quick accesse,
My blessed Lord, art thou! How suddenly
May our requests thine eare invade!
To shew that state dislikes not easinesse.
If but I lift mine eyes, my suit is made:
Thou canst no more not heare, then thou canst die.

Of what supreme almightie power
Is thy great arm which spans the east and west,
And tacks the centre to the sphere!
By it do all things live their measur'd hour:
We cannot ask the thing, which is not there,
Blaming the shallownesse of our request.

Of what unmeasurable love
Art thou possest, who, when thou couldst not die,
Wert fain to take our flesh and curse,

And for our sakes in person sinne reprove,
That by destroying that which ty'd thy purse,
Thou mightst make way for liberalitie!

  Since then these three wait on thy throne,
Ease, *Power*, and *Love*; I value prayer so,
  That were I to leave all but one,
Wealth, fame, endowments, vertues, all should go;
I and deare prayer would together dwell,
And quickly gain, for each inch lost, an ell.[18]

A whole chapter and more would not be sufficient properly to unpack this verse, so I will restrict myself to a few pertinent observations under four headings, recognizing that this poem is a conversation of the soul with God, to be understood both as a private devotion and as a communal prayer.

1 The poem is based upon a biblical premise: 'And all things, whatsoever ye shall ask in prayer, believing, ye shall receive' (Matthew 21.22, KJV). Biblical phrases and resonances sound throughout and within the language of the poem. 'If I but lift mine eyes' in verse one echoes the psalms set for the office of Morning Prayer on Day 27 each month in the *Prayer Books* of 1559 and 1662 – Psalms 121.1 and 123.1.
2 The vocabulary is simple and suspended somewhere between oral and written language. On the other hand, by careful use of figures of speech, above all metaphor, Herbert, in true 'metaphysical' manner, is continually challenging, defamiliarizing the everyday in riddles and shifting images. In verse one God's court is contrasted with the highly formal protocol of the Elizabethan and Stuart English court by its ease of access through prayer, by which my 'suit is made'.[19] And there is the use of 'invade' – a violent warlike quality, even in prayer (ushering in the theme of the second verse, which is 'power' and its military overtones).
3 In the final couplet of the poem, Herbert takes a familiar and ancient proverb of the inch and the ell, used in Anglo Saxon to translate Matthew 6.27, and which Herbert uses elsewhere in his poem *The Church-porch*[20] then, by chiasmus, reverses its normal use, developing further the theme and metaphors of measuring that run through the whole poem.
4 Verse three embraces the theology of the incarnation and the redemption achieved through it. Good prayer, in Herbert, is always soundly theological, embedded in language of dramatic metaphors and images.

These brief observations will serve to indicate the carefully crafted language of Herbert's poetry as, in his poetic art that is rooted in the Bible but above all the daily office, it bleaches into prayer and worship. The developing themes and images of the poem, echoing Scripture and resonating dramatically, challenging and creative, are motivated by rhetorical tropes – there are examples in these four short verses of metaphor, oxymoron, asyndeton, apostrophe, anaphora and chiasmus, used deliberately and effectively but carefully hidden, requiring few technical words or theological obfuscations. It is the language that carries the theology.

And so I turn now to some examples of liturgical prayer and language in the twentieth century, their difficulties and their success when compared with the elements and crafted form of Herbert's verse. It needs to be emphasized that liturgical language requires to be both taught and learnt. It is not the language of common social communication and intercourse. Reflect on these two statements:

> I saw Brian at the station this morning.
> I saw Eternity the other night.

Quite clearly they refer to two very different human experiences of 'seeing', the latter expressed in a poem by Henry Vaughan (1621–95), and it is perfectly possible for anyone to 'learn' the different uses of common words, although 'seeing eternity' needs practice in prayer and worship. One of the limitations of liturgical reform in the twentieth century has been in its repeated insistence that the language of the liturgy should be clear, simple and understandable. In the Constitution on the Sacred Liturgy of the Second Vatican Council, the first of its completed documents, we read:

> The rites should be distinguished by a noble simplicity; they should be short, clear, and unencumbered by useless repetitions; they should be within the people's powers of comprehension, and normally should not require much explanation.[21]

I think that this statement was a mistake. In the Anglican *Book of Common Prayer*, the Athanasian Creed (*Quicunque vult*) speaks of 'the Father incomprehensible, the Son incomprehensible: and the Holy Ghost incomprehensible'. It does not mean, of course, that the Trinity cannot be understood (even if this is the case): rather it is that the Trinity cannot be bounded or embraced. That is something very different. In this sense is liturgical language properly 'incomprehensible' and that, linguistically, requires a fine art. And so we turn to Thomas Cranmer.

One of the few prayers in the Anglican tradition of the Eucharist that can be safely ascribed to Archbishop Cranmer is that which we have come to know as the Prayer of Humble Access, spoken, in the 1662 *Book of Common Prayer* (and first finding this form in 1552), by the congregation immediately after the utterance of the Sanctus. Here it is in modern spelling.

> We do not presume to come to this thy Table, O merciful Lord, trusting in our own righteousness, but in thy manifold and great mercies. We are not worthy so much as to gather up the crumbs under thy Table. But thou art the same Lord, whose property is always to have mercy: Grant us therefore, gracious Lord, so to eat the flesh of thy dear Son Jesus Christ, and to drink his blood, that our sinful bodies may be made clean by his body, and our souls washed through his most precious blood, and that we may evermore dwell in him, and he in us. Amen.

Here we find a form of prayer that was part of the liturgical school for Revd George Herbert. It is rooted in Scripture – the incident of Jesus and the Syrophoenician or Canaanite Gentile woman (Mark 7.24–30; Matthew 15.21–28) who seems to upbraid Jesus with her insistence that 'even the dogs under the table eat the children's crumbs'. Its vocabulary is quite simple, and within it is deeply embedded the theology of atonement. But now we see how, in the *Alternative Service Book* of 1980 (and before that the experimental services known as Series 2 and Series 3), is proposed the omission of the words 'that our sinful bodies made be made clean by his body, and our souls washed through his most precious blood'. The omission is continued in the simplified proposal in *Common Worship* (2000), which reads:

> So cleanse us and feed us
> with the precious body and blood of your Son,
> that he may live in us and we in him.[22]

The difficulty in this clipped abbreviation, as Professor David Frost (a long-time member of the Church of England Liturgical Commission and a professor of Renaissance English Literature) commented, lies in our contemporary 'desperately literal approach to all language'.[23] In short, we have lost the linguistic capacity to engage properly with metaphor in our radical distinction between the literal and the metaphorical. In Frost's sharp words, written not long after the publication of *Honest to God* (1963), 'John Robinson would never have got a hearing in Cranmer's day, because few then took images quite so literally.'[24]

The point is, of course, that we seem to have lost the capacity to engage at a deep level with theology through liturgical language. It is, above all, a failure of the ear for metaphor and the complexities of rhetoric. The problem with the Prayer of Humble Access seems to have begun early in the Age of Reason with the Latitudinarian Bishop of Salisbury, Gilbert Burnett, who argued in his three-volume *History of the Reformation* (1679–1714) that the words ('that our sinful bodies may be made clean by his body, and our souls washed through his most precious blood') cause grave disquiet to many people inasmuch as they appear to indicate that the bread cleanses the body while the wine washes the soul.[25] This was a theological issue, the question of the doctrine of concomitance, that can admittedly be traced back as far as Anselm and Thomas Aquinas; and so the words were omitted, for safety's sake (a good Anglican motive), from the early Anglican liturgical revisions of the Eucharist, known as Series 2 and Series 3 during the period of final preparation of the *Alternative Service Book*. But this change was, in fact, a victory for literalism and the death of liturgical language which, while deeply theological, is very capable of breaking the rules of safety. As David Frost expressed it:

> [The phrase] was thought to mislead the simple into thinking that the Bread cleansed one's body, and the Wine washed one's soul. To which my answer has always been, if so, *so what*? Was anyone ever seriously led astray by thinking that?[26]

The point is, of course, that if liturgical language (like its cousin, poetry) is to have the capacity to move us, it must employ the resources of image, metaphor and the careful tropes of rhetoric. When Paul Ricoeur embarks upon his discussion of metaphor in his book *The Rule of Metaphor* (1975), he acknowledges that when 'metaphorical discourse says something about reality [this] collides with the apparent constitution of poetic discourse, which seems to be essentially non-referential ...'[27] The point about referentiality is essential. Metaphor thus necessarily both 'is' and 'is not', a redescription of reality that dissolves common boundaries of time and place. Ricoeur continues:

> From [the] conjunction of fiction and redescription I conclude that the 'place' of metaphor, its most intimate and ultimate abode, is neither the name, nor the sentence, nor even discourse, but the copula of the verb *to be*.[28]

In short, liturgical language that is properly inspired by the life of metaphor takes us to the very heart of being itself. This is a truth deeply known to the early Church Fathers and as late as the poetic sermons of St Bernard of Clairvaux (1090–1153), and it explains, at least in part, their fascination with the Song of Songs. In his *Commentary on the Song of Songs*, Origen in the third century reverses the modern understanding of literal and metaphor in what, for us, is a chiasmic move that regards the metaphorical as literal and the literal as 'mere metaphor'. 'This book', Origen begins his *Commentary*,

> seems to me an epithalamium, that is a wedding song, written by Solomon in the form of a play, which he recited in the character of a bride who was being married and burned with a heavenly love for her bridegroom, who is the Word of God.[29]

But the language of the Song is to be learnt and adopted only in maturity, for there is danger in such powerful words, in taking *literally* that which is a *mere metaphor*, that is its description of erotic love. The language and its living power should not be given to the immature or those who have not had (here Origen quotes from the Epistle to the Hebrews) 'their faculties trained by practice to distinguish good from evil'.[30]

My point is that Origen actually *thought liturgically*, and with this we return to the work and thesis of Catherine Pickstock. We catch a glimpse of such thinking in the fiduciary language of Samuel Taylor Coleridge for whom the symbol (expressed in metaphor) 'abides itself as a living part in that Unity, of which it is the representative'.[31] But the retreat from the liturgical in modernity is forewarned even in Plato's suspicion of text, writing and 'written speech'[32] in the *Phaedrus*, and the long decay of the living power of words, a power that Pickstock finds still exemplified in the language and shape of the medieval Roman Rite. My concern here (as has been seen in the poetry of George Herbert) is not with vocabulary and the choice of words so much as with the *form* of language and its shaping power. Nor is simplicity or even clarity (in a rational sense) the issue. Liturgical reform during and after Vatican II seemed to work upon the argument that over Christian centuries liturgy has had a tendency to develop in mazy complexity from an original, simple text (Hippolytus' *Apostolic Tradition* is held up as such, although it does not actually provide any precise written 'text' for the liturgy). Thus Louis Bouyer writes in his influential book *Eucharist* (1966) of the medieval Roman Mass:

> Concurrently with the melodic and soon to be polyphonic developments of the old chants, interpolative words came to be introduced into the

> flowery vocalizations which had begun by indefinitely extending the individual syllables. Either in Latin or the vernacular, they started out as a paraphrase of the *basic text*. But from paraphrase a transition to free amplification was soon to be made, and this became less and less connected with the *original text*.[33]

This presupposes, of course, that there actually was an original, basic text (Hippolytus, for one, as I have already noted, does not provide one), and that the liturgy, indeed, is a 'text'. For it may rather be seen as a communal utterance between the oral and the written, always in the process of making and reinvention within the eschatological vision of the Church. Pickstock then defends the complexity of the Roman Rite, dismissing the idea of its mere decadent accretions and confusions. She writes that:

> ... the many repetitions and recommencements in the mediaeval Roman Rite can be situated not within a context of secular interpolation, but rather of oral provenance conjoined with an apophatic reserve which betokens our constitutive, positive, and analogical distance from God, rather than our sinfulness and humiliation. According to such a perspective, the haphazard structure of the Rite can be seen as predicated upon a need for a constant re-beginning of liturgy because the true eschatological liturgy is in time endlessly postponed.[34]

This does, of course, set liturgical revision in a rather new context, a resituation in time and place, from the pragmatic, ecumenical movement engaged in by many churches after Vatican II. As regards language, what is required is an acknowledgement of the strangeness of the words of worship, their stretched quality setting them apart from everyday speech, though this does not necessarily imply the deliberate use of archaic or dated forms.[35] But, as Pickstock has suggested, there is a need to give attention to those tropes and rhetorical devices, so beloved of the Renaissance, that have the capacity to expand the living power of words in the forms of poetry and oral speech. For example:

1 *Asyndeton* is a rhetorical device wherein conjunctions and connecting words are omitted. It can be seen as a characteristic of contemporary clipped and utilitarian language, but it is also used to great accumulative effect by Herbert in the poem we have reviewed ('Wealth, fame, endowments, vertues ...'). Asyndeton is also used effectively by such twentieth-century poets as W. H. Auden, Robert Lowell and John Berryman.[36]

2 *Anaphora* is the repetition of a word or phrase in successive clauses.[37] Its frequent use in medieval literature – it is a favourite device of Chaucer and Sir Thomas Malory (1415/18–71), author of *Le Morte D'Arthur* – may account for its presence in the sixteenth-century English vernacular liturgies of Cranmer and the Reformers. An obvious example of it in liturgy is the *Agnus Dei*.

3 *Oxymoron* is a rhetorical device wherein incongruous and apparently contradictory terms are brought together for effect.[38] 'Living death' would be a good example in colloquial English. Better still is Milton's description of hell in *Paradise Lost* as 'darkness visible', taken by William Golding as a title for one of his novels. A more complex but powerful oxymoron can be found in Gerard Manley Hopkins' poem *The Wreck of the Deutschland*:

> [She] Was calling 'O Christ, Christ, come quickly':
> The cross to her she calls Christ to her, christens her wild-worst
> Best.[39]

I have chosen this last example precisely because it is not easy. It requires us to slow down, think, absorb, contemplate its strangeness and its power to arrest.

To such forms liturgical language might, indeed should, aspire. I could go on to consider the resources in rhetoric of *chiasmus*, *ambiguity*, *apostrophe* or the genre of *satire*. The list is extensive.[40] This last suggestion of *satire* might seem an odd one until one returns to its origins and etymology in the Latin *satira*, a later form of *satura* which means 'medley'.[41] The complex, polyphonic texture of the Roman Rite, the multiplicity of voices available in the liturgical action, the complexities of action and changes of mood (from the Sanctus abruptly to 'On the night that he was betrayed ...') allow a liturgical celebration that requires daring and imagination, flexibility and defamiliarization. The origins of the term *satire* seem to have been in a dish of various fruits, a medley, offered to the gods ...[42] Perhaps already we are not so far from the eucharistic, sacramental offering.

As I draw near to the close of this preliminary chapter concerning the nature of liturgical language, a chapter that probably raises as many questions as it resolves, I will give some attention to a twentieth-century liturgical prayer that, in some ways, bears comparison with Archbishop Cranmer's Prayer of Humble Access. For like its predecessor in the sixteenth century, David Frost's post-communion prayer which begins 'Father of all, we give you thanks and praise', has gained a place in the affection of worshippers in the Anglican tradition, the vast majority of whom will have no idea of its origin or have thought about why it 'works' so well at this point at the conclusion of the liturgy. Just as Cranmer wrote very few original Collects or prayers, so this prayer (written by one who is professionally neither a theologian nor a liturgist, but a professor of English Literature) is one of the very few 'original' prayers that have taken their place in contemporary Anglican worship. Oddly, perhaps, it is susceptible to the same theological criticism as the Prayer of Humble Access, its contravening of the doctrine of concomitance, though in the modern case no one seems to be very concerned about it or even to have noticed it: more of this in a moment. Here is the prayer in full.

> Father of all, we give you thanks and praise that when we were still far off you met us in your Son and brought us home. Dying and living, he declared your love, gave us grace, and opened the gate of glory. May we who share Christ's body live his risen life; we who drink his cup bring life to others; we whom the Spirit lights give light to the world. Keep us firm in the hope you have set before us, so we and all your children shall be free, and the whole earth live to praise your name; through Christ our Lord. Amen.

Frost's prayer is, like the Prayer of Humble Access, based on a biblical passage, the so-called parable of the Prodigal Son (Luke 15.11–32). It also follows the four elements of Herbert's poem 'Prayer (II)': the biblical foundation, simple vocabulary, challenge to thought and theological content in the theology of incarnation and redemption.

All prayer properly begins in praise ('Father of all, we give you thanks and praise'). The address to the Father draws together both God as Father and the human father of the Gospel parable, who is then merged with God. 'You met us in your Son' offers a nicely complex convergence with the Son of the parable – who here becomes the Father, met in Christ the Son. 'Dying and living' is a good instance of oxymoron, while the centre of the prayer makes fine dramatic use of asyndeton, drawing us forward in our Christian commitment as we prepare, after communion, to go out into the world at the end of the liturgy. The dramatic narrative is suspended on a simple structure of verb and noun (back to *The Diversions of Purley*!):

> He declared your love
> gave us grace
> opened the gate of glory.

This final metaphor of the gate of glory (with its nice use of alliteration) opens the eschatological dimension of the prayer – liturgy is always anticipatory – and prepares us for undertaking the task of each member of the Communion body. We pray that we may live his risen life (as Maximus the Confessor and many others in the early Church insisted, we are already now living the risen life in Christ); bring this life to others; and give light to the whole world (Matthew 5.14). The final sentence, requesting that we be made firm in our hope, expands the light from ourselves, to the body of the Church and finally to the whole earth, concluding, as it began, on a doxological note of praise.

Just a brief further word about the doctrine of concomitance. You will recall that the Prayer of Humble Access has suffered in present times the loss of the words 'our sinful bodies may be made clean by his body, and our souls washed through his most precious blood'. The issue was the division made between the effect of the body and the effect of the blood, in contradiction of the doctrine of concomitance between body and soul. But we have seen how a powerful sense of metaphor can dismiss the dilemma of literalism, and it is in this dramatic and unified sense that Frost's post-communion prayer, in its distinction between Christ's body and the cup and their effects, should be said.

It is perhaps indicative of the crisis in contemporary liturgy and its language that the fine prayer that we have just considered itself suffered diminution through the political processes of synodical approval in the Church of England. Liturgical language, like the language of its relative poetry, is not encouraged by dealings in the corridors of church power even though it is certainly subject to the discipline of theology and tradition. The sentence beginning 'Keep us firm in the hope you have set before us' originally began with an image drawn from the Epistle to the Hebrews 6.19, 'Anchor us in this hope.' This reference to Hebrews caught nicely the paradox of free will, emphasizing that as we may be kept in the living hope of Christ, so we may be – as his slaves – truly free. The anchor was, in the early Church, a familiar symbol of hope, mentioned by Clement of Alexandria as often engraved on Christian rings and frequently found in conjunction with the symbol of the fish.[43] It is a pity that the more energetic and densely allusive phrase originally suggested by Frost is now replaced by the weaker 'keep us'.

This final point is worth mentioning, not only to illustrate the dangers of seeking simplicity and the wrong kind of clarity in our liturgy, but to indicate the synchronic density of liturgical language, its rootedness in history and tradition without any abandonment of the demands of contemporary speech and context. And if we Anglicans are tempted to think that nothing can replace the sixteenth-century glories of the *Prayer Book*, composed and compiled when English was on the point of producing the genius of William Shakespeare, then we should perhaps recall that every age has a tendency to look back to times of earlier glory, not least in its language. After all, even Sir Thomas More found it necessary to defend the English of his day against its detractors.

> For as for that our tong is called barbarous, is but a fantasye. For so is, as euery learned man knoweth, euery strange language to other. And if they would call it barayn of words, there is no doubte but it is plenteous enough to expresse our myndes in anye thing wherof one man hath vsed to speke with another.[44]

So we in our own time may, and indeed must, also speak in defiance of the decay of language. In the Appendix to George Orwell's *Nineteen Eighty-Four* (1949) Orwell writes on 'The Principles of Newspeak'. 'The purpose of Newspeak', he says, 'was not only to provide a medium of expression for the world-view and mental habits proper to the devotees of Ingsoc, *but to make all other modes of thought impossible*.'[45] 'Newspeak', as contemporary politics frighteningly reminds us, is about utter control – while the language of the liturgy is about freedom and hospitality to the other. It is the language of praise and worship, and of life not death. It seeks to make all things possible. Above all it is a living language. Archbishop Cranmer would have been dismayed at the survival of his *Prayer Book* more or less intact for four hundred years. For the language of prayer and the Bible must be integrated with the living development of words, occupying a place that challenges and yet speaks to the language of everyday a poetics that is at once 'common' and also defamiliarizing. As early as 1540, in his preface to the *Great Bible*, Cranmer affirms that regular re-translation is the 'more ancient custom' of the Christian Church.

> For it is not much above one hundred years ago, since scripture hath not been accustomed to be read in the vulgar tongues within this realm; and many hundred years before that it was translated and read in the Saxons' tongue, which at that time was our mother's tongue ... And when this language waxed old and out of common usage, because folk should not lack the fruit of common reading, it was again translated in the new language.[46]

Thus it is also with the language of the liturgy of the Church. And yet, as the language of praise and doxology, it is also conservative, strange and stretched, as in ancient rhetoric. Liturgical language follows the devices of the poetic, and yet it remains the language of the common person in the community of the Church seeking communion with God.

As an Anglican, I would suggest that the glories of Cranmerian liturgy partake also of an element of what the eighteenth-century dissenting hymn-writer Isaac Watts pursued (in the term of Pope and the Scriblerus Club) – that is the 'art of sinking'.[47] It is the art of 'sinking' language to the level of a whole congregation, and yet it also takes a genius to sustain this in a form of words, in an age that has limited both philosophically and practically the mystery of language,[48] that glorifies the incomprehensibility – the unboundedness – of God in an eschatological vision that stretches, in the very tropes and liveliness of words, between heaven and earth.

And so we move on to a consideration of the poetics of liturgy.

2

The Poetics of Liturgy

> Really great poetry only exists when man radically faces what he is. In so doing, he may be entangled in guilt, perversity, hatred of self and diabolical pride, he may see himself as a sinner and identify with his sin. But even so he is more exposed to the happy danger of meeting God than the narrow-minded Philistine who always skirts cautiously the chasms of existence, to stay on the superficial level where one is never faced with doubts – nor with God.[1]

In the exploration of a poetics of liturgy the present chapter will take a somewhat different form from other chapters in this book. It will be by way of an extended reflection on a recent collection of essays entitled *Poetry and Prayer* (2015), edited by Francesca Bugliani Knox and John Took. This is the second in a series of excellent volumes under the general title of 'The Power of the Word'.[2] From this beginning I will suggest that the study and practice of liturgy and worship can never ignore the demands of poetics or the language of poetry, though these are not to be confused. Their complex relationship has been little recognized or understood by the liturgical reformers of the last hundred years or so, and the contemporary almost universal insistence on writing in liturgical language that is simple, everyday and understandable is a profound mistake that results in words and a grammar in worship that are quite unable to bear the necessary theological or indeed spiritual weight and mystery of corporate prayer. Furthermore there appears to be an assumption that, simply because we live in an age when relatively few people read much poetry, they are therefore quite unable to respond to the delicate and stretched language of a liturgical poetics. My own experience in a parish community suggests that this is simply not the case. The fact that people rarely read poetry does not mean that they cannot be alive to its mystery, power and beauty, and the same can be said of the language of the liturgy.

Karl Rahner's words with which this chapter began might suggest the close association that exists between 'really great poetry' and the self-exploratory engagements of liturgy and its profound 'capacity to open the heart and mind ... to the mystery of God'[3] through self-examination and a movement into the depths of being and the self where God, it may be said, is truly to be found. It is not my intention here to review the complex history of discussions of the relationship between prayer and poetry since the early twentieth century, beginning with important works like Henri Bremond's *Prière et poésie* (1926, English trans. 1927) or the influential work of Evelyn Underhill 'who defined the poet as innate mystic and an exemplar of humility and innocence'.[4] She was not, of course, entirely correct. But I begin with the thought of the theologian Karl Rahner in his essay 'Poetry and the Christian' (1966), which lays emphasis on the power of the word and the particular relationship between three things – faith, the presence of mystery and the word of poetry. Rahner writes:

> The first requisite for man's hearing the word of the gospel *without misunderstanding it* is that his ears should be open for *the* word through which the silent mystery is present ... For in this word comes what is incomprehensible, the nameless, silent power that rules all but is itself unruled, the immense, the abyss in which we are rooted.[5]

Liturgy that fails to acknowledge this requisite for hearing the word of the gospel, even in a largely un-poetic age obsessed with literality, quickly loses any sense of the mystery of faith, and soon withers away. But this does not mean that we Anglicans remain solely committed to the ancient language of a distant, admittedly more poetic, Renaissance age or, indeed, that the poetics that we seek is limited to the poetry of 'religious literature'. As T. S. Eliot, writing as a literary critic, suggested long ago in his essay 'Religion and Literature' (1935), we 'are not concerned here with religious literature but with the application of our religion to the criticism of any literature'.[6] This, nevertheless, is not to suggest that great poetry does not have the capacity to transcend the passage of history within which a language inevitably changes. A brilliant example is the capacity of great actors to speak, apparently quite naturally, Shakespearean blank verse in Ralph Fiennes' brilliant film of *Coriolanus* (2012) which is set in an utterly convincing contemporary context of political strife, war and bloodshed. The film might act as a reminder that those who lead worship, far from stumbling through language that has been reduced to the simplest syntax and vocabulary, and even if they are not trained actors, should at least learn to speak coherently, thoughtfully and with the ability to cope expressively with complex grammar. A recent experience of the capacity of a congregation to respond to the language of poetry occurred in an Advent course that I led in my church when I read aloud Christina

Rossetti's poem 'A Christmas Carol'. Familiar enough when sung as the hymn 'In the bleak midwinter', it had a quite different effect when read as a poem, and the difference was noted by a number of people. When *read* aloud the words came alive in a new and powerful way.

The liturgy, like most great poetry, places words, even familiar words, under the strain of profound mysteries. Liturgical language is primary, unlike the necessary but still secondary language of theological articulation upon which the liturgy both draws and feeds. It nourishes the imagination, of which the best description in English remains that of the poet S. T. Coleridge from the early nineteenth century as 'the living Power and prime Agent of all human Perception, and as a repetition in the finite mind of the eternal act of creation in the infinite I AM'.[7] How can this liveliness and creativity be recovered for the 'finite' mind in prayer and in the language of our liturgy?

Let us take a moment or two with R. S. Thomas' poem entitled 'The Prayer'.[8] He begins with an all too familiar experience and the difficulty of starting our prayer.

He kneeled down
  dismissing his orisons
as inappropriate.

The suppliant finds it easiest to fall back on old, well-known prayers, uncertain of where to begin and hearing nothing by way of response. It is all so predictable, the answers the same each time, the 'casualties of his past intercessions.' The prayer is arid, devoid of sacramental reality and empty of real meaning. Praying is a wilderness experience, as dry as the desert sand in both word and mind. But from the desert itself and in the drought of the prayer, the living response begins to form from the cry of anguish itself.

  the prayer formed:
Deliver me from the long drought
  of the mind. Let leaves
from the deciduous Cross
  fall on us, washing
us clean, turning our autumn
  to gold by the affluence of their fountain.

Thomas' poem follows an experience that, if we are honest, we recognize only too well. We, like the suppliant in the poem, kneel to pray but nothing happens – prayer is not an easy thing. So – we, like the disciples before us (Luke 11.1), fall 'back on an old prayer' and ask to be taught to pray and what to pray for. We listen for a response – for the still, small voice, almost without breath or sound, that spoke to Elijah on the mountain (1 Kings 19.12). But there is nothing except all the old wordy demands to God, the habits of intercession, the familiar ways of prayer. Thomas then turns to the sacramental image of the blood of Christ for which we hold out our hands in our prayers: and out of nothing 'the prayer formed'. It comes graciously. Thomas ends his poem with a vivid, dramatic image – the tree of the Cross sprouts leaves,[9] in a baptismal image, washing us clean in a plenteous fountain, as the Bible itself is described in the essay by the translators prefatory to the King James Bible: 'a fountain of most pure water springing up unto everlasting life'.[10]

Prayer, then, is answered in the attempt to pray – from out of our silence and our stumblings there comes revelation and transformation.[11] In liturgical prayer also we should not expect too much of ourselves, which is too often the case, though through our very 'inappropriateness' words are revealed in mysterious and (for some) familiar images that burst upon the imagination. For the prayer begins in the listening and the waiting. We should never underestimate the capacity of poetry to come even to us in the complex relationships of a liturgical poetics. Though there should never be false or simple conflations between poetry and liturgy, we remain guided by the poet as one, in the words of Jay Parini, 'feeling tossed out of Eden, forced to "make do" with whatever frail embodiments in language he or she can muster'.[12] This condition of the poet is brilliantly perceived by Seamus Heaney in his lament upon his task in the poem 'Exposure' which begins in post-lapsarian Ireland:

It is December in Wicklow:
Alders dripping, birches
Inheriting the last light,
The ash tree cold to look at.[13]

In this bleak landscape, the poet aspires to great heights, but instead remains, in his own sense of himself, earthbound.

And I sometimes see a falling star.
If I could come on meteorite!
Instead I walk through damp leaves,
Husks, the spent flukes of autumn,

Imagining a hero
On some muddy compound,
His gift like a slingstone
Whirled for the desperate.

How did I end up like this?
I often think of my friends'
Beautiful prismatic counselling
And the anvil brains of some who hate me

As I sit weighing and weighing
My responsible *tristia*.
For what? For the ear? For the people?
For what is said behind-backs?

Heaney, the poet, has much in common with Thomas the priest, the one with his poetry the other with his prayers. Each has his aspirations, each knows failure, each feels himself to be casting, we might say, pearls before swine – Heaney describes this as like throwing out words like stones from a sling for the 'desperate'. The poet, like the priest at prayer, feels himself to be a failure beside others who succeed, taking himself perhaps too seriously – for what end?

And yet the point is that 'Exposure' is a wonderful poem, as is so often the case when poets lament their worthlessness and inability to write. It is precisely then that they compose some of their greatest verse – one thinks of Coleridge's 'Dejection Ode' or Gerard Manley Hopkins' tragic 'terrible sonnets', poems written out of despair. And so it is with prayer – an affiliation that liturgy has found it hard to assimilate into corporate worship. For the poem and the liturgy are essentially places of articulate listening wherein, it may be, within the question lies the answer – the poet might call this inspiration, in prayer, revelation, when we find the leaves

... turning our autumn
to gold by the affluence of their fountain.

Now, of course, this is precisely the moment in Thomas' poem when we have to pay the closest attention. The task is not easy and we must work hard at the language and its images to allow them to work on us. It is the same with God in our prayers and in language of the liturgy of the sacraments. We reach that moment of uncertainty, or worse, that is yet somehow wonderful if we are but patient. Compare this with the rather despairing sentence from the 1985 report of the Archbishop of Canterbury's Commission on Urban Priority Areas, *Faith in the City*: 'We have heard calls for short, functional service booklets or cards, prepared by people who will always ask "if all the words are really necessary".'[14] Even, or perhaps especially, in the bleak conditions of the UPA such people are, to the poet Heaney, possessors of 'the anvil brains of some who hate me'. For it is at this moment, when the question about the unnecessary words is asked, that language simply disintegrates into dreary platitude, a replication of deadly urbanization instead of its transformation, fearful of a loss of the 'language or culture of faith'.[15] But we should not be thus fearful for in fact such words may be expressive of something far deeper, far more persistent and less obsessed with economy, if it can only be salvaged. As another contemporary poet (and an Anglican priest), David Scott, has discovered it in his poem 'The Book of Common Prayer 1549':

> This is just what you might expect
> a Prayer Book to be like. This is
> what we always thought about rain;
> about dying, and marriage, and God.
> We needed only the help which
> the right placing of a relative pronoun
> could manage. Words, then, said what they meant;
> they bit. A man was a houseband
> until death departed him.
> And all was for common use:
> printed in Fleet Street,
> at the sign of the sun,
> over against the conduit.[16]

But why should it be, for Anglicans at least, simply 'then' – in words locked into the sixteenth century? Today as well we are bound to seek the recovery of such meaningfulness in language that is precise and grammatical – the right placing of a relative pronoun – where poetry both begins and ends. Even without faith it originates in a seriousness that still demands the precise articulation of what the *Alternative Baptism Texts* of 2015 leave merely rather vaguely as 'a deep spiritual yearning'. This is a yearning that needs a moment of revelation and a proper utterance that lies beyond immediate comprehension precisely because it is so deeply felt, so serious. Even that old poetic reprobate Philip Larkin recognized this in his poem 'Church Going', entering the musty church building without faith and yet realizing that:

A serious house on serious earth it is,
In whose blent air all compulsions meet,
Are recognized, and robed as destinies.
And that much never can be obsolete,
Since someone will forever be surprising
A hunger in himself to be more serious.[17]

A church then becomes a place that is 'proper to grow wise in' – a wisdom that begins in worship with compulsions that we all share, maybe with or without recognition or belief, if they can only be brought to our attention again. Karl Rahner knows that in poetry, as in our worship, we are often 'entangled in guilt, perversity, hatred of self and diabolical pride'[18] and perhaps it is here that the language of our liturgy, embedded as it always is in the ancient traditions of the Church and sacrament, must be content to begin, 'exposed to the happy danger of meeting God' and facing doubts *de profundis*. Writing on Rahner, David Lonsdale proposes two kinds of words:

> Typically, human words distinguish, define and separate, especially in technical or purely functional contexts. But there are also words which unite, reconcile and liberate. Poetic metaphors bring together into a unity different and sometimes apparently incompatible layers of meaning. Words of truth, love and forgiveness, reconcile, unite and set free.[19]

Such words begin in the familiar everyday and with 'what we always thought about' things. When liturgists turn to poets for help, though recognizing their differences, they should not turn simply to those who have written within the Church or on clearly 'religious' matters. Though Herbert, Donne and, in his sermons, Bishop Lancelot Andrewes are certainly poetic treasures within the Anglican tradition, we still need to be reminded by Eliot that 'Corneille, or Racine, even in those of their plays which do not touch upon Christian themes, are great Christian religious poets.'[20] Or we can come closer to home, instructed by Claudius in Shakespeare's *Hamlet* in his great soliloquy when he admits 'Pray can I not.'[21] For Claudius' speech, saturated as it is in the biblical texts of the penitential psalms and the biblical story of Cain and Abel, learned in the distinction between frail humanity and God's impartial justice, remains a poetic lecture *on* prayer – and not prayer itself. Małgorzata Grzegorzewska links Claudius with the Pharisee of Luke 18.11 who, in Jesus' parable, 'stood and prayed thus with himself' (KJV)[22] (σταθεις προς εάυτον ταυτα προσηυχετο), a prayer directed inwards and not to God, and thus an 'idiotic' prayer.[23] For all of his cleverness, Claudius' prayer lacks substance, and he knows it all too well.

> My words fly up, my thoughts remain below.
> Words without thoughts never to heaven go.[24]

All prayer and all the words of the liturgy carry our thoughts heavenward on language, even when that thought is more than we can know ourselves and is masked in incomprehension of the mystery. Liturgical language, furthermore, is word that is indeed saturated in history and tradition yet still embodied in the life of the contemporary everyday – the life and the word feeding one another at the core of our being, a truth acknowledged by that most intelligent of Victorian doubters, George Eliot, at the very beginning of her novel *Adam Bede* (1859). Here we meet Adam hard at work and singing Bishop Ken's morning hymn, the words and their thought merging with the brisk activity of the workshop upon which the labourer concentrates, the words sometimes blurring into pure activity.

> It was to this workman that the strong baritone belonged which was heard above the sound of plane and hammer singing –
> 'Awake, my soul, and with the sun
> Thy daily stage of duty run;
> Shake off dull sloth ...'
> Here some measurement was to be taken which required more concentrated attention, and the sonorous voice subsided in a low whistle; but it presently broke out again with renewed vigour –
> 'Let all thy converse be sincere,
> Thy conscience as the noonday clear.'[25]

Adam Bede's integration of Bishop Ken's late seventeenth-century hymn with his physical labour – the words submerged yet still present when close attention to his task must take first place – seems in a way reminiscent of the place of the psalms in Christian worship, rooted in the everyday. At the centre of what Jean Leclerq has called 'the poem of the liturgy'[26] is the ancient liturgical repetition of this collection of songs and poems that sound the full range of human emotion, from the deepest despair to exultant joy. The psalms remain at the heart of the Anglican daily office, as they were the heart of the early monastic liturgy, because they are finally rooted in the complex, sometimes incoherent experience of what it is to be human – but all before God. The ancient questions are beyond our solution. Why do the good suffer and the wicked flourish (Psalm 73)? What can condemn the godly person to utter the cry of despair, 'My God, my God, look upon me; why hast thou forsaken me?' (Psalm 22.1, *BCP*). Can praise ever be more exultant than in Psalm 150? Has any poem offered more comfort than the words of Psalm 23?

Professor David Frost, a member of the Church of England Liturgical Commission and who was responsible for the version of the Psalms that was included in *The Alternative Service Book* (1980) and *An Australian Prayer Book* (1978),[27] has correctly written:

> The psalms take us through the reality of human emotion: we grouse against God, we protest our innocence, we demand the blood of our enemies. The psalms could be called 'the Sinner's Prayer Book': there is one part of Christian worship where we don't have to act, where a Sunday-best suit is not required. The psalms expose the reality of our feelings: our emotions come out into the open, where, since they are no longer suppressed, they can be dealt with by the transforming and healing power of Christ.[28]

Frost's correct sense of the earthiness of the psalms perhaps goes some way to explain the relative failure of the 1963 *Revised Psalter*, produced under the literary guidance of T. S. Eliot and C. S. Lewis. It was simply *too* literary, simply *too* poetic even and too remote. It seems a pity then, that Frost rather undercuts his proper sense of the universality of the Psalter in human experience when he suggests, a little too donnishly, that 'we need a congregation that understands good typology, and can cope with metaphorical and analogical interpretation'.[29] Such is certainly unlikely to be the case with most congregations with which I am familiar (though by no means all) – and that is, perhaps a good thing. For they value the psalms in their worship in a different way. It was something that St Benedict in his Rule understood when he writes of the 'psalmi cum antiphonas',[30] psalms being sung in the Benedictine monastic office 'against' the framing of short poems that contextualized them in both time and eternity. And the remarkable translator Miles Coverdale (1487/8–1569), whose English psalms remain with us in the *Book of Common Prayer*, though he was no Hebraist, is one of the largely unremarked great poets of the English language, with a genius for the common phrase that states exactly what is meant and required. One of my favourites is Psalm 105.18: 'the iron entered into his soul'. The image is hard, precise – and just right. It 'bites'. It is now part of the English language.[31]

Getting it 'right' by the original (a modern obsession in translation) is not always true to the heart of liturgical poetics. The spirit of the psalms is greater than simply academic correctness (and there are other kinds of precision). Many years ago I was struck by a story told by the distinguished Jewish American poet and academic John Hollander. It was of the child brought up to know the Psalter, and for whom the penultimate verse of Psalm 23 (in the familiar King James Version: 'Surely goodness and mercy shall follow me all the days of my life') was, indelibly, 'Surely good Mrs Murphy shall follow me all the days of my life.'[32] It is only with what the poet Wallace Stevens called 'a later reason' that we realize that there is something profoundly *right* about the child's (mis)construction. For her the psalm gave the assurance of a benign Mrs Murphy following and protecting her, unseen, every step of the way – a far more powerful sense and image of a guardian angel than any later theological abstraction. As John Hollander puts it: 'The child rightly attended to the trope set up by the intense verb "follow me" and supplied an appropriate subject for it, thereby turning mechanical allegory into poetic truth.'[33]

Academically, of course, the child does no such thing. She turns an abstraction into something that to her is as intensely and precisely real as anything can be – endowed as she is with the wonder and imagination of childhood. John Hollander, a poet, has the good sense to respect this, and captures it, for us, in the language of his academic trade. It is a process in which nervous liturgical revisers have been woefully deficient, failing in what Paul Ricoeur, in a way similar to Wallace Stevens, once named a 'second naïveté', reached only after we have crossed the necessary 'desert of criticism'.[34] We are here back to the power of the imagination in our liturgical language and action, a power that needs to be fed, with infinite care, by word and image.

Institutionally the Church does woefully little to prepare its ministers to engage in such a task – to bring Mrs Murphy to life in language that is not reductive, stripped down and easily accessible but rather pregnant with life for the imaginations of those for whom the technical language of tropes and grammatical constructions is not meaningful – though its careful structures are at the very heart of good liturgy, needing only the right placing of a relative pronoun, an adverb or an adjective for words to say what they mean. I am not convinced by the suggestion in the Church of England's *Patterns for Worship* (1995) that all our service books need to do is provide dry bones and skeletons, after the manner of Ezekiel's valley, with 'working instructions or hints to make it all work'.[35] That has at least three faults: it is lazy, it overestimates the training of most ministers and worship leaders, and it underestimates the power of the imagination – which is why, it may be suggested, many people prefer to go the cinema, with all its immensely careful and brilliant technology to stimulate the imagination, rather than go to church. It is to neglect the resources we actually have to hand in language and worship – as Archbishop Cranmer knew so well.

Let us consider, for a moment, the place of hymns that have been so much part of our Anglican worship from the nineteenth century. In 1928 that old reprobate D. H. Lawrence, a poet and novelist, wrote an essay entitled 'Hymns in a Man's Life'. He looked back to the nonconformist hymns that he sang as a child, and that had remained with him even as his Christian faith and adherence to the Church withered away. Here is one of them.

> Each gentle dove
> And sighing bough
> That makes the eve
> So fair to me
> Has something far
> Diviner now
> To draw me back
> To Galilee.
> O Galilee, sweet Galilee,
> Where Jesus loved so much to be,
> O Galilee, sweet Galilee,
> Come sing thy songs again to me!

It isn't much as poetry, perhaps, though its images are strong, working from the particular and familiar as a doorway into a mythic world, and they remain as powerful in the adult imagination as good Mrs Murphy did to the small child. Lawrence writes:

> To me the word Galilee has a wonderful sound. The Lake of Galilee! I don't want to know where it is. I never want to go to Palestine. Galilee is one of those lovely, glamorous worlds, not places, that exist in the golden haze of a child's half-formed imagination. And in my man's imagination it is just the same. It has been left untouched. With regard to the hymns which had such a profound influence on my childish consciousness, there has been no crystallising out, no dwindling into actuality, no hardening into the commonplace. They are the same to my man's experience as they were to me nearly forty years ago.[36]

His first sentence captures the essence of what he is saying – the word has a wonderful sound. It creates a world, a living word, a word that bites.

Lawrence, for all his rhetoric, sees with a perspicacity that eludes all of that dry Victorian search for the historical Jesus, for facts and evidence. Many years ago a professor of English in Durham University, Dick Watson, gave his audience, of which I was a member, at his Inaugural Lecture a lesson on the power of hymns in worship. He linked Lawrence with another old reprobate writer, Thomas Hardy, and his poem 'Afternoon Service at Mellstock' (*c.* 1850), looking back to his own religious childhood:

> On afternoons of drowsy calm
> We stood in the panelled pew,
> Singing one-voiced a Tate-and-Brady psalm
> To the tune of 'Cambridge New'.
> ...
> So mindless were those outpourings! –
> Though I am not aware
> That I have gained by subtle thought on things
> Since we stood psalming there.[37]

Professor Watson's point, of course, like Hardy himself, is that these outpourings were not so 'mindless', whatever the attention or intellectual ability of the children might have been. They dug deep into the soul, and remained there. For they were built upon the fine foundation of the psalms, and Watson patiently unpacks why such a familiar hymn as Henry Francis Lyte's 'Abide with me' has endured and still has the power to console us, a hymn of sentiment that eschews sentimentality. It is, in fact, a well-crafted piece of writing, exploiting to the full the power of chiasmus and syntax and the end-stopped lines of the verse form. Here is just one example from the beginning of the hymn.

> Abide with me, || fast falls the eventide;
> The darkness deepens, || Lord with me abide.

It is familiar enough. Two heavily caesura'd lines that reverse at beginning and end 'Abide with me: with me abide.' Between them the eventide is given greater precision by the deepening darkness. And there is just one word left hanging, standing on its own – Lord; what Watson calls a 'free agent'.[38] It is not great poetry, but it is carefully written to develop its theme in a working poetics through an overarching image of the tide whose movements would have been perfectly familiar to Lyte's congregation – he was perpetual curate of the coastal town of Lower Brixham. The poetry draws upon the familiar.

'Abide with me' is a good example of what in the eighteenth century the poet Alexander Pope and the Scriblerus Club called 'the art of sinking'. The great hymn-writer Isaac Watts (1674–1748) was a master of this quite modest but far from easy art, which is why his hymns remain so familiar in our churches today – 'When I survey the wondrous cross', 'There is a land of pure delight', 'O God our help in ages past', and so on. Watts himself underestimates the power of his hymnody, its careful syntax and composition and its powerful images when he writes:

> In many of these composures, I have just permitted my verse to rise above a flat and indolent style; yet I hope it is everywhere supported above the just contempt of the critics: though I am sensible that I have often subdued it below their esteem; because I would neither indulge any bold metaphors, nor admit hard words, nor tempt the ignorant worshipper to sing without his understanding.[39]

Watts does not altogether do himself justice as a poet, but the point is well made, with one reservation. Hymns, indeed, are a particular poetic form that demands, within the context of corporate worship, stability of rhythm, sound doctrine and an immediacy of reception within the time it takes to sing the words. This does not preclude a largely concrete, but rarely abstract, imagery that carries the singers forward in a dramatic participation that is, or may be, deeply liturgical, just as the Thanksgiving of the Eucharist sweeps us forward, with angels and archangels, into the Sanctus, transcending time and space even as we sing. A good example in hymnody is the final verse of Charles Wesley's 'Love divine, all loves excelling':

Finish then thy New Creation,
  Pure and spotless let us be;
Let us see thy great salvation
  Perfectly restored in thee,
Changed from glory into glory
  Till in heaven we take our place,
Till we cast our crowns before thee,
  Lost in wonder, love, and praise!

It is that word in the last line – 'lost' – that is the key to the whole hymn. Beginning in the first verse with the kenotic mystery of God's presence among us in 'humble dwelling', the singers are drawn through the wonder of salvation until they are finally, indeed, 'lost' in wonder and in the glory of heaven. Dick Watson, who links the hymn with the story of Jupiter and Mercury in Ovid's *Metamorphoses* Book VIII (which, he suggests, Wesley would have known as a boy), writes of this vision:

> We are lost in [it]: it is so magnificent that we find ourselves totally unlike our normal selves. We have a sudden vision of ourselves, yet not ourselves, casting down our crowns before the throne of God like the four and twenty elders in Revelation 4.10.[40]

The very precise words of Wesley's hymn, especially if they are sung to the right music, are transformative, or perhaps better transfigurative, not with intellectual challenge, but with imaginative possibilities. They give us hope in mysteries beyond our comprehension – and, in a largely unbelieving age, that might be enough even in the liturgy. I doubt if we can actually put much substance onto the hopelessly vague idea of the 'deep spiritual yearning' of our time, as found in the Introduction to the 2015 *Alternative Baptism Texts*, even if such yearning might be the case. I actually rather doubt it. But the liturgy's task is to draw us through word and image, entangled in guilt and perversity (as Rahner suggests), towards the concrete possibilities that in imagination grant us hope. Wesley's hymn does this. Or, Thomas Hardy, again, speaks eloquently of this when, as an old man and in the midst of the miseries of the First World War, he looks back to the Christmas story of his childhood, and it still draws him.

> So fair a fancy few would weave
> In these years! Yet, I feel,
> If someone said on Christmas Eve,
> 'Come; see the oxen kneel
>
> 'In the lonely barton by yonder comb
> Our childhood used to know,'
> I should go with him in the gloom,
> Hoping it might be so.[41]

The key word here, of course, is 'hoping' – and it is not easy to unravel. That is why it is just right.

In this chapter I am anxious not to seem to establish too easy a relationship between poetry and prayer or the liturgy. In the next chapter I will consider it more precisely. But so far, what I have sought to suggest is the absolute necessity of a liturgical poetics that runs quite counter to the current liturgical obsession with accessibility and with simplified language for those who, it would appear, cannot understand (a rather patronizing idea) and have no sense of the traditions of worship. A brief survey of poets will remind us that often the relationship in one person of the vocations of the poet and the priest can be problematic or worse, though there are clear exceptions to this, above all for Anglicans in the life and work of George Herbert. But being a poet and a priest almost broke Gerard Manley Hopkins;[42] it is there as a tension in the often curmudgeonly priest/poet R. S. Thomas; and it is clearly evident in the vocational dilemma of the American Trappist monk Thomas Merton who for eight years between 1949 and 1957 wrote no poetry in an otherwise prolific life as a poet. Most specifically, as a monk, Merton declares a 'radical difference between the artist and the mystic':

> When the poet enters into himself, it is in order to reflect upon his inspiration and to clothe it with a special and splendid form and then return to display it to those outside ... but the mystic enters into himself, not in order to work but to pass through the centre of his own soul and lose himself in the mystery and secrecy and infinite, transcendent reality of God living and working within him.[43]

I can see the difference, and it is real, but I am not convinced that it is anything like as absolute as Merton seems to suggest. In poetry, in the liturgy (rather than as mystics), in contemplation, we enter into ourselves to depths that we rarely if ever reach in normal, everyday life. Each requires a stretching of language from the quotidian norm – but it is also from that normality that we begin to be, in Rahner's phrase, 'exposed to the happy danger of meeting God' in both sorrow and joy.

The Lukan parable of the Pharisee and the Publican (Luke 18.10–14) has hovered just below the surface in much of the writing of this chapter. It is a story of two people who go to the temple to pray, much as some of us go to church to pray and engage in the liturgy. Each of us knows, if we are honest, which of the characters in the parable fits us best. It is also a story of two different languages – the one self-obsessed (like Claudius in *Hamlet*), the other desperately seeking reconciliation with God. In his book *Meditations on Liturgy* (1965),[44] Thomas Merton reflects upon the nature of the 'sacramental consciousness' entered into by contemplative exercises in words, delving into the depths of words until they yield new insights and mysteries. It can never be found in a flight from language, but in sometimes desperately seeking ways into language, even and perhaps especially for those for whom such exercises are difficult and rare. It was many years ago that I first encountered A. D. Nuttall's book *Overheard*

By God: Fiction and Prayer in Herbert, Milton, Dante and St. John (1980). Reading it again today I am quite persuaded that it should be compulsory reading for all who embark upon the tasks of liturgical revision, the writing of new liturgies, or guiding a congregation in liturgical worship.

Overheard By God is all about the language we use in prayer. It is written by someone who readily admits that he is not a believer yet at the same time is 'exasperated by the enervate professions of believers'.[45] That, in my view, is at least a promising start. The last chapter of his book begins with a literary analysis (Nuttall was a professor of English) of John 18.33–38, the dialogue between Jesus and Pilate, which Nuttall describes as an example of 'discontinuous dialogue' – where questions (by Pilate) are answered by other questions (by Jesus). Nuttall makes the point that Jesus is so outrageous at his trial that he appears to offer us the ancient alternatives – *aut deus aut malus homo* – either he is indeed God, or else a wicked and blasphemous man. But there is a third possibility, and one to which Nuttall himself subscribes: that Jesus was simply mad. Our shocked response to this – and I assume that most readers of my book will be shocked – is based, Nuttall suggests, upon two false presumptions: 'first, that madness is the opposite of intelligence and second that madness is incompatible with goodness'.[46] It is certainly true that most extremely dull people are quite sane, and that very often mad people are highly intelligent, even charitable. Thus, even if a sceptic might wish to accuse Jesus of megalomania, then one at least, Tony Nuttall, is prepared to admit that 'his real claim upon our reverence is immense'. Jesus is mad and yet the best of men.

Thus, Nuttall concludes, we need to 'see what a knife-edge thing the Gospel of John is'. Its claims are extraordinary. Does the possibility that Jesus was mad finally and irrevocably invalidate those claims? Nuttall concludes his book with a confession.

> This barbarous reader took no belief to his reading of the Gospel. But the first thing he encountered was a frontal challenge to that unbelief.[47]

For Nuttall it is all a question of language, which is the fine knife-edge upon which everything is balanced. That is why I have chosen to finish this chapter on liturgical poetics with this odd moment in the writings of an unbeliever or, perhaps in the end, he was not so much of one after all. For it is a moment concerned with the power of words – which is where, after all, the Gospel of John begins – Eν ἀρχη ἠν ὁ λογος, 'In the beginning was the Word.' It may be that we are all deranged, singing our hymns and endlessly entering into the repeated words of the Eucharist week after week. Perhaps it does not matter. But if we once lose faith in language, if we curtail and simplify it for the sake of a particular sense of clarity, if we fall prey to literalism and forget the power of the imagination in words – then we have lost the very vehicle by which God created all things, and redeemed them in Jesus Christ who in his discourse with Pilate held the initiative in word. Or perhaps he was just someone with a constitutional inability to answer a straight question, and therefore upon whom, like Pilate (who was not very good with words), one gives up. It is for us to choose by an act of faith, or not.

3

A Ritual Poetics and the Demands of Liturgical Language

Liturgical revision in the later twentieth century in the Church of England, primarily in relation to the publication of *The Alternative Service Book* (1980), resulted in a great deal being said, largely in lamentation, about the linguistic decline from the rich Cranmerian heights of the *Book of Common Prayer*. Much was written by conservatives that was nostalgic and inexact in its understanding of liturgical language while, on the other hand, revisionist demands for clarity and simplicity in the language of worship have, as we have already seen, seemed to be rooted in a misunderstanding of the particular poetic demands of the language of the liturgy. David Cockerell's essay 'Why Language Matters' in David Martin and Peter Mullen's conservative book of essays *No Alternative: The Prayer Book Controversy* (1981) rather typically confuses the more general term 'religious language' with liturgical language, and rests upon a number of vague and ill-defined principles such as 'transparency' and 'vitality'.[1] But I do not wish to anticipate the politics of such debates that are dealt with at more length later in this book.[2]

In the present chapter I want to develop a suggestion about the nature of ritualistic aspects of poetic language made to me by the fine Jewish scholar Ariel Zinder of the Hebrew University of Jerusalem,[3] whose work is concerned with similar issues in the language of his own liturgical tradition (a comparative study about which, as far as I know, almost nothing has been acknowledged by Christian liturgical scholars), and with reference to a remarkable book recommended to me by Zinder, Arthur Greene's *Post-Petrarchism: Origins and Innovations of the Western Lyric Sequence* (1991). I will take Greene as my starting point, developing his largely literary concerns in directions of my own.

I begin with the somewhat obvious observation that the Elizabethan *Prayer Book* of 1559, with its origins in Cranmer's 1549 *Prayer Book*, should be seen as an English Renaissance text more or less contemporary not only with the flowering of drama that was to find its peak in the plays of William Shakespeare, but with English post-Petrarchan lyric sequences such as Edmund Spenser's *Amoretti and Epithalamion* (1595), Sir Philip Sidney's *Astrophil and Stella* (written 1581–2, published 1591) and others rather less well known by such poets as Sir Thomas Wyatt and Barnabe Barnes. They all looked back, of course, to the fourteenth-century *Canzoniere* of Petrarch in a poetic lyric tradition that emphasizes the textual rather than the contextual aspects of language, forging a distinction between, on the one hand, lyric fictions as agents of diachronic change and, on the other, myth and ritual as agents of synchronic stability. In the sixteenth century there is a clear distinction between this elegant Petrarchan lyric tradition and the far more widely read poetry of the Psalter of Thomas Sternhold and John Hopkins, whose first collection of 44 metrical psalms appeared in 1549, but which, in Greene's words, 'has never prospered with critics and theorists, and accordingly has not been received as literature'.[4] But my point here is not in distinction but rather that there is actually far more in common between the language of the lyric tradition in literature and the liturgical language of the *Book of Common Prayer* than has been recognized, while at the same time within this commonality there is also a clear contrast to be made between fictional lyric poetry and the 'lyric ritualist'. But it is precisely this commonality that suggests a necessarily far more complex sense of the nature of liturgical language that has simply not been so far acknowledged by liturgical scholars. It should, after all, be remembered that if the poetic fictions of Petrarch cannot be appreciated without acknowledging among his sources psalms and Song of Songs,[5] Wyatt, Sidney, George Gascoigne, and after them George Herbert also produced English translations of the psalms.[6] In the flowering of Renaissance English writing Thomas Cranmer and his Elizabethan and Jacobean liturgical successors (and behind all of them the late medieval Bible translators Coverdale and Tyndale) cannot be entirely excluded from this poetic company.

As we pursue the distinction between the fictional and the ritual aspects of lyric poetry we need to emphasize at the outset the two fundamental poetic elements of time and space. The characteristic of the Petrarchan lyric sequence in its creation of a fictional world is the locating of the first person of the narrator in the present, around which time both past and future revolve, the fiction a specific agent of 'sense-making change'[7] in a world of mutability.[8] Thus we find in Petrarch's *Canzoniere*, Part I: 'Before Laura's Death':

> O you who hear within these scattered verses
> the sound of sighs with which I fed my heart

in my first errant youthful days when I
in part was not the man I am today ...[9]

It is the final word, 'today', that provides the temporal perspective for the whole sonnet, the point in time from which all anticipation and past suffering stem. The poem is written in a form of speech that is potentially common to any of us in both its concerns and its vocabulary, but even as common speech it is also poetically 'pure language', for a poem is not to 'mean' but to 'be', avoiding what Hans Robert Jauss has termed 'referential illusion'.[10] It aspires to pure fiction, pure invention. Myth or ritual, on the other hand, seeks stability in a broad time that is collectively inhabited and unhampered by the instabilities, the mutability, of the personal present. In Arthur Greene's words, 'ritual tends to imagine a reversible immanence, where each of these worlds [the real and the hypothetical] dwells inside the other'.[11] In the ritual world, that is, the world of the liturgy, we move into what Mircea Eliade called 'sacred time' in which a 'primordial mythical time [is] made present ... *ab origine, in illo tempore*',[12] undisturbed by the vicissitudes of the fictive 'I'.

Apart from time, mythic space also is distinct from the locatable precisions of the fictive. In Greene's words, 'fictions, lyric or otherwise, tend to give the illusion of occurring in a knowable place, while ritually oriented poems are supposed to happen anywhere the reader or auditor might be'.[13] When we link this synchronic understanding of space to the 1559 service of Holy Communion both its links with and differences from the Renaissance lyric sequence will become clear, as will its complex nature within the event of a language that refuses simplification. Furthermore, its distinctive nature as 'sacred space' becomes clear in a literary comparison with the secular world of Victorian fiction in which time and space exist within a self-sustaining society that tolerates no transcendent point of view beyond that of a collective consciousness conveyed to the reader, in George Eliot's novels for example, by the device of the omniscient narrator.[14] Such a secular literary device entirely absolves the text of the complex, transcendent relationship with 'Almighty God' as addressed by the priest (speaking in the plural – 'our' – on behalf of the congregation) at the beginning of the Communion prayer of 1559.

Before turning to a close reading of that prayer – read as a literary intrusion into a ritual text – a few more comments should be made with regard to ritualism and poetic language. This will, I hope, make it quite clear why the invariably abortive recourse to contemporary practising poets by twentieth-century liturgical reformers was rooted in a misunderstanding. For the poets, T. S. Eliot or W. H. Auden perhaps – generally writing even in the twentieth century in the broad literary and poetic tradition of the Petrarchan lyric – seek to produce personal fictions, as in, for example, 'The Love Song of J. Alfred Prufrock' ('Let us go then, you and I') or even the *Four Quartets*, in the opening of 'Burnt Norton' that concludes with 'My words echo / Thus, in your mind.'[15] The liturgical will always be awkward for the lyric poet as it seeks, in Ariel Zinder's words, 'the forming of a community through the magic of words'.[16] Yet, at the same time, this is not to deny the profound poetics of the liturgy, and it is precisely these poetics that I am seeking to uncover and present as a necessary and intrinsic part of all liturgical language. Certainly there are poets who move close to a liturgical intensity. Greene offers us close readings of the American pastor and poet Edward Taylor's (1642?–1729) *Preparatory Meditations* and Walt Whitman's *Leaves of Grass* (first edition 1855) as examples in poetry of 'ritual sequences', shunning poetic fictions, synchronic more than diachronic, and realizations more than descriptions. As Charles Feidelson once said of Whitman, the 'I' of his poems, far from asserting itself, is lost and becomes absorbed into the vision.[17] In what is perhaps Whitman's best known poem, the 'I' is absorbed both in time and space so that its mourning is situated in no precise moment or place but in a mythic time, perennial and ever-returning with the turning seasons:

When lilacs last in the door-yard bloom'd,
And the great star early droop'd in the western sky in the night,
I mourn'd – and yet shall mourn with ever-returning spring.[18]

Whitman, it might be argued, in his way knows the context of liturgical language better than either Eliot or Auden.

Such ritual worlds do not provide fictive alternatives, but approach Eliade's sense of sacred time, the time of myth made present and singularity made collective. The 'I' of Whitman's verse is everyone. If in fictional narrative the event always dominates utterance, in liturgical poetics the utterance – the Word – controls and realizes the event.[19] In a sense, it might be said after all that it is this that is truly *pure language*. Here there is no passage of time, while in the Petrarchan *Canzoniere* there is endless process and time passing though without progress:

Seventeen years the heavens have revolved
since I first burned with fire that rages still;
when I think of the state that I am in
I feel a chill within those flames of mine.[20]

Western poetics since Petrarch have struggled with the cultural fading of sacred history, from *Hamlet* to *The Waste Land* (1922), in spite of the problematic insistence of the sacred in verse that is drawn by the fictional narratives of secularization. That is why contemporary poets have had so little to offer to the specific demands of the liturgical. Rather, it is the case that we have forgotten the particular poetics of liturgy itself, known for a brief moment in the second half of the sixteenth century when Sidney could compose *Astrophil and Stella* as well as translate the psalms, and Cranmer only a little earlier could write theologically and with a classical assurance that yet has never prospered in literature (because it is liturgical).[21] Thus, in the history of poetry after Petrarch, Arthur Greene, citing only Edward Taylor[22] and Whitman, writes of the 'nearly clandestine history of the ritual sequence',[23] while the careful demands of liturgical poetics, enacted before God, became forgotten or else lost in the vague and poetically imprecise nostalgia of defenders of the *Book of Common Prayer* in the later twentieth century and beyond.

And so we turn to the Holy Communion liturgy of the Elizabethan *Prayer Book* of 1559, taken substantially from the text of 1549 and, in Judith Maltby's words, 'one of the most ubiquitous texts in Elizabethan England ... a performed and participatory text. It was therefore a text open and accessible to the literate and illiterate, cutting across the boundaries of class, education, and gender.'[24] It was, indeed, probably better known to Shakespeare's audiences than any other text. It is also a supreme achievement of liturgical poetics, an art of language in common speech that is almost entirely now forgotten. It begins:

> Almighty God our heavenly father whiche of thy tender mercye, diddest geve thine onely Sonne Jesus Christ to suffer death upon the Crosse for our redemption ...[25]

Speaking on behalf of the community, the priest addresses God the Father *in heaven*, thereby establishing a *space* that is already theological, between heaven and the earthly life of Jesus Christ at his crucifixion, and a *time* that cannot be identified with our present moment, yet relates to it through the agency of Christ and in his suffering. Time and space here are those of ritual, not fiction, being anywhere where the participants in the liturgy might be, and yet not knowable except theologically.

> Who made ther (by his one oblation of himself once offered) a ful, perfect and sufficient sacrifice, oblation, and satisfaction for the synnes of the whole worlde, and didde institute, and in his holy gospel commaunde us

> to continue a perpetual memory of that his precious deathe, untyll his comminge againe ...[26]

Cranmer's theology demands – for the sacrifice cannot be repeated – that our relative space[27] be anchored in the moment of Christ's crucifixion, a moment that is at once within history and yet transcends the historical. In a perfectly balanced and repeated threefold structure, looking *back* to Christ ('ful, perfect and sufficient'), and *forward* from the particular to the universal 'whole worlde' ('sacrifice, oblation, and satisfaction'), Cranmer places redemption in the widest possible space. This, then, is anchored (and instituted) in the particularity of our worship, based in Scripture, that ensures the moment of Christ's death, once for all, but that also transcends time in a 'perpetual memory', yet still enacted in time until the final eschaton of Christ's second coming. If the Petrarchan lyric continually draws us back to the fictive, specific 'I', in the poetics of the liturgy we are continually being taken, through the instant of Christ's redeeming sacrifice, into the universal that is guaranteed by our continuing, perpetual and communal ritual.

> Heare us O merciful father, we beseech thee, and graunt that we receiving these thy creatures of breade and wine, according to thy sonne our saviour Jesu Christes holy institution, in remembraunce of his death and passion, may be partakers of his moste blessed body and bloude ...[28]

The prayer of the Church now returns and anchors its petition in a further address to God, at this point focused from the broad 'heavenly father' of the beginning to the more personal 'merciful father' whom we now beseech as the attention is upon the particular and specific elements of the bread and wine, linked with the particular event and moment of the Last Supper of Jesus and his disciples. The broad reaches of time and space are governed now by this one moment and occasion, entered into in the action of the Communion, done in remembrance and according to Scripture (Matthew 26.26–28; Mark 14.22–24; Luke 22.19–20; 1 Corinthians 11.23–26). In the action and words spoken in the liturgy, the bread and wine become the 'creatures' by which we partake of the body and blood of Christ.

> Who in the same night that he was betrayed, toke bread, and when he had geven thankes, he brake it, and gave it to his disciples, saying: Take, eate, this is my bodie, which is geven for you. Doe this in remembraunce of me. Likewise after supper, he toke the cuppe, and when he had geven thankes, he gave it to them, saying: Drinke ye all of this, for this is my

> bloude of the new Testament, which is shedde for you and for many, for remission of sinnes: doe this as oft as ye shall drinke it, in remembraunce of me.

The closeness of this text to the wording of William Tyndale's 1534 New Testament translation of 1 Corinthians 11.23–26 is clearly apparent, while F. E. Brightman indicates Cranmer's closeness here also to the *Liturgy of St James*, the ancient liturgy of Jerusalem.[29] The anaphora of St James has been described by Louis Bouyer as 'the most accomplished literary monument of perhaps the whole of liturgical literature',[30] and Bryan Spinks has traced its careful and delicate linguistic shifts in the epiclesis and prayer of consecration.[31]

However, my point here is neither directly liturgical nor scriptural. It concerns the complex liturgical *poetics* of the *Prayer Book* Communion Service. Archbishop Cranmer was a writer of prose and a poor poet. He readily admits as much himself. 'Mine English verses', he wrote, 'want the grace and facility that I wish they had.'[32] Nevertheless this very statement itself, as C. S. Lewis pointed out, 'shows more loyalty to poetry than a wilderness of sonnets'.[33] And this is just my point. Cranmer's liturgy, nurtured by the work of the earlier Continental Reformers,[34] was written on the very edge of the great age of the English Renaissance Petrarchan sonnet and Elizabethan poetry and drama. Lewis emphasizes exclusively Cranmer's genius for translating medieval Latin, and we shall see in a later chapter the close continuity between medieval vernacular traditions of prayer and the Cranmerian liturgy.[35] But what is rarely if ever acknowledged is that, at the same time, Cranmer was perfecting a subtle and complex liturgical poetics that occupies its place alongside, though in liturgical distinction from, the Renaissance lyric poetics of Sidney, Spenser and their fellow poets. And it is precisely this poetics that renders the language of his liturgy so powerfully and subtly reflective of the careful theological demands being made upon it within the shifting liturgical life of the English Church.

But to return to Petrarch for a moment: it has often been remarked that Petrarch's influence on European poetry effected a shift from objective to subjective modes of thought.[36] This is certainly true, but it needs to be taken a little further. Like Cranmer, Petrarch was profoundly educated in classical rhetoric. Indeed, it could hardly have been otherwise. As Lewis once remarked:

> While Tudor education differed by its humanism from that of the Middle Ages, it differed far more widely from ours. Law and rhetoric were the

> chief sources of the difference ... In rhetoric, more than anything else, the continuity of the old European tradition was embodied.[37]

In education and culture the makers of the Anglican liturgy were at one with the broad traditions of humanist scholarship that stretched from Petrarch to Erasmus and of which the primary concern was 'to restore an Augustinian exegesis which is directed to religious feeling rather than the intellect'.[38] But this ran in two directions – on the one hand there is the fictive poetic tradition that built upon the individual and emotion and, on the other, there are the ritualists with their textual liturgical concerns for the communal and the reiterative. Yet although they are distinct, these poetics cannot altogether be separated. Dominic Baker-Smith has called attention to the way in which the theologian and humanist Jacques Lefèvre d'Etaples, sometimes known to us as Jacobus Faber (*c.* 1455–1536), in his *Quincuplex Psalterium* (1509) replaces medieval fourfold exegesis with what he calls the *true* literal sense.[39] Just as Petrarchan sonnets focus upon the singularity of the erotic passion and the suffering poet who weeps and speaks, ritual engagement with the text includes the interpretative response of the reader in the sufferings of love, but also – in the ritual mode – participation as 'partakers of his moste blessed body and bloude'.

In the golden world of Sidney's *Apology for Poetry* (1595), theological colouring gives way to poetic singularity and erotic suggestion in such phrases as 'erected wit' or 'infected will'.[40] Fifty years later Archbishop Laud, at the speech made at his execution on 10 January 1645, speaks within the same textual world of Renaissance metaphysical poetics when he affirms his adherence to the Protestant Church of England in his 'metaphysical' connection between his condition and the passing of the community of the Israelites through the Red Sea.

> I have prayed as my Saviour taught me, and exampled me, *Ut transiret calix ista*, That this Cup of Red Wine might passe away from me, but since it is not that my will may, his will be done; and I shall willingly drinke of this Cup as deep as he pleases and enter into this Sea, aye and passe through it, in the same way he shall be pleased to lead me.[41]

Laud's identification of himself with Christ in the Garden of Gethsemane is possible for him both by his approaching martyrdom and by his theology of Holy Communion – his participation in the liturgy. For a particular moment on Tower Hill, London, time and space are opened upon history and eternity: the crossing of the Red Sea, the agony in the Garden of Gethsemane, and Laud's execution in 1645 are drawn together and open upon eternity within the fiction-turned-liturgical-poetics.

We have seen in this chapter how the fictions of the Renaissance lyric sequence and the dramatic fiction of a character such as Hamlet struggling to invent himself as the revenger with the closing of Purgatory in the Articles of the Church of England[42] render the secularizing traditions of Western poetry awkward for the language of the liturgy. Herein have lain a mistake and a misunderstanding of much liturgical revision in the twentieth and twenty-first centuries concerning language. Liturgical poetics, while being deeply related to the post-Petrarchan tradition, actually follow a profoundly different expression of time and space in the ritualistic and communal rather than the fictive and personal. Keats, writing in 1818 of Wordsworth and the 'egotistical sublime',[43] was setting himself at the Romantic antithesis to any communal liturgical poetic. Much closer to this poetic, as we have suggested, is the poet of *Leaves of Grass*, 'a speaker who participates in every phase of time, to whom no date is closed'. As Arthur Greene continues:

> ... it is much more common for *Leaves of Grass* to depart from evidently Petrarchan designs to find fresh ways of self-definition. Whitman explicitly scatters the tensions of the Petrarchan retrospective topos, for example, to create a work that does not continually define its present moment against a differently colored past and future.[44]

It is not my intention or purpose here to pursue further a discussion of the poetry of Walt Whitman. But it may be worth reflecting on the strangeness that is felt in reading *Leaves of Grass* as a ritual sequence with closer ties to liturgical poetics than we find in almost all other modern poetry except perhaps the Ezra Pound of the *Cantos*. This, to the contemporary reader, slightly unnerving oddity lies in their textual (rather than any contextual) closeness to the poetics of the Elizabethan *Book of Common Prayer*. It is not, in the first instance, a question of theology or belief (though these cannot be, disturbingly, entirely absent even in Whitman), but rather a commonality with Renaissance poetics that is, at the same time, a radical ritual divergence in a sense of time and space, a shift perceived in the movement from Sidney, to Archbishop Laud (a literary man who is also saturated in the language of the *Book of Common Prayer*), and finally to the theologically preoccupied genius of Archbishop Cranmer.

My fundamental point is quite simple. Contemporary obsessions with simple and understandable language in the liturgy miss entirely a fundamental truth about the nature of the complexity of liturgical language and its poetics. Going back to Thomas Cranmer and the *Book of Common Prayer* is not, and cannot be, simply a nostalgic return to a moment when the English language was flourishing in an extraordinary interstice between the late Middle Ages and the Renaissance, but something far more than this. Cranmer's theological battles during the Henrician Reformation in England were carried out and articulated through a sophisticated and educated understanding of textuality and poetics that is then moulded into the liturgical and theological demands of the Church both alongside and apart from the poetry of Spenser, Sidney and later William Shakespeare. When the French humanist Jacques Lefèvre d'Etaples speaks of the *true* literal sense of the psalms he, like Archbishop Laud after him, makes no simple distinction, as later ages have done, between the literal and the metaphorical, a failure, as Samuel Taylor Coleridge observed in *The Statesman's Manual* (1816) of 'the present age'.[45] Coleridge, it may be, is the last serious thinker in the English tradition truly to have understood the peculiar poetics of liturgical language and its necessary theological immersion in a poetics of time and space. Neither the study of literature nor that of theology have acknowledged that truly to understand the genius of Cranmer we must also place him alongside the late medieval/ early Renaissance humanism of Petrarch and, in England, the poets Wyatt, Spenser and Sidney. But we must never forget that they, unlike Cranmer, were not churchmen or theologians.

PART II

Language and Performance in the Liturgy of the Early Church

4

Liturgy and Performance

In his book *The Early Liturgy* (1959), Joseph Jungmann remarks that prayer in the Gospels is characterized by Jesus' insistence that the devotions of his followers should be said in private and in contrast to the great public liturgy of the temple in Jerusalem. In the Sermon on the Mount of St Matthew's Gospel, Jesus emphatically warns against public display and the Gentile habit of 'heaping up empty phrases' (μη βατταλογησητε) or repeating words idly (Matthew 6.7), for many words are of no advantage. Prayer ought not to be ostentatious but private: '...whenever you pray, go into your room and shut the door and pray to your Father who is in secret (ἐν τω κρυπτω); and your Father who sees in secret will reward you' (Matthew 6.6). The particular form of prayer proposed by Jesus, slightly longer in Matthew than in Luke, is the brief and 'characteristically Jewish'[1] Lord's Prayer, a prayer, in the words of Rowan Williams, 'that asks God to sustain in us the sense of our humanity in its fullness and richness'.[2] In the early life of the Church, Jungmann suggests, 'Stephen the Protomartyr shed his blood for the concept that the liturgy of the Old Testament at Jerusalem had to cease and that a new sort of worship which is inward and spiritual must take its place.'[3]

By definition, of course, the language of such inward and private prayers is largely unavailable to us. There are moments in the Gospels when Jesus does pray in community with his disciples, as in the accounts of the Last Supper, but it is somewhat odd that liturgical scholarship has devoted itself almost entirely to the forms and formal language of Christian liturgy and almost entirely neglected the even more elusive language of devotion on the private, and perhaps also more 'popular' and even apparently more primitive, fringes of public worship and its effect upon the formal language of the liturgy and spirituality of the community of the Church as we have later received them. This is all the more strange given the incessant arguments about the nature and form of liturgical language in many churches since the Second Vatican Council, not least within the Anglican Communion, and these will occupy us at length in later chapters of this book (Part IV).

In his recent book *Ancient Christian Worship* (2014), Andrew B. McGowan devotes an early chapter to the 'word' in early Christian reading and preaching.[4] Insisting upon words as not only the medium for the transmission of ideas but also a source of revelation,[5] McGowan nevertheless pays scant attention to the origin and nature of such words beyond the formal texts of Scripture and the Torah in synagogues. What might be of more interest, for our present purposes and for reasons that will become clear, is to look briefly, at the outset, more closely at Hebrew liturgical poetry as it develops in the early centuries CE, and as it has recently been studied by the Jewish Ariel Zinder. Zinder remarks that the term for such poetry is 'Piyyut', which is taken from the Greek *poesis*.[6] Although Zinder dates the flourishing of such Piyyut in the fourth century, it is clearly practised earlier during the series of benedictions known as the *Amidah* (standing), and Zinder suggests:

> It is in the course of this repetition by the precentor that most liturgical poems were recited. These poems would have been written by the precentor himself or by a local poet, or inherited from an older poet or from an unknown source. Naturally these poems were replaceable. If the precentor wrote or found a better poem, the old Piyyut was replaced by a new one.[7]

Existing alongside the more formal liturgical utterances, what is important here is to note the fluidity, informality and capacity for change in such Piyyut as it draws on local poetic practices. Later in his thesis Zinder suggests that this is an example in liturgical practice of what Jacques Derrida would identify in texts as the 'supplement' – that is, the double agent on the fringe of textual formality that is both a supplement to the central text and at the same time itself a central presence, a 'plenitude enriching another plenitude'.[8] Zinder suggests that the relationship between Piyyut and the liturgy is an instance of Derridean supplement:

> The poem indeed adds a 'plenitude upon plenitude' yet it also goes much farther than the liturgical text, thus proposing not an addition but an alternative. Piyyut goes along with the prayer, but also constantly asks: Is prayer enough? Can the communication with God be so compact and restrained? Is it addressing what's really important? As such these poems act as supplements: they seem helpful and indispensable yet are also violent, in constant danger of overflowing, of over-doing what prayer does, of exposing the whole logic of prayer to unanswered questions.[9]

If such vigorous and even violent 'supplement', found on the fringe of worship, is the case in Jewish prayer, how does this impact upon the origins of Christian worship and liturgy in the Jewish tradition? In what sense is the language of the liturgy informed by both the private and the public in the act of worship? Ronald Jasper and Geoffrey Cuming have suggested that the roots of the Christian anaphora lie not so much in the synagogue but in the family and domestic blessing (*berakah*) and above all in the thanksgiving after a meal, the common grace (*birkath ha-mazon*) or blessing over food.[10] Jasper and Cuming emphasize, though this is debatable, the difference between blessing (*berakah*) and thanksgiving (*tōdah*), stressing that prayers of thanksgiving are followed by intercession, and in the *birkath ha-mazon* suggesting the three themes of the blessing of God for creation and for the gift of food and prayer for the restoration of Jerusalem.[11] To the matter of intercessory prayer we will return later. For now it is important to note that all of these themes are apparent in early Christian prayers, linking them, and particularly in the Eucharist, to the family prayers of the Jewish community at Passover, somewhere between the private and the public.

And so, if the synagogue services certainly did contribute to the early Christian language of prayer and the liturgy, perhaps of even more importance are the domestic prayers of blessing and thanksgiving. This would, perhaps, make best sense of the much debated chapters IX and X of the *Didache*, or *The Teaching of the Twelve Apostles*, a work of ethical principles, directions, and liturgical ordinances, dating from possibly as early as the first century,[12] which clearly contain strong echoes of Jewish meal prayers. Thus, it may be suggested that if chapter XIV of the *Didache* offers very broad directives for the formal assembly on the Lord's Day to 'break bread and offer the Eucharist',[13] then chapters IX and X offer much fuller instructions for table prayers at domestic Eucharists, containing the themes of thanksgiving for creation, for food and drink both for refreshment and that of a 'spiritual' nature, and for the perfection of the Church (the new Jerusalem). In chapter IX an instruction is given to pray for 'the holy Vine of thy servant David',[14] to be linked to John 15.1 ('I am the true vine ...') which C. H. Dodd, with reference to the *Didache*, connects with both Old Testament vine symbolism and the early Christian Eucharist.[15]

The point is that these responsorial prayers, with their repeated formula 'Glory be to thee, world without end', appear to be in the nature of table prayers in the Jewish tradition of domestic celebration, and that the words we have in the text of the *Didache* are not prescriptive but allow for the creative freedom of the 'celebrant'. In Staniforth Maxwell's translation, the last sentence of chapter IX reads, 'Charismatists, however, should be free to give thanks as they please.'[16] Such informality in early liturgical language and expression might be set alongside the observation made by Jasper and Cuming that as the earliest liturgies became more formal and prescriptive there was a 'tendency to preserve archaic modes of speech'.[17] This, in the Western tradition, becomes more evident towards the end of the third century as Latin begins to dominate over Greek in the language of the cities of the West. Theodor Klauser has argued that even at the beginning of the third century, while clergy and theologians in Italy were still using Greek, it was only in North Africa, and above all Carthage, that the liturgical transition to Latin was taking place.[18] If we accept Klauser's dating of the predominance of Latin over Greek in Italy as coming at about 300 CE, a time when popes began to use Latin in the inscriptions on the tombs of the predecessors, then:

> We must necessarily conclude that for at least eighty years, *the language of the liturgy in the West was at variance with that of the people.* In those days, too, there had already come into being that cleft between the language of the liturgy and the language of the people which is giving us such trouble today.[19]

For our purposes there are two issues to be taken from this. First, that the formal structures and language of the early liturgies of the Church were already, in their time, becoming more or less remote from the common language of the people, in much the same way as the Latin of the Roman Rite in England in the sixteenth century was remote from the vernacular of the common man or woman. In our own time the same may be said of the English of the *Book of Common Prayer*, but nor should contemporary liturgical English neglect this strangeness. Second, at the same time as a similar process was happening in the Jewish community, around the third or fourth century, a creative common language, perhaps with its origins in the Christian Church in the privacy of Jesus' teaching in the Gospels, was flourishing on the fringes of the formal liturgy of the Church yet still part of it, a 'supplement' which was very much an element in the devotional life in Christianity and the *plebs sancta Dei* – the holy common people of God.[20]

However, this should not be misunderstood as simply allowing freedom of creative expression even in extempore prayer, though this, as we shall shortly see in our reflections upon Amalarius of Metz (*c.* 780–850/1) and the early Middle Ages, may have developed later. Although actually little is really known about Roman liturgical practice before the sixth century,[21] the evidence of the *Apostolic Tradition* generally ascribed to St Hippolytus of Rome, which is usually dated from the first half of the third century, is both that liturgical practice was essentially conservative, Hippolytus' work being written 'to guard the tradition which has remained until now' in the face of recent innovations brought about 'through ignorance or error',[22] and restrained. It is clear that liturgical language is regarded as the expression of a community, not the outpourings of the individual before God, and thus, as far as it can be recovered, the liturgy in Rome avoided any emotional excess in preference to clear speech and ordered prayer.[23]

As we turn to the *Apostolic Tradition*, which remains a central source for our knowledge of the life of the Church and its liturgy in the third century, we need to bear in mind that its original Greek text no longer exists except in a few small fragments. The work was first discovered in 1848 in a manuscript written in the Bohairic dialect of Coptic, and has been subsequently found in Sahidic Coptic, Arabic, Ethiopic, and finally Latin, the last of which exists in only one incomplete late fifth-century manuscript in the form of a palimpsest in the Verona Cathedral library.[24] Our most familiar texts in English, until recently those of Burton Scott Easton (1934) and Dom Gregory Dix (revised by Henry Chadwick, 1968), therefore work largely from a 'vernacular' translation in Latin of a text whose original Greek was probably already becoming remote to the common Christian worshippers in Rome, and which has not survived for our scrutiny.

It might be assumed from the evidence of the *Apostolic Tradition* that the ancient liturgies in Rome were far from fixed in their form. In its most extended comment on extempore worship, taking Dix's translation (without his Greek interpolations) we read:

> And the bishop shall give thanks according to the aforesaid <*models*>. It is not altogether necessary for him to recite a prayer according to a brief form, no one shall prevent him. Only, let his prayer be thanksgiving to God; but let each one pray according to his own ability.
>
> If indeed he is able to pray suitably with a grand and elevated prayer, this is a good thing. But if on the other hand he should pray and recite a prayer according to a fixed form, no one shall prevent him. Only let his prayer be correct and right [*in doctrine*].[25]

The injunction for the bishop to pray to the best of his ability is found in a text as early as Justin Martyr's *First Apology* (67.5), which is addressed to Emperor Antoninus Pius in the second century.[26] In the same work Justin notes that the Greek anaphora in the Eucharist in Rome at about 150 CE was extremely long, whereas, as Henry Chadwick succinctly put it, 'the Latin genius was for brevity'.[27] In the mid third century, St Cyprian of Carthage in *De Dominica Oratione* discourages high-flown words in public worship, preferring instead restraint and quiet in the prayers of the Eucharist.

Thus, in many respects, we find ourselves back to something like the teaching of Our Lord in the Sermon on the Mount in such evidence as we have of the early Roman liturgy, promoting quietness, restraint and succinctness in the words of the liturgy. Yet if the bishop is encouraged to use his own words under the guidance of the eucharistic forms proposed in the *Apostolic Tradition*, it has to be acknowledged that the Eucharistic Prayer itself (Dix, pp. 11–12) has a fluency and grace that is absent elsewhere in the prayers of Hippolytus, suggesting perhaps that its forms and language were beginning to become fixed and formalized even at this early date, though this must remain somewhat speculative. It might seem, therefore, that the bishop was free to find his own language, yet within the formal limits of liturgical tradition – in short, the language of liturgy already was balanced between a conservatism that already was tending towards a somewhat remote medium of liturgical formality, and a creative, somewhat more private, freedom for the bishop, at least, to articulate doctrine and devotion.

At the end of the second century Tertullian, writing in Carthage, in his *Apologeticum* (*c.* 197 CE), suggested to the Church that:

> We gather as one body and congregation so that we might wrestle with God in our prayers, a violence pleasing to him. We also pray for our rulers, for their ministers and for those in power, for the state of the world, for peace, and for the end to be delayed.[28]

The idea here of violence returns us to something like the Jewish Piyyut as described by Ariel Zinder. Common prayers linked with the Eucharistic liturgy are evident also in the *First Apology* (*c.* 150 CE) of Justin Martyr, though without the element of 'wrestling with God' that we find in Tertullian, which suggests an energy and a striving for words as well as the concern for including everyday matters – 'the state of the world' – that indicates how such prayer was both flexible and timely. Within the Eucharist itself there are no prayers of intercession in Hippolytus' *Apostolic Tradition*, though Justin Martyr reports that the 'prayers of the faithful', named after the diptychs – that is the two lists of names, one for the living and one for the dead, read by a deacon at the Eucharist – were uttered between the sermon and the preparation of the gifts.[29] The derivation of these prayers was almost certainly from the informal Jewish *berakah*, or prayers of domestic blessing, to which reference has already been made.[30]

The similarity of such prayers to those in the Alexandrian *Liturgy of St Mark* has been noted by Jasper and Cuming. They suggest an origin for this liturgy as early as the second century.[31] Thus, if in the Western liturgy there seems little evidence of free intercessory prayer at the time of the *Apostolic Tradition*, the anaphora of the liturgy of Alexandria in the Eastern Mediterranean from an early date has lengthy, and developing, intercessory prayers immediately after the preface, the language of which embraces every aspect of political and daily life. After prayers for 'the emperor, the army, the princes, councils, townships, neighbourhoods', prayers are then extended to the sick, those in prison or the mines, travellers by land and sea, a good harvest, the poor and orphaned, the military and finally the departed.[32] Characteristic of the language of these prayers is the manner in which the everyday concerns give rise to a metaphorical form of prayer for this life – the literal giving rise to the metaphor. For example:

> Give a good journey to our brothers who have gone abroad or are about to go abroad in every place, whether by land or by river, on lakes or on roads, or travelling by any means; bring them all back from everywhere to a quiet harbour, to a safe harbour; vouchsafe to sail and to journey with them; return them rejoicing to their rejoicing families, in health to healthy families. And also, Lord, keep our sojourn in this life free from harm and storm until the end.[33]

Such transition from the language of the commonplace into the metaphorical and theological is characteristic also, it may be noted, of the 'Prayers and Thanksgivings upon several occasions' added to the Litany, Morning and Evening Prayer in the 1662 *Book of Common Prayer*.[34]

Evidence of this pattern of common prayer in the West from the middle of the third century is found in Cyprian's treatise on the Lord's Prayer, which is clearly based on the earlier work of Tertullian. Behind all such intercessory prayer is the language of the everyday, though there is clear evidence of the fear and danger of this becoming disordered and personal. Cyprian writes, again with clear echoes of the Sermon on the Mount:

> When we gather as one with the brethren and celebrate the divine sacrifices with God's priest, we are to be mindful of moderation and proper order. We are not to bandy about our prayers with disordered voices nor to beseech God with confused wordiness when we should do so with modesty since God hears the heart, not the voice.[35]

Cyprian continues to insist that the Church's prayer is never private or individual, but public and communal, for the Church is one. Furthermore, prayer is to be understood both spiritually and literally, rooted in the realities of life yet also concerned with the things of God. Liturgical language, like the language of poetry, does not work simply at one level.

Here a brief mention should be made of the place of hymns in Christian worship and liturgy. It is clear that St Paul promoted the singing of hymns as he encouraged the Christians in Colossae: 'with gratitude in your hearts sing psalms, hymns and spiritual songs to God' (ψαλμοις, υμνοις, ᾠδαις πνευματικαις) (Colossians 3.16). In classical Greek a ὕμνος is a festive song in praise of gods or heroes, and thus, by derivation in the Christian tradition, a song of praise addressed to God.[36] Jungmann in *The Early Liturgy* has indicated how early Christian liturgy and worship adopted (and adapted) many elements in pagan religion, not least the language and style of prayers and hymns.[37] But Theodor Klauser has argued that, at least in Rome, 'the growth of Latin liturgical poetry [and hymnody] ... met with strong opposition' in the face of liturgical practice that 'was on the whole almost puritanical in its severity and brevity'.[38] Nevertheless, there is some evidence that two early Greek hymns, the still familiar *hymnus angelicus* or *Gloria* and the *Agnus Dei*, were known at an early date in Rome, though in the case of the former its use was restricted to high festivals. Such severity was less prevalent in the East, and hymns like the *Phos Hilaron* (still sung in English in John Keble's nineteenth-century translation, 'Hail, gladdening Light'), which was regarded by St Basil the Great (*c.* 330–79) as extremely ancient,[39] were sung during the evening office as early as the second century.

In the later Latin West, Augustine, in his commentary on Psalm 148, describes a hymn as 'the praise of God in song', and attributes four hymns to St Ambrose of Milan (*c.* 339–97): *Aeterna rerum conditor*, *Deus creator omnium*, *Iam surgit hora tertia*, and *Veni redemptor gentium*. These Latin hymns are all characterized by a simplicity of iambic metre, clarity of meaning and simple language that is easy to memorize, and this is suggestive of congregational use. Thus the first verse of *Veni redemptor gentium* reads:

Veni, redemptor gentium,
Ostende partum Virginis;
Miretur omne saeculum:
Talis decet partus Deum.

(O come, Redeemer of the earth,
and manifest thy virgin-birth.
Let every age in wonder fall:
Such birth befits the God of all.)

(Trans. J. M. Neale)

This hymn's popularity is evidenced by the mention of it by Pope Celestine in a sermon preached against the Nestorians in Rome in 430. It is also quoted by Bishop Faustus of Riez (d. 490 CE) and Cassiodorus (d. 757 CE), both of whom attribute it to Ambrose. According to tradition, Ambrose's hymns were sung by the people in Milan during the night vigils in the bishop's church.[40] After the fourth century Latin hymns grew in number, and clearly indicate a Latin that is designed to accompany the liturgy of the Church that was very much of and for the people.

The characteristic severity of the Roman liturgy remained, however, until at the end of the seventh century Pope Sergius (d. 701 CE) made the singing of popular hymns (above all the *Agnus Dei*) formally part of the preparation for communion. Significantly, Sergius was not himself a Roman, but a native of Antioch in Syria, elected by popular acclaim and active also in the English church.[41] He thus combined the liturgical energy of the East with an exposure to the more flamboyant style and language of the Gallican liturgy and the worship of the Celtic and Germanic churches before the time of Charlemagne. It was largely through St Sergius that 'the Roman liturgy was enriched by a series of prayers which were both less austere in their ideas and less reserved in their language'.[42]

It is with this turn to the Gallican Church of the far West that we move finally to a figure in the Church of the early Middle Ages, and a greater personality in the history of the Western liturgy than has been properly recognized: that is to Amalarius of Metz, who was probably Bishop of Trier from about 809 to 813, dying in 850 [851]. It is not insignificant that Henri Cardinal de Lubac devoted the second part of his great liturgical work *Corpus Mysticum: The Eucharist and the Church in the Middle Ages* (1949, trans. 2006) to the liturgical theology of Amalarius, though de Lubac begins with a violent quotation from his arch-enemy Deacon Florus of Lyons as he denounces Amalarius in his work *Adversus Amalarium.*

> Arian! Nestorian! False prophet! Man of unheard-of audacity, puffed up with carnal ideas, worse than Pelagius! Enemy of the faith, of Scripture and of the Church! Ridiculous and sacrilegious opinions! Confused and muddle-headed words! Perverse dogmas, foolish fables! Monsters of absurdity! Books full of stupidity, folly, delirium and profane novelties,

> full of pernicious errors, lies, blasphemies and heresies! Books inspired by demons, books that absolutely must be burned![43]

Florus did not mince his words. De Lubac's concerns in *Corpus Mysticum* are primarily with Amalarius' liturgical theology and his understanding of the *threefold body* in the Eucharist. My concerns here are somewhat different. In his major work, the *Liber Officialis*, and also in his *Eclogae de Officio Missae*, Amalarius outlines and then describes in detail his understanding of what O. B. Hardison Jr has called 'the rememorative allegory of the Mass'.[44] That is, following in a tradition that leads us back at least to the travels of the Spanish nun Egeria to Jerusalem between 381 and 384 CE in which she describes the dramatic liturgical following of the events of Holy Week in the holy places of the ancient city,[45] Amalarius understands the Eucharist as a dramatic, allegorical enactment of the life and Passion of Our Lord. A careful distinction needs to be made, however. The Anglican scholar Kenneth Stevenson, in his work on the liturgy of Holy Week,[46] distinguishes between what Hardison calls the 'rememorative' from the 'representational'. It is, in fact, the latter term that should properly, and more problematically, be applied to the liturgical writings of Amalarius, while the former sustains a more strictly liturgical sense in which the events within the liturgical action (the Last Supper, etc.) are recalled liturgically within the drive to portray them literally or act them out. This distinction is clarified in Douglas Jones' Introduction to the Church of England liturgical book *Lent, Holy Week, Easter: Services and Prayers* (1984) which anticipates the later Church of England *Common Worship: Times and Seasons* (2006). Jones writes:

> … we have distanced ourselves from every attempt simply to reconstruct past events. This is of special importance in these services, where the temptation is strong to encourage an imaginative representation of the events of our Lord's life. We do not think of assisting worshippers by mental efforts to go back to the first Palm Sunday and Good Friday. We think of assisting them to make a present liturgical celebration. The cross and the resurrection are inseparable.[47]

This distinction is a proper one, but indicates what might best be described as a creative fracture between the properly liturgical and the living, imaginative worshipping life of the Church. To put this more simply, it is a creative fracture between liturgy and performance, and it was this creative fracture over which Amalarius and Florus were debating in the ninth century. In Book III of the *Liber Officialis*, which is given entirely to a discussion of the Eucharist, Amalarius makes it quite plain that for him the liturgy is to be celebrated as ritual drama involving both clergy and people through word, gesture and action. In the Preface to his great work Amalarius writes:

> Sacraments should have likeness to the things for which they are sacraments. Therefore the celebrant should be like Christ, just as the bread, wine and water are similar to the body of Christ.[48]

Amalarius appreciates the power of the dramatic and the imaginative in liturgical celebration even though we might, at the same time, acknowledge the liturgical propriety of Douglas Jones and Kenneth Stevenson's more cerebral statement on rememorative liturgical celebration. In short, Amalarius is sensitive to the 'literal' and role-playing element in the liturgy of the Eucharist that involves a lively use of common, culturally embedded language, a perception that was perhaps the missing element in the language debates of the later twentieth century in the Church of England – to which we will give closer attention later – and was certainly present in the early liturgical acknowledgement of the dramatic (and theological) power of language and style in pagan worship as it was adopted into the Christian liturgy.[49]

Clearly Amalarius was far from unlearned in liturgical matters. He had been a pupil and admirer of Alcuin of York (*c.* 740–804) and was well aware of the work of Christian theologians and historians from Augustine to Bede, and his understanding of the delicate relationship between the inner and outer senses (which, for him, emerges in the dramatic celebration of the liturgy) bears close analogy to the cosmic-negative theology of his great contemporary at the Carolingian court, the theologian John Scotus Eriugena (*c.* 810–*c.* 877).[50] He was also perfectly well aware of the power of the Church's fourfold interpretation of Scripture – that both the Bible and the liturgy work (like all good poetry) on a number of simultaneous levels as we read and participate dramatically in them. As Hardison has pointed out, Amalarius is often closer in spirit to what we would now understand as a literary critic rather than a theologian[51] and this is by no means insignificant in any debates, then and now, concerning the subtleties of liturgical language and practice.

In his liturgical instructions Amalarius is ever sensitive to the living context of language and culture – returning not to abstract issues of accessibility to the understanding, but rather to its rootedness in native song and custom that are meaningful at far deeper, even more private, levels. In the *Eclogae de Officio* he writes (though the Latin is far from clear):

Idcirco precor cantores ut non prius despiciant nostra, quam discutiant ea iuxta ordinem librorum at rotunditatem rationis. Et si invenerint minus congruere ea ordini librorum et rationi alicui, dent indulgentiam meae emperitae; sin autem non despiciant edere nostra olera, qua rubra testas illis ministrat ...

(Therefore I beg the singers not to despise our [proposals] before they consider them in relation to the arrangement (rule?) of the books and the sphere of reason. And if they find them less appropriate to the arrangement of the books and for some particular reason, please excuse my lack of expertise. But do not despise our fruits with their rustic skins ...)[52]

Amalarius then justifies his position by referring to Pope Gregory's advice given to Augustine of Canterbury in which he recommends the use of the living native tradition, not least in the development of a liturgical language.

It may be said, then, that Amalarius was the first churchman in the Western tradition to apply fully the allegorical exegesis of Scripture to the liturgy and develop this in a representational form.[53] The response to Amalarius by his opponents has something of the liturgical hesitance and nicety of Stevenson and Jones in our own day as they prefer the more sober liturgical 'rememorative' to the more dramatic and engaging 'representational' in the celebration of the Eucharist. They may in a sense be right, but something has been lost. Amalarius was denounced as a heretic at the Synod of Quiercy in 838 and removed from the see of Lyons. Deacon Florus accuses him of corrupting the churches in France, not least in his stimulating the *simpliciores* to improper practices. These are described more precisely by Bishop Agobard of Lyons in terms of 'theatrical mannerisms and stage music', and much later in the twelfth century, in wildly overstated terms, by Aelred, Abbot of Rievaulx (1109–67), who complains in his *Speculum Charitatis* of feminine singing, dramatic sighs and priests who 'contort the whole body with histrionic gestures' which 'amaze the common people' but are more of 'the theatre, not the oratory'.[54]

Nevertheless, in his careful and detailed description of the Mass in Book III of the *Liber Officialis*, Amalarius is very precise in his theological sense of the complex combination of word and symbol, both embedded in a recognition of popular sensibility. And, as Joseph Jungmann has been careful to point out, in his liturgical proposals for the Latin Mass Amalarius 'marked out the trend for the future'.[55] Thus, some 150 years after Amalarius we find St Ethelwold, Bishop of Winchester in his *Regularis Concordia* (*c.* 965–75) proposing dramatic liturgical tropes to his clergy as part of his attempt to revive English monasticism after the dark days of the Danish invasions. For these he was drawing directly on continental practices, particularly those of the abbey of Fleury.[56] The effect of the exposure of the austere Roman liturgy to the Gallican tradition of the Frankish and Celtic churches was a new creativeness in liturgical language that finally rediscovered itself again, if it was ever entirely lost, in the lay liturgical language of the Middle Ages, to which I shall turn in some detail in Chapter 6. Even as the formal Latin Rite, as is perhaps inevitable with the formal tendency, noted as we have seen by Jasper and Cuming, of all liturgies to preserve archaic modes of speech, remained embedded in a language and form ever more remote from the language of the people, the energy of the liturgical spirituality of Amalarius remains within popular devotion and liturgy. For a time, in the Carolingian epoch, Jungmann suggests, this energy was apparent, despite the conservative opposition in the Church, in 'a spiritual life which sparkled especially in the monasteries and in the cathedrals', where scholarship was also recovering the study of Greek culture and the ancient creative energies of the Antiochene liturgy of the Eastern tradition.[57] It is a question whether such sparkle remains today.

Thus, in this brief review of some of the early liturgies of the Church and their language, I would seek to add a somewhat different tone to what might be termed the more 'purely' liturgical concerns of scholarship that extends from Deacon Florus to the present day. For example, in his widely read and respected book *Eucharist: Theology and Spirituality of the Eucharistic Prayer* (1966, trans. 1968), Louis Bouyer writes of the Eucharist in the Roman Catholic Church during the period of the Reformation and after.

> Here, obviously, with the eucharistic canon and its retinue of prefaces, the ancient eucharist still subsisted. However, even though it was not necessary to retrieve it, a pressing need still existed to *divest it from much incongruous veneer*, and to return it to an intelligent manner of being observed.
>
> ... The modern Roman missal, without excluding completely the apologies and the other medieval devotional prayers, restricted them to the preparation of the celebrant and his ministers, to the offertory and the communion. Furthermore, it generally retained only the best of these. As for the tropes, they disappeared completely, only to return, unfortunately, in our own day in a still less felicitous form with too many inadmissible paraphrases of the chants of the ordinary and trivial commentaries.[58]

My unease with this is not precisely with its liturgical claims as such. I suggested in Chapter 1 that Catherine Pickstock has rightly defended the complexities of the Roman Rite against the arguments of Bouyer.[59] All practice will, in the course of time and repeated use, require refreshment and a return to early principles. But apart from Bouyer's somewhat pompous tone, the difficulty lies with his assumption that the liturgy is ultimately a rather disembodied, theological concept that requires a kind of purity of practice that is carefully governed from on high in the Church with, it has to be said, vague overtones of the patriarchal Grand Inquisitor of Dostoevsky. In fact, its language is more living and with a greater poetic complexity than Bouyer seems to admit. All liturgical revision faces the delicate challenge of balancing proper scholarship, as it seeks to preserve the careful traditions of the Church, with a sense of the living, poetic language and culture of spirituality and true worship. The tropes which Bouyer so quickly dismisses, as I have already suggested in Part I, are part of the life of the liturgy as Amalarius and Ethelwold clearly recognized, and it is a life that can be traced back even as far as St Paul and his encouragement of the singing of hymns, and even, perhaps, to the spirit of the Sermon on the Mount itself with its suspicion of the dangers of the over-formality of public worship and its sense of prayers said, perhaps, on the edge. This is what Tertullian calls a violence and a wrestling with God in our prayers in a tentativeness, an energy and perhaps an uncertainty in extempore and changing forms of words that is 'pleasing to him'.[60] It is an interesting example, and in an unlikely place, of the Derridean concept of the supplement.

5

Hippolytus and *The Apostolic Tradition*

The present chapter will develop the theme of theatre and performance in liturgy and its language, but in a rather different way from the previous chapter. I will continue to give attention to Hippolytus' *Apostolic Tradition*, but now in dialogue with a remarkable book published many years ago that has never received the attention it deserves. The book is Peter Malekin and Ralph Yarrow's *Consciousness, Literature and Theatre: Theory and Beyond* (1997),[1] and its concerns are with spirituality and a particular model of consciousness and what Malekin and Yarrow call 'spirit in performance'. This is rooted in a profound sense of underlying unity in true consciousness – non-sequential and a-temporal – that begins with lines from T. S. Eliot's *Four Quartets*:

> Time past and time future
> Allow but a little consciousness.
> To be conscious is not to be in time.[2]

It is this model of the mind, this 'spirit in performance', that I seek here to apply to the primitive Christian eucharistic liturgy with particular attention to *The Apostolic Tradition*, attributed to St Hippolytus of Rome.

As I noted in the last chapter,[3] the origins of this work are complex and debated and it has often been remarked that it presents the outline of a liturgy that was never actually celebrated or that it was on its way to be obsolete even when it was written.[4] Literally this may perhaps have been the case, given the particular nature and possible purpose of Hippolytus' writing, but there are larger issues of performance and text to be considered and it is not my intention here to engage in the historical and indeed theological issues that are the customary trademarks of liturgical scholarship. Suffice it to remind ourselves that *The Apostolic Tradition* is extant in Latin, Coptic, Arabic and Ethiopic versions and, although it has generally been regarded as reflecting practices in Rome towards the end of the second century CE, more recent scholarly opinion places it in Egypt and more precisely Alexandria. The work as a whole constitutes what is known as a Church Order (an alternative title that was sometimes given to it in the nineteenth century is *The Egyptian Church Order*), a form of document that first appeared in the second century and reached its full development by the end of the fourth century as 'systematic manuals of disciplinary and liturgical rules for which the collective authority of the whole apostolate was claimed'.[5] As a text, therefore, *The Apostolic Tradition* offers intriguing possibilities for questions of performance as the celebrant is not given a precise text but merely guidelines, suggesting a creativity and variety in 'performance' that was later restricted as the liturgy of the Mass became textually rigid and theologically and more dogmatically controlled. Certainly what Gregory Dix calls the Paschal Mass is dramatically described by Hippolytus in terms of its 'effect' upon those present as the bishop gives thanks

> and milk and honey mixed together in fulfilment of the promise which was <*made*> to the Fathers, wherein He said I will give you a land flowing with milk and honey; which Christ indeed gave, <*even*> His Flesh, whereby those who believe are nourished like little children, making the bitterness of the <*human*> heart sweet by the sweetness of His word (λογος);
> water also for an oblation for a sign of the laver, that the inner man also, which is psychic, may receive the same <*rites*> as the body.
> And the bishop shall give an explanation (λογος) concerning all these things to them who receive.[6]

The reasoned intelligence, the merging of soul and body into one (Dix's rather odd word 'psychic' could also be rendered 'soul'[7]), the realizing of the promise (the entry into Canaan, Christ's Passion) in present experience – all draw us closer to the sense of consciousness or mind as understood by Malekin and Yarrow without the demanding overlay of theology and doctrine as they accumulated in the later Middle Ages.

Moving on some one hundred and fifty years after *The Apostolic Tradition* we return to the Spanish nun Egeria's vivid descriptions for her sisters back in Spain of the Passiontide liturgy in Jerusalem that dramatically embeds theology in the often exhausting 'performance' of Jesus' last days in the city. But this performance, led by the words of the bishop, is not for any audience but rather for the realization of the 'effects' of the participation in events that are at once rooted in the past, experienced entirely in the present, and bring time itself to a halt in an eschatological sense of eternal truth. Finally, to be conscious is not to be in time. Egeria writes dramatically:

> Then the bishop speaks a word of encouragement to the people. They have been hard at it all night, and there is further effort in store for them in the day ahead. So he tells them not to be weary, but to put their hope in God, who will give them a reward out of all proportion to the effort they have made ... And in this way they continue the readings and hymns ... It is impressive to see the way all the people are moved by these readings, and how they mourn. You could hardly believe how every single one of them weeps during the three hours in which the Lord suffered for us.[8]

From scriptural text, at the reading of which the people weep, the weeping becomes nothing less than a participation in the text itself, and a felt sense of the drama of salvation that is being enacted.

This sense of sacred drama, lived simultaneously at different levels, was to continue up to the high Middle Ages via, as we saw in the last chapter, the controversial figure of Amalarius of Metz. The sense of drama in the liturgical descriptions of Amalarius lead O. B. Hardison Jr to comment that it communicates a mode of existence that can finally only be known by the felt experience of it. The bishop's enemies at the Synod of Quiercy condemned him for 'corrupting' the Church throughout France, Bishop Agobard complaining of his '*theatralibus sonis et scenicis modulationibus*' ('theatrical mannerisms and stage music'),[9] though it is quite clear that the sense of the dramatic performance, the significance of church vestments as, in a sense, costumes and the paten, candles, thurible and so on as stage properties were part of a dramatic tradition which saw the Mass as the archetypal drama within the mould of which, by speech and action, each guiding the other, the individual dramas of people's lives may be shaped. Theology is realized not as doctrine but through and within language in performance.

But we must return to the work of Malekin and Yarrow and its relationship with the liturgy of Hippolytus at the beginning of the third century CE. There are two points to be made. To start with, Malekin and Yarrow's model of mind and their holistic sense of consciousness (which for them looks back also to Indian spirituality as well as the plays of Shakespeare in performance and Heideggarian modes of thinking[10]) allows us access to Amalarius' sense of theology in performance in the Mass as actually entering into (without precisely explaining) the matter of Christology and the doctrine of the Trinity, known through and across time and space. Peter Malekin, a lecturer in English literature who was not himself a professing Christian, as we shall see, actually uses 'trinitarian' language in his descriptions of consciousness, and catches his own sense of the unity of all being in an essay on Wordsworth writing 'Lines written a few miles above Tintern Abbey' in which the 'mind of man' seeks to grasp the 'spontaneous unarticulated awareness of the divine ground of its own individual being'. It is an awareness in the words of the poet, and found also at moments within the language of liturgical performance that, as Malekin remarks,

> is again commonly recorded among the mystics, and the Christian mystics, if they placed it within a theological framework, tended to interpret it as an awareness of the individual within the transcendence of the Godhead, rather than the experience of the manifest personal God. Wordsworth seems to feel the same, though he leaves the word 'God' without further definition.[11]

The impersonality of the remark is important. Within such dramatic poetics it is finally transcendence that reaches out to us rather than we seeking to articulate anything of the personal God.

Now the second point: in the text of *The Apostolic Tradition* we read an ordinance that, if the precise words of the text themselves were never actually 'celebrated', the spoken word of the liturgy clearly arises out of a performance that in its multilayered complexity gives rise, in the first instance, to the text (rather than the other way around). Modern liturgists should, perhaps, take note of this status of the text. Hippolytus breathes the air of spirit in rememorative performance which links him with the later Amalarius and results in the characteristically sharp and perceptive, if not entirely fair, portrait of him by Dom Gregory Dix (which might almost be a portrait of himself as a liturgist) as 'a wide rather than a deep or accurate scholar, an exegete and commentator rather than an original thinker, with a mind awake to theological difficulties, but not sufficiently balanced or profound to contribute adequate solutions ...'[12] But the observation could be turned around. In *The Apostolic Tradition* we encounter a form of theological thinking through the experience of the liturgy which, to theologians and liturgists, might seem to miss the point precisely because the point has been reached by another route and without the need for what becomes too often pedantic over-articulation, a too anxious demand for plain sense in words. Within the hospitality of proper liturgical expression we may be continually surprised by our felt agreements, even while differing in matters of articulated doctrine and creed. Though perhaps driven by political necessity, Cranmer was a master of the felt agreement in liturgy, of words and a grammar which have a capaciousness that should characterize Anglican worship at its best but is often lost in our smaller squabbles.

As we turn to the eucharistic text of *The Apostolic Tradition* an exercise of the imagination is immediately required. If we assume that the work does indeed reflect the practice of the church in Rome perhaps in the middle to later years of the second century CE or, as the text states, 'the tradition which has continued until now',[13] we can also assume that any such liturgical celebration, presided over by the bishop, was not in some spacious basilica but rather in a house-church of domestic proportions. There is no evidence in Rome of any larger buildings until the last decades of the third century, and even then the original sense of church building was being expressed by the North African Christian apologist Arnobius of Sicca (d. *c.* 330) as late as the Diocletian persecution, when he demanded, 'Do we honour God with shrines and by building temples?'[14] Until the early fourth century, the Eucharist was almost certainly celebrated as, in J. G. Davies' words, 'a domestic gathering, relatively informal, with sacred and secular united',[15] and it is in this context that we must seek to appropriate and understand *The Apostolic Tradition*, a self-confessed work of conservatism.

Thus we must begin with an act of the imagination – seeing the universe in small room, eternity in the moment and not on the great stage of a magnificent cathedral but in a drama played out within domestic confines. Malekin and Yarrow begin their chapter on theatre and drama in *Consciousness, Literature and Theatre* with this statement: 'If the essential spiritual function of narrative is to locate and activate the impulse to narrate – telling the story of meaning – the fundamental of drama is to enact and embody that story.'[16] Drama and its words work through bodies and in such a way that there is no clear distinction between mind, consciousness and body. In other words, there must be a move away from the text-object ('the play', or indeed the liturgy, as text) into a different mode of being and into a new model of consciousness.[17] Now let us turn, then, to the *sursum corda* of Hippolytus. (The English text used will be that of Jasper and Cuming in *Prayers of the Eucharist*, pp. 34–8, as being the simplest and clearest.)[18]

[*Bishop*]
The Lord be with you.
And all shall say:
The Lord be with you.
And with your spirit.
Up with your hearts.[19]
We have (them) with the Lord.
Let us give thanks to the Lord.
It is fitting and right.

From the very beginning, through the action of the 'heart', the worshippers are transported so that before the bishop even begins to speak properly they are placed liminally between two realms, the earthly and the divine, speaking, as is right, thanks to God. Here then body, mind and spirit are one.

And so we return to Malekin and Yarrow as they address the question of theatre and spirit.[20] Understanding spirituality as the condition of consciousness beyond duality, they grant it 'equivalence with cosmic play in its potential state'. In more theological language this might be said to be an eschatological understanding of consciousness. Spirituality, in other words, is never static but can only be 'known' as a progressive and dramatic process. Meaning is made, both individually and collectively, by closely interrelated verbal and non-verbal sign systems, the spirit performative. Such performance transcends time and space (Malekin and Yarrow refer us to the Prologue[21] of Shakespeare's *Henry V*, a play that in three hours embraces, by a willing suspension of disbelief, five years of history), the spiritual dimension known in the theatre in speech, actions and the interweaving of 'states' of space and time such that theatre itself 'can be used to bring about a spiritual transformation in the individual and the community'.[22] In particular, as an actor enters into a role, the possibility offered for improvisation within the adopted role creates opportunities to create new worlds and to transcend the limitations of our present mode of being. Amalarius in his liturgical proposals, one feels, would have understood this.

In *The Apostolic Tradition* the bishop begins to speak on behalf of the gathered people. His words are addressed to God the Father who could be said, therefore, to be a singular 'audience' for a performance of the whole gathered Church, and yet it is God who 'acts' in the sending of his Son, Jesus Christ, as our saviour and redeemer. It is the Son, in what might be described as 'enacted Christology', who overcomes and embraces in his being the duality of human and divine, flesh and spirit, drawing the people towards God through the drama of the Passion, and thus, in the bishop's words, 'gaining for you a holy people'.[23] As St Athanasius (*c.* 296–373) was to articulate it a century later in his great work *De Incarnatione*, it is in the action of God in the Son (the λογος) whereby fallen humanity is restored to the image of God, the drama leading us towards a conclusion that is the realization also of the beginning, a realization of what Malekin would have called 'fullness of consciousness' or 'an awareness of immortality'.[24] As to the question of the epiclesis in the Eucharist of *The Apostolic Tradition*, it is clear that this is not theologically driven to bring about some change in the elements, as would be the case in the fourth century,[25] but is called forth 'for the strengthening of faith in truth'. It is thus in the Spirit, and through the language of the liturgy, that the community is reunited and becomes one in a singularity of being that is echoed in Peter Malekin's own non-Christian spirituality. But in *The Apostolic Tradition*, as in an even earlier Christian work which provides us with an outline of the eucharistic action, the *Didache*, it is through the action of the Holy Spirit and the broken bread that the Church is 'brought together from the ends of the earth into thy kingdom'.[26]

I am not wishing in any sense to imply that there is a sort of fugitive Christianity in Malekin's thinking on the nature of consciousness and spirit. He would rightly have resented that. My point is about the particular nature of this form of poetic language. And I would certainly wish to suggest that Malekin would have clearly understood the dramatic force of the proposed Eucharistic Prayer of *The Apostolic Tradition* and its 'eschatology'. This is not least the case as we reach the most complex part of that prayer.

According to Malekin and Yarrow the pivotal condition of consciousness in spiritual development is characterized by a certain 'neutrality', a sense of detachment[27] that results in a condition of liminality that is a state of giving and being given and in which 'a different status for the Self becomes available'.[28] This would seem to describe well, at least, what Hippolytus knows as the Spirit-filled unity of the eucharistic community, that is the whole Church in its eschatological participation in the risen life of Christ. And such a condition is to be considered in relation to four elements: performers, character, audience and performance-text. Before we return to the anaphora of *The Apostolic Tradition* we need to give brief attention to each of these elements, inasmuch as the complex (and often textually ambiguous) structure of the Eucharistic Prayer mingles each element in the dramatic 'performance', as performer becomes audience and character is merged between the different participants until all become one in anticipation under the direction of the performance-text.

Performance, first, demands a shedding of self, an embracing of neutrality that Malekin and Yarrow describe in terms of an ancient tradition of Christian theology and spiritual formation, that which is known as the negative way. They write:

> The exercise is an exploration, an attempt to recreate the first awakening to the experience of being alive. There is no need to do anything (most performers start to try, however ...). There is no script or score. That is the condition which Grotowski also sought through his *via negativa*: a kind of wiping clean of that which is known, a return to the ground of knowingness.[29]

As a Christian priest myself I recognize immediately the experience of 'celebrating' in the Eucharist which is the very opposite of any intention or histrionic performance, but a sense of being led and sustained by the words of the liturgy (or rather the drama within the words) to a state of neutrality in which, at best and very occasionally, one loses the sense of being present altogether.[30] From such renunciation stems an endless exchange of 'character' – roles merge in performance, the speaker and the listener, the dancer and the dance,[31] become one. At this point the impossible, we might say, is realized in utterance. Malekin and Yarrow speak of this in relation to the performance of Shakespeare (*The Winter's Tale*) and Bertolt Brecht (*The Good Person of Szechwan*), but it is equally, and even perhaps more, the case with the dramatic offering and receiving of the gifts of the Spirit in Hippolytus' liturgy.

> The impossible, which is one of the realms of theatre (and Paulina [in *The Winter's Tale*] is working a particularly theatrical, but none the less deeply significant trick[32]) can occur only if you are open to it: not rejecting, not anticipating, simply available ...
>
> But the essential moment from our point of view here is not the successful outcome but the state of preparedness ...[33]

In such a state, character and audience merge, each drawn together in the stillness of waiting – a liminal waiting upon God or (and the difference is not, after all so great, if we had but the sense of humour to realize it) a *Waiting for Godot* (*En attendant Godot*). The despair of Beckett's play is, after all, only a hair's breadth away from the breathlessness of Simone Weil's *Waiting on God* (1950). And the stillness is all – liturgy has always properly known, though all too rarely observed, the necessity for silence in language,[34] of allowing the words spoken to create the dramatic space as a passage into the unknown, delicately balanced between the private and the collective in a spirit of generosity.

The performance-text is the beginning, each action unique as an opening up *towards* meaning projected in both sound and silence. In a key sentence, Malekin and Yarrow write of the words as spoken by the actor that 'they require not pointing to make a meaning clear, but self-abnegation to avoid impeding it'.[35] The priest knows this also. Meaning, properly, is waiting to be found. It is not present for all to see in words made too literal, simple and plain. However, within the development of the Mass as it entered into the high Middle Ages, the words became fixed, hung upon theological frameworks that struggled to *define* meaning, and there was lost, at least in the Roman Rite, that early, more improvisatory freedom that looked *towards* meaning as it was offered in word, gesture, movement and silence. And it was this freedom, as we shall see in the next chapter, that Thomas Cranmer captured in his liturgy as he drew also upon the lively traditions of vernacular worship in late medieval England. In *The Apostolic Tradition*, the bishop's words addressed to God gradually draw us from the cosmic creation of all things through the divine Word to the particularity of the Christ of the Last Supper and the Passion. From this point in the anaphora 'character', time and place begin to merge. *We* are present at the Supper of Bread and Wine as the bishop speaks the dominical words, flowing from which, and in their 'historical' origin, are the purposes, cosmic and eschatological, of the action: that Christ might destroy death; break the bonds of the devil; tread down hell; shine upon the righteous; and manifest the resurrection.

Everything centres upon the key words and actions – the eating of the 'broken' body and the drinking of the shed blood, in bread and wine,[36] and the statement, 'When you do this, you make my remembrance.' It is, of course, a key moment in Reformation theological debate. Gregory Dix renders this in Hippolytus, 'When ye do this [ye] do My "anamnesis".'[37] More provocatively Burton Scott Easton suggests, 'As often as ye perform this, perform my memorial.'[38] In this 'performance' the effects are brought to life and, in the power of the Holy Spirit, the unity of consciousness and being within the gathered Church is realized. In a passage of admittedly almost untranslatable Latin (the impossibility reaches deep into the very words of the text themselves), the gathering together of the entire complexity of the action that is present, in history and in eternity, both received and offered, observed and participated in for a moment that transcends the distinction between human and divine, we 'receive the holy things for the fullness ... in truth, that we may praise and glorify you'.[39] That with which we began – the praise of God – is only now fully realized in its total unity through the dynamic action of the words in 'performance'. Within this the sense of the divine or Godhead, which as Malekin and Yarrow pointed out is also the case for the notion of kingship in Shakespeare's dramas of *Richard II* and *Henry IV*, 'is neither merely the role nor merely the person: it has to be worked out from the dialogue between them'.[40] God is known and entered into only dynamically in the interlocutory medium of the Spirit.

Scholarship has reached no agreement as to whether Hippolytus concludes his anaphora with the singing of the Sanctus, the great anthem in which the people join with angels and archangels and all the company of heaven in a shout of praise drawn from Isaiah 6.1–3, a gathering of all into one in a great moment of supreme consciousness of being.[41]

Most scholars would regard this as anachronistic, an imposing of a later development on an early liturgical text. The most persuasive advocacy for its presence in *The Apostolic Tradition* remains that of the great liturgical scholar E. C. Ratcliff,[42] for it is in the coming of all together in the Sanctus that the 'theatre' of the Eucharist, in the words of Malekin and Yarrow in their understanding of spirit in performance, 'operates across all channels and, in functioning as an integrated whole, provides more than the sum of the parts, so opening into the realm of the more than ordinary, the magical'.[43] The conclusion of their chapter on theatre and drama in *Consciousness, Literature and Theatre* describes, though in the context of Shakespeare's plays, with uncanny accuracy, the performance as memorial of the anaphora of Hippolytus, a performance-text which avoids established theological prescription, but which brings about in enactment, in actuality and in anticipation, that process of salvation as one of unification and transformation from reduction. As player (bishop) and audience (God/congregation) shift roles and places, the pattern of renunciation and return (as is also the case, dramatically at least, in *King Lear*, *The Winter's Tale* and *The Tempest*), finds its final embodiment in Christ and the Church which becomes his body in performance.

Robert M. Torrance, in a book that was a key text for Malekin and Yarrow in their work, *The Spiritual Quest: Transcendence in Myth, Religion, and Science* (1994), writes of spirit in a manner of which Christian theologians concerned with the nature and work of the Holy Spirit should take note.

> Spirit (like Aristotle's *form*) is distinct from matter not by difference of substance but as potential actualization from given condition, future from present, indeterminate from determined ... Only when it is consciously represented does the future inherent in life become spirit; it therefore partakes of the differentiation of subject and object, self and world, in which consciousness is grounded.[44]

Malekin's lifelong concern for a proper understanding of the nature of 'consciousness', and a model of the mind which would go beyond the divided and limited notions of consciousness that now tend to govern our sense of what it is to be fully and truly human, has never adequately been explored by Christian theologians or liturgists within the wisdom of the early Church Fathers and the dynamic, eschatological spirituality of the early Christian liturgy before they became overwhelmed by the philosophical theological debates of the third and fourth centuries CE. One of the treasured items in my own library is a copy of Peter Malekin's translation of some of the writings of Jacob Böhme, the seventeenth-century German Lutheran theosophical writer and mystic.[45] As Peter points out in his Introduction, Böhme never abandoned his professed Lutheranism, though he challenged the Church with the question, 'Where do you want to look for God?'[46] The key sentence in Peter's summary of Böhme's thought, it seems to me, links him both with Plotinus and with the Buddhist tradition. It links him also with our present discussion and with *The Apostolic Tradition* as evidence of the early Eucharist as spiritual performance known only in a unity and balance of a form of consciousness through words that later Christian theology, locked as it was into institutions and power structures, found almost impossible to maintain.

> In one experience at least, that which appears to lie behind Böhme's conception of the *Ungrund* or Absolute (compare Plotinus's ultimate One, or that which is beyond number, the Buddhists' Void, etc.) no interpretation takes place 'during' the 'experience', since in it the trinity of all manifest or relative experience, subject, object, and action or perception, is entirely lacking. It is the mercy of God that there is such a rest from the ego and its busy-ness.[47]

Peter's choice of language in his references to the trinity and to the 'mercy of God' is significant. Literary criticism since Harold Bloom's *The Anxiety of Influence* (1973) has acknowledged that at the very heart and centre of all interpretation and hermeneutical activity lies the uninterpretable moment – for example, the moment of Christ's death on the cross, or the moment when the eucharistic elements are received and consumed – that can only be spoken, 'performed' and experienced in enactment. From this all possibility of understanding flows. It is that moment of one-ness that is possible only in *quies*, detachment or 'neutrality', that 'crucial and pivotal condition of consciousness in the unfolding of the spiritual'[48] which, by the mercy of God, is a release from the ego and its busy-ness.

This might begin to explain why in the anaphora of *The Apostolic Tradition* we find a particular stress on redemption[49] and release from suffering, and why the Eucharist can finally only be known as an action, a 'performance' in memorial. The Greek word in the biblical tradition which lies behind this is ποιεω – to make, produce, create or cause to be.[50] In the fragmentary evidence that we have of Hippolytus as witness of the Christian liturgy of the early third, or even late second century CE (and if Rome is indeed its origin there is little, as Geoffrey Cuming has pointed out, to connect it with later Roman services[51]), we find what Anthony Gelston has described as a sense of 'balance'[52] such as Peter Malekin, in his own way, would have readily acknowledged.

Peter was always hesitant in his use of the word 'mystic', especially with respect to that good Lutheran Jacob Böhme. But he is never hesitant in his linking of the language of different religious traditions – the Christian not only with Plotinus but with Mahayana Buddhism, with the Vedas, or with Daoism. He sought unity through forms of consciousness that never relinquished or denied the vigorous life of the mind in all its particularities, though like Böhme he often regarded conventional scholarship as simply a mixture of arrogance and ignorance. In the glimpse that we have of the early Christian Church at worship in Hippolytus' *Apostolic Tradition*, in words that direct rather than prescribe, from the dialogue that we know as the *sursum corda* to the possibility, no more than that, of the concluding Sanctus, that hint of the glorious hymn of praise sung here on earth but an anticipation of the unity of all things in heaven and earth, we find an intelligent spirituality of redemption, known only in performance, that Peter would I think have understood. This observation reflects my memory of our conversations when we would enjoy a unity in our differences from which Peter would go on to his practice of meditation while I would say the daily office of the Anglican Church.

Before we move forward more than a thousand years in the history of the Western Church, to the late Middle Ages and the eve of the English Reformation, this chapter has paused for a moment and sought to intertwine with literary and non-Christian thinking to suggest further the ritual poetic complexity of the language of the liturgy. It may be that the middle years of the sixteenth century in England, riven though they were by political, social and religious divisions, were a moment to catch a consciousness sustained by a vital sense of language that was at once culturally alive, intellectually subtle and theologically braced. It is a moment, perhaps, that we have lacked in our own time and that has shaped the difficulties and misunderstandings in our more recent debates about liturgical language. But perhaps lessons can be learnt again if we but listen.

PART III

Medieval and Reformation England

6

Liturgical Language and the Vernacular in Late Medieval England

I move forward now some hundreds of years to England on the eve of the Reformation as Latin and English sat side by side in the liturgy. The particular focus of the present chapter will be upon the relationship between the English vernacular and the liturgy of the Church in later medieval England before the great watershed of the work of Archbishop Cranmer in the middle of the sixteenth century and the publication of the 1549 first *Book of Common Prayer* of King Edward VI. This, and its successor in 1552 together with the Elizabethan *Prayer Book* of 1559, deliberately sought to impose liturgical uniformity upon earlier diversity in worship. At the beginning of the sixteenth century there were at least five 'uses' in England – those of Sarum (Salisbury), York, Hereford, Bangor and Lincoln – of which Sarum (upon which Cranmer heavily depended) and to a lesser extent York were by far the most widespread.[1] In contrast to these local usages the Reformers sought to bring about what they believed to be a return to the 'Godly and decent ordre of the auncient fathers, [that] hath been so altered, broken and neglected, by planting in uncertein stories, Legendes, Respondes, Verses, vaine repeticions, Commemaracions, and Synodalles'.[2] In the Act for the Uniformity of Common Prayer that prefaces the Elizabethan *Prayer Book* of 1559, there is express prohibition of the use of 'any interludes, plays, songs, rhymes, or ... other open words' in the authorized liturgy.[3]

What has been described by Bruce Holsinger as 'a kind of historical monopoly on liturgical vernacularity'[4] that is frequently ascribed to the sixteenth century English *Book of Common Prayer* needs to be firmly contested in the literature and liturgical life of the preceding centuries, beginning with Eamon Duffy's reminder in his influential book *The Stripping of the Altars*, a study of lay religion in England between *c.* 1400 and *c.* 1580, that 'in the liturgy and in the sacramental celebrations that were its central moments, medieval people found the key to the meaning and purpose of their lives'.[5] If liturgy was at the very heart of medieval life, then its expressions can hardly be simply consigned to the remote Latin of the Church or excluded from the vernacular of everyday speech and exchange. Nor can liturgical study exclude, as is too often the case, the careful attention of literary scholars and be restricted to the work of liturgists, theologians and historians. For, as Holsinger has asked, 'in what sense might literature (which would include poetry and drama) be seen as in part an *effect* of liturgy'[6] or, to go further than Holsinger, liturgy and the poetics of ritual, indeed, an effect of literature? And as we consider this and its implications for liturgical study, how might such reflections alter or revise our attention to Cranmer and the liturgical events of the mid sixteenth century?

As demonstrated by the debates over liturgical language in the later part of the twentieth century leading up to the publication of *The Alternative Service Book* (1980), though without much further serious reflection, it is not only language in its grammar and vocabulary that changes but also how language is used and understood, not least in its relation to religion and theology. As we have seen in Chapter 1, in discussing Cranmer's Prayer of Humble Access Professor David Frost has remarked on the 'desperately literal' nature of contemporary English.[7] This has not always been so. Quite simply, the medieval age was not only an age of metaphor but, even more, all experience was bound together in a metaphorical understanding that was quite different from our contemporary bifurcated and highly 'literal' universe. In the words of Andrew Hass,

> With the turn to the modern, the metaphor becomes simply that, a literary metaphor, a trope, no longer with any practical connection. So that the discipline of modern astronomy now no more applies to the discipline of literature than, say, theories of poesy apply to theories of quasar activity.[8]

To the medieval and sixteenth-century mind no such distinctions were conceivable. The language of metaphor embraced all things in heaven and on earth, and this unity overcame even the differences between one language and another.

Since so much hinges on the shift from Latin into the vernacular, not only in the liturgy but in the matter of biblical translation largely, in the first instance, from the Latin Vulgate, from Wycliffe, Coverdale and Tyndale up to the King James Bible of 1611, some understanding of medieval models of translation is necessary. Rita Copeland, and more recently Annie Sutherland, have traced the history of translation theory in the European tradition to the classical, and more specifically Ciceronian, position in the translation of Greek into Latin. Most famously in his treatise *De optimo genere oratorum*, on translating the speeches of Demosthenes and Aeschines, Cicero asserts, '*In quibus non verbum pro verbo necesse habui reddere, sed genus omne verborum vimque servavi*' ('And in so doing, I did not hold it necessary to render word for word, but I preserved the general style and force of the language').[9] But this principle of *non verbum pro verbo* in Cicero, Copeland points out, allows an appropriative process in translation founded upon a sense of the *disjunction* between Greek and Latin culture and language. Translation, for Cicero, is an appropriation of what *has* been Greek into what *now* becomes Latin. Jerome, however (and after him the tradition of medieval Christianity), while sustaining the principle of *non verbum pro verbo* uses this as a model for what Copeland describes as 'textual fidelity rather than of difference, as a theory of direct conservation of textual meaning without the impediment of linguistic multiplicity'.[10] This does not, of course, mean that medieval translation might not appear at times more like exegetical commentary or expansive gloss. For example, the translation of Psalm 50 in the Auchinleck Manuscript (*c.* 1330) does not set out to be 'a precise, evocative terminology of the original' but, in Annie Sutherland's words, 'the poet's goal appears to be the distillation of the psalm's penitential essence into a piece of easily memorable rhyming vernacular devotion accessible to a wide audience'.[11]

No longer, then, is translation a matter of linguistic disjunction – between Latin and English – but an acknowledgement, above all in biblical or religious texts, that a communality of meaning exists beyond all linguistic particularities, and for Jerome the 'native genius' of any language is an opportunity to pursue dynamic equivalence rather than difference.[12] This is, of course, to simplify what becomes, in later figures such as Boethius (*c.* 480–*c.* 524) and John Scotus Eriugena (*c.* 810–*c.* 877), a highly complex history of translation; but nevertheless, if it remains substantially the case as a Hieronymian formula, then its consequences for our understanding of the relationship between the use of Latin and the growth of the vernacular in liturgy, biblical translations and religious texts, up to the key date of 1549, need to be taken seriously. To begin with, the stark division between the two languages of Latin and English needs to be broken down. Furthermore, this is what underlies Jerome's arguments against literalism in the language of the Bible and liturgy. Finally, this is an acknowledgement of the sense of theology as being *within* the structures and rhythms of language itself, and above all the language of the liturgy, rather than simply a matter of doctrine understood and imposed from without.

The implications of such theories of translation for contemporary liturgy lie beyond the boundaries of this chapter and will be taken up in later chapters. For now it may be noted, as Margaret Deanesly indicated in her influential work on the Wycliffite Bible and the Lollards, that the provisions of the Council of Oxford in 1408 and the Arundel Constitutions of 1409 did not forbid English Bibles as such. They were commonplace enough anyway in both English and French and, as Cranmer was later to point out, 'many hundred years before that it was translated in the Saxons' tongue, which at that time was our mother's tongue'.[13] It was rather that such Bibles should require the approval of a diocesan bishop or provincial council as the tendency was, in Lollard hands, for the individual translator, if not properly supervised and authorized, to fall into heresy.[14] But the language itself – English – was not the issue. Second, it becomes clear that the doctrinal disputes that heated the fires of Reformation controversy in England as the sixteenth century progressed from the reigns of Henry VIII to Elizabeth I and beyond often lay within the forms and structures of language itself, intensifying and complicating the arguments over the liturgical shift from Latin to English. The principle of *ex opere operato*, which maintained that the efficacy of the rites and sacraments of the Church was independent of any individual disposition among those present (including the priest), extended to the very language used, whether it was understood or not. It was this principle, among others, that motivated the rebellion in the West Country in 1549, to the fury of Cranmer, as people feared the loss of 'the mass in Latin' and the sacrality inherent in its words even if they could not be understood.[15] The poor people of the West Country did not appreciate, however, the Hieronymian principle of communality between languages, of dynamic equivalence rather than dynamic difference between Latin and English.

Turning now to the use of the vernacular in lay devotions known through such texts as those of the Primers and the *Lay Folks Mass Book*, we need to delve first back somewhat earlier to the *Ancrene Riwle* (*Ancrene Wisse*), a handbook for anchoresses of noble birth written in the earlier part of the thirteenth century.[16] Written in English, Part I of this handbook begins with a discourse on devotions: 'This is the beginning of the first book, the book of hours and other good prayers.'[17] Presented as a red rubric in the most authoritative manuscript in Corpus Christi College, Cambridge, this sentence can be read as 'Here begins the *first* Book of Hours', and it is followed by instructions for prayer both in English and in Latin. The first act of the anchoress on rising in the morning is to repeat the *English* words, making the sign of the cross, 'In the name of the Father and of the Son and of the Holy Ghost,' followed by the *Latin* of the *Veni Creator Spiritus*. Such practice would appear to contradict the general assumption, as expressed by Roger Wieck, that 'until around 1400, Books of Hours were entirely in Latin'.[18] In fact, the *Ancrene Riwle* suggests a far more fluid interchange in devotion and liturgical practice between Latin and English even in the early thirteenth century, establishing a clear linguistic model that survived until what Geoffrey Cuming calls the 'reforming Primers' printed in the sixteenth century between 1530 and 1545, culminating in the Primer of Henry VIII, the *King's Book*, which was published on 29 May 1545.[19] These later Primers, up to the publication of the first *Book of Common Prayer*, were a mixture of the traditional Hours of Our Lady with material drawn from Lutheran sources and, in the words of the injunction expressing the royal purpose in the *King's Book*, published 'to haue one vniforme ordre of al suche bokes throughout all our dominions, bothe to be taught vnto children, and also to be vsed for ordinary praiers of al our people not learned in the Latin tong'.[20]

However, if we return to Henry Littlehales' edition of the earlier manuscript (G.24) Prymer of St John's College, Cambridge (*c.* 1400) we find, in very much the manner of the *Ancrene Riwle*, the Hours in English with an interspersion of Latin.[21] Thus the Hours of the Blessed Virgin open with the Latin 'Domine labia', followed by the English 'Lord thow schalt opene my lippes.' Only one manuscript version of the Primer (Glasgow MS. V 8, 15) is in both Latin and English and, against the suggestion that the Primer in Latin may be considered as 'the Prayer-Book of the Middle Ages',[22] Littlehales suggests that it is far more likely that this was the Primer in English both because of its general invariability and because of its distinction from material to be found in the Breviary and Manual. The English Primer, in other words, upon which Cranmer so heavily depended as 'a convenient method of introducing Lutheran ideas into England under the guise of traditional piety',[23] had been the staple of English piety outside the official liturgical provision of Latin service-books for some hundreds of years, sometimes not as books of private devotion but as part of the property of the parish church itself,[24] and their language formed the basis of lay devotion and theology. Two instances of the close connection between the domestic devotion of the English Primer and the liturgy of the Church may be drawn. First, there is a brief image in the *Paston Letters* of the fifteenth century: as Sir John Heveningham comes home in the summer of 1453 from attending three Masses in his parish church, he informs his wife that he will 'sey a lytyll devocion' in the garden before dinner. In fact he died in his garden, his Primer in his hand and his prayers being said, finally, in English.[25] The second is the image of the Catholic Sir Thomas More praying with his Primer in his imprisonment in the Tower of London and awaiting his death by execution.[26] If More's book, as one might expect of a devout Catholic who had aspired in his youth to be a

Carthusian monk, is in Latin, his own private prayers, written in the blank spaces in the book, are in English, and he would have known that it was this devotion that connected him in his isolation to his family at prayer from the same Book of Hours at home in Twickenham. As a record of the united More family we have Hans Holbein's fine drawing from 1527 of them all at prayer, holding their books of devotion.

If even the learned and devoutly Catholic More was praying in both Latin and English, for the majority of the medieval population of England (and More himself estimated that about half the people could read English[27]) the language of prayer was predominantly English and drawn from the Primer, a 'religious handbook' which, 'though not an official ecclesiastical publication ... was based on the usage of the Church'.[28] In addition to the Primer, the *Lay Folks Mass Book* provides clear evidence of the devotional life of medieval England upon the axiom that the *lex orandi* is also the *lex credenda* of a devout people of any age and therefore important as an 'estimate of ... personal belief and spiritual condition'.[29] Indeed, it was even argued, as late as the reign of Queen Mary, that to understand the service of the Church in Latin was actually a hindrance to devout people who, though present at an inaudible Mass (which, it was suggested in the fourteenth century by Johannes Andreas, ought to be said in Latin and *in silence*), should at the same time be occupied with their own prayers in a language understood by them.[30]

The *Lay Folks Mass Book* was originally written in French around 1150, being translated into English in about 1300.[31] The prayers of the Mass itself are not translated in the book, but the layperson is told what to do at each point of the Mass as the service is explained, meanwhile prayers being provided in English. It is expected that something as familiar as the Lord's Prayer (the *Paternoster*) should be learnt by rote and repeated in Latin. As the priest begins:

And whils he saies, hold thee stille,
Bot answere at temptacionem
Set libera nos a malo, amen.
Hit were no need thee this to ken
For who con not this are lewed men.[32]

The Gospel is read in Latin and should be attended to with proper 'dread', even if not understood, for:

Men aght to haue ful mikel drede,
When thei shuld here or else hit rede.[33]

Thus Latin and English remain together in the lay participation in the Mass, the awesome and fearful truths of the Gospel and Creed remaining properly veiled in the mystery of the Latin words while private devotions are said in English. The poet John Lydgate's verse manual for the laity, to be used while Mass is celebrated, the *Merita Missae* (*c.* 1400), makes it clear that grace is received merely by the hearing of the Gospel in Latin, whether understood or not, while the layperson is encouraged in devotion by sometimes dramatic poetic images, in this case drawn from chivalry:

And whan the gospille shalle be rede
Lestene as thou were adred,
For Euvry talle of a kyng
Wold haue dredfulle lestnyng;
And what man saye it is not soo,
Be redy to fight or thou goo.
Than dare I saye thou arte a knyghte,
That dare fight in thi lordis right.[34]

John Lydgate (*c.* 1370–1449/50) was one of the most prolific of late medieval English poets, spending almost all of his life first as a monk in the monastery of Bury St Edmunds and later in Bury in Lancashire, drawing people to their devotions in the liturgy by his English verse. The eighteenth-century antiquary Joseph Ritson dismissed him as 'a voluminous, prosaick and driveling monk',[35] yet Lydgate nevertheless stands with Geoffrey Chaucer and Boccaccio as a major literary figure of his time both in the religious and the courtly realm.[36] In the writings of clerical poets like Lydgate and his near contemporary, John Skelton (*c.* 1460–1529), tutor to Prince Henry who was to become King Henry VIII, we encounter in the English language a refutation of Johan Huizinga's suggestion that the literature of the late Middle Ages in Europe was the 'servant of an expiring mode of thought'.[37] Indeed, quite to the contrary, in them we find what Bruce Holsinger has described as 'the productive medieval symbiosis of literary writing and liturgical culture'[38] that Archbishop Cranmer rejected, for example in his 'Sermon of Good Works' in the *First Book of Homilies* of 1547,[39] even as he inherited in his own liturgical compositions the very poetic language that had been inspired by precisely such a conjunction.

Between 1317 and 1360, the Franciscan Richard de Ledrede, Bishop of Ossory in Ireland, sought to wean his minor clergy from their indulgence in popular songs in the vernacular by composing Latin and occasionally macaronic verses (in Latin and English) to be sung to the same tunes.[40] Nor was the bishop the first English lyricist to compose religious verse, for in the mid twelfth century no less a figure than St Godric of Durham was writing poems to the Virgin[41] and the monk Thomas of Ely in the *Liber Eliensis* records songs of his fellow monks at Ely, which he attributes to King Canute himself, and which were sung publicly in dances:

> Merye sungen the muneches (*monks*) binnen Ely
> Tha (*when*) Cnut King rew ther by;
> 'Roweth, knites, noer the land,
> And here we thes muneches saeng.'[42]

It is not clear how 'liturgical' were the macaronic lyrics dating as far back as the early thirteenth century such as the fine intercessory hymn to Mary:

> Of on that is so fair and bright,
> *Velud maris stella*,
> Brighter than the dayes light,
> *Parens et puella*:
> Ic crye to thee – thou se to me –
> Levedy, preye thy sone for me,
> *Tam pia*,
> That ic mote come to thee,
> Maria.[43]

As Douglas Gray has written of such verses, 'We do not really know what purposes these were intended to serve; probably they were to be used in preaching, possibly as private poems for devotion.'[44] What seems very clear is that poems composed in English or translated from Latin, especially by Franciscans, were familiar in preaching, public or private worship.[45] Praying in English, often of a sophisticated poetic quality, both in church and in private, was central to the culture of late medieval devotion. St Francis of Assisi (1181/2–1226) had, after all, described his disciples as *joculatores Dei* (God's minstrels) and writers of fine English lyrics such as William Herebert and James Ryman were Franciscans.[46] Herebert's 'What is he, this lordling, that cometh from the fight?' is a paraphrase of Isaiah 63.1–7, part of the readings for Wednesday in Holy Week from the *Sarum Missal*.[47] It is a theme perhaps better known today in the Scottish court makar and priest William Dunbar's (?1460–1513/30) 'Done is a battell on the dragon blak', with its final line in Latin of each verse, '*Surrexit dominus de sepulchro*.'[48] In such poets the close connection between vernacular poetry and the liturgy is quite clear.

As G. R. Owst made clear long ago, religious lyrics were also common in collections of sermon material in the fourteenth and fifteenth centuries.

The sermon-encyclopedia of the Franciscan, John of Grimston, written about 1376, contains an assortment of vernacular lyrics that draw upon both biblical and liturgical themes and materials,[49] and it was within this tradition that William Langland (*c.* 1362–*c.*1380) was writing in his great *Vision of Piers the Plowman*, in which 'the messages of the preacher and poet are fundamentally the same'.[50] The close correlation between liturgy and literary invention in medieval England is well illustrated by the fact that Text F of the *Lay Folks Mass Book* is written, in a separate hand, on eleven blank pages at the end of the Text B manuscript of *Piers Plowman*, dated about 1450, and this is the only text of the *Lay Folks Mass Book* in which the rubrics (written in red) are given in full.[51] The language of lay prayer in church and ritual, it may be said, and the language of poetry lie side by side on the page. Indeed, Langland explicitly avows that the roots of his vision and poem originate in the lay liturgy, both Latin and English, of the Primer and the Psalms, for 'the lomes that y labore with'

> Is *pater noster* and my primer, *placebo* and *dirige*,
> And my sauter som tyme and my seuene psalms.[52]

In Passus 5 of *Piers Plowman*, Accidia (Sloth) admits that he knows idle tales and the secular romances of Robin Hood and Earl Randolf of Chester, but cannot repeat his *Paternoster* in Latin, nor even prayers (presumably in English) of Our Lord and Our Lady, actually falling asleep over his devotions and omitting to perform his penances.

> I can noughte perfitly my *pater-noster* as the prest it syngeth,
> But I can rymes of Robyn hood and Randolf erle of Chestre,
> Ac neither of owre lorde ne of owre lady the leste that euere was made.[53]

Langland's intention is clear. The central purpose of *Piers Plowman* is the sustaining of the spiritual welfare of England and the search for true Christianity in the face of ecclesiastical, and as a result societal, corruption,[54] and ordinary decent folk were expected to know their prayers, both in Latin and English, from the Primer or the *Lay Folks Mass Book*. Poets like John Lydgate in his *Merita Missae* and William Langland in *Piers Plowman*, among many other writers and lyricists, were writing in a sophisticated English poetic tradition that was rooted in a lay liturgical practice and language that reaches directly into the liturgies of the English Reformation, their language part of a common cultural inheritance that belies any 'historical monopoly on liturgical vernacularity'[55] for Cranmer or the *Books of Common Prayer* after 1549.

Nor can a brief mention of the role of the medieval stage and the drama of the medieval Church be omitted.[56] Even as the medieval English pageant cycles did not die out of their own accord but rather under suppression by the Protestant Reformers,[57] their continuity was in some sense ensured in the supreme outburst of dramatic and linguistic energy of the Elizabethan and Jacobean stage. In the words of O. B. Hardison Jr:

> As they [the pageant cycles] disappeared, dramatists turned from solely religious subjects to secular ones. Classical history and the history of the national state replaced sacred history as prime sources for dramatic plots. Ethical, political, and protopsychological doctrine vied with, and for some authors replaced, the older sacramental psychology.[58]

Closer comparative study between two of the greatest literary jewels of English in the later sixteenth and early seventeenth centuries – the *Books of Common Prayer* and the great plays of, above all, William Shakespeare – have only recently begun to emerge in the work of such scholars as Stephen Greenblatt and Daniel Swift.[59] Both Swift and Greenblatt emphasize the political, ecclesial and theological *discontinuity* between late medieval and Reformation England and, at the same time but more usually forgotten, the profound *continuity* in language and even ritual form, especially in the case of tragedy. As Hardison has expressed it:

> If it seems strange to speak of comic structure and tragic tonality in *Romeo*, *Hamlet*, and *Othello*, a parallel can be found in the shifting tonalities of the Mass itself, which is joyful on Christmas and deeply somber on Passion Sunday, although the same comic structure is used on both occasions.[60]

It is now more than forty years since Hardison offered a critique of the continuing authority of E. K. Chambers and Karl Young with respect to medieval religious drama. At the heart of Chambers' vision of the medieval stage there is a profound anticlericalism that sets the clergy and liturgy against the 'mimetic instinct' of secular theatre and poets. In his words, 'the minstrels braved the ban of the Church and finally won their way', and 'the *ludi* of the folk, based upon the observances of a forgotten natural religion, and surviving side by side with minstrelsy, broke out at point after point into *mimesis*'.[61] According to Chambers, liturgical drama began as 'a mere spectacle, devised by ecclesiastics for the edification of the laity' that eventually 'broke the bonds of ecclesiastical control' and came 'in time to appeal to a deep-rooted native instinct of drama in the folk and to continue as an essentially popular thing, a *ludus* maintained by the people itself for its own inexhaustible wonder and delight'.[62]

This, Hardison suggests, is simply a mistake. In fact, it seems clear that the allegorical interpretation of the Mass in the Western tradition, and its consequent dramatic 'performance' as liturgy, began at least with Alcuin of York in the later eighth century and was more fully, if controversially, developed, as we have already seen in Chapter 4,[63] by his pupil Amalarius, Bishop of Metz, in his major work, the influential *Liber Officialis*.[64] To return for a moment to Amalarius, the dramatic sense of the Mass is made quite explicit in his shorter *Expositio* (813–14):

> The prayer which the priest says from the *secreta* to the *Nobis quoque peccatoribus* signifies the prayer of Jesus on Mount Olivet. What occurs later signifies the time during which Christ lay in the grave. When the bread is immersed in the wine, this means the return of Christ's soul to His body. The next action signifies the greetings offered by Christ to His Apostles. And the breaking of the bread of the offerings signifies the breaking of bread performed by the Lord before the two at Emmaus.[65]

The priest and participants in the Mass are clearly seen as playing roles, and each action is a mimetic presentation of a biblical moment. I have already suggested that Amalarius is actually closer to a literary critic than a true theologian in his work, his concern being to make the Mass in its dramatic mystery 'ever more widely known to the *simpliciores*'.[66]

Such allegorical interpretation of the Mass as drama endured despite the theological opposition and the denunciation of Amalarius as a heretic at the Synod of Quiercy in 838.[67] For it is clear that the dramatic performance of the Mass by priests continued and, through the development of liturgical tropes such as the Easter dialogue *Quem Quaeritis*, with its origins quite early in the Middle Ages, eventually gave birth to vernacular tropic equivalents that remained deeply rooted in the religious life of the people. The poetics of the *Quem Quaeritis* trope lie on the very cusp of ritual and representational drama in an uneasy complexity that liturgy cannot, finally, avoid.[68]

As with vernacular verse, the dramatic history of the ritual of the liturgy and its 'performance' proceeds within a continuity, rather than the discontinuity between sacred and secular as described by Chambers, which the English Reformation does not finally sever. As the work of Judith Maltby in her book *Prayer Book and People in Elizabethan and Early Stuart England* (1998) suggests, the poetics of the devotional language and the 'performance' of the liturgies of Cranmer and the *Books of Common*

Prayer are to be seen deeply within the devotional life of the people, in both Latin and the vernacular, maintaining a far greater degree of linguistic coherence than the severances of doctrine and politics could ever bring about.

Before moving on from the drama of the medieval Church, a brief word on the matter of tropes is necessary. Karl Young states that 'in its broadest sense a trope may be defined as a verbal amplification of a passage in the authorized liturgy, in the form of an introduction, an interpolation, or a conclusion'.[69] Young notes not only the *dramatic* form of many tropes, such as the Latin dialogue used at the beginning of the introit for the third Mass of Christmas (as we find in the so-called Winchester Tropers[70]) which concludes with the words of the *incipit* of the introit of the Mass, *Puer natus est*, or indeed the *Quem Quaeritis* trope itself,[71] but also the profound influence of such quasi-liturgical material upon European verse and lyric poetry more generally.[72] The language of medieval popular devotion, as it moved between liturgical Latin and the vernacular, coexisted with vernacular poetry and lyricism in a particular poetics and form of language that informs the language of the English *Books of Common Prayer* to an extent that is still far too little recognized.

As a brief exercise in exploring this continuity, let us turn to Archbishop Cranmer's Collects in the 1549 *Prayer Book*, and one in particular, an almost (this qualification is important) completely new composition, that for the First Sunday in Advent. It has been noted that the Roman Collects, many written in the fifth and sixth centuries, were fine Latin compositions, written with notable economy at a time when classical rhetoric was flowering.[73] Writing in 1549 Cranmer drew heavily upon the Latin prayers of the *Sarum Missal*, and of the 84 Collects for Sundays and holy days for that year, only seven have an earlier English form.[74] As has been noted by Geoffrey Cuming, Cranmer did not draw upon the English Collects of the Primers to any great extent, partly because such a large number of these were for saints days that were omitted from the new liturgies of the Reformation. Only a very few of the Primers' Collects appeared in 1549.[75] However, if, in his work of translation, it was to the Latin collects of the *Sarum Missal* that Cranmer turned to a very large extent, it may be suggested that ordinary folk, accustomed to the vernacular prayers of the Primers, and the steady stream of devotional material that has been reviewed in this chapter – in lyrics and poetry, in drama with its roots in the liturgical tropes and the Mass as filtered through the *Lay Folks Mass Book* – were not as radically affected by such liturgical changes in the earlier part of the sixteenth century as might have been expected.[76] Primers continued to proliferate up to the last of the reforming Primers which sought to impose a degree of uniformity in worship, the *King's Primer* (or *King's Book*) of 1545,[77] but the simple fact that is largely ignored is that Cranmer was writing, in translation or in his original prayers, in a vernacular language of devotion that was firmly rooted in the worship of preceding centuries. His genius was not radical but conservative, and if his theology demanded a uniformity that sought a broad stability in liturgy unknown to the Middle Ages, his sense of language tapped deeply into the poetics and rhetoric of that earlier period. Scholars have long agreed that to overemphasize the presence and use of the *cursus*, a system of prose rhythms for the close of Latin phrases and sentences, in the first *Prayer Book* of Edward VI is a mistake. C. S. Lewis puts it most succinctly, writing that the *cursus* 'does not hold the secret of the Prayer Book's music'.[78] Rather, the secret of that music lies more deeply in the complex traditions of Medieval English language and religious poetry.

Cranmer's first great liturgical achievement was the English Litany of 1545, written at the behest of Henry VIII during his wars with Scotland and France to intercede for 'the miserable state of all Christendom'.[79] Described by Diarmaid MacCulloch as 'an ingenious effort of scissors and paste out of previous texts',[80] Cranmer's magnificent Litany, which remains in liturgical use in the *Book of Common Prayer* to this day, was evidence of what F. E. Brightman called his 'extraordinary power of absorbing and improving other people's work'.[81] But even when translating from the Latin, largely drawing upon the Sarum rite, Cranmer is profoundly conscious of the power of the English language. Returning for a moment to the theme of translation, Cranmer was quite relaxed in his use of a 'more than liberty of a translation' to grant a richness in English where Latin words 'were but barren as meseemed, and little fruitful'.[82] But I am not entirely convinced of the truth of Geoffrey Cuming's suggestion that 'one obvious feature of Cranmer's work is the psychological need which he seems to have felt to use someone else's work as a starting point' for his English liturgical prayers.[83] Rather he was deliberately writing, in his scholarly manner, in the tradition of medieval literature and poetry which continuously drew upon sources both directly and indirectly – vernacular religious verse, often a quilt-work of Latin and English texts, and liturgical material from the Roman Rite.

Let us now consider one of the few Cranmerian collects that Cuming describes as 'completely new compositions'[84] for the 1549 book, that is the Collect for the First Sunday in Advent. This claim to originality is true inasmuch as this collect is not a translation from any Latin original, but it is still built out of earlier material, most particularly a quotation from the Epistle of the day from the Letter to the Romans, chapter 13: 'let vs therefore cast away the dedes of darkenes, and let vs put on the armoure of light.'[85] The translation from Greek originates in William Tyndale's 1534 New Testament.[86] Here is the full collect in the 1549 version:

> Almighty God, geue vs grace, that we maye cast away the works of darkenes, and put upō vs the armour of light, now in the time of thys mortal lyfe, (in the which thy sonne Iesus Christ came to visite vs in great humilitie) that in the last daye, when he shall come againe in hys glorious maiestie, to iudge bothe the quicke and the dead: we maye ryse to the lyfe immortall, through him, who liueth and reigneth with thee and the holy gost, nowe and euer. Amen.[87]

The poetic structure of the collect both governs and is governed by its careful theology, based upon the central antithesis of Christ's first coming, in great humility, and his second coming, in his glorious majesty. Cranmer, though a writer of prose rather than verse, possessed a sense of literary structure which is also that of his medieval predecessors, Langland, Lydgate and others in the Franciscan tradition of poetry who thought 'theologically' in literary balances. The use of rhetorical devices such as chiasmus is here not classical but rather follows the patterns of medieval poetry, using essentially simple vocabulary (after the genius of Tyndale) in careful balances and the use of antithesis. The description of Christ in his second coming is taken from a source that would already have had the ring of familiarity, the *King's Primer* of 1545, the authorized Primer of Henry VIII: 'Christ shall come ... in his majesty and glory ... and shall judge all, quick and dead.'[88] But the key to the power of the collect lies in the fact that Cranmer is not content with what Cuming calls the 'strict collect form',[89] which would begin with description and conclude with petition ('give us grace ...'), but turns this around and more dramatically opens with the petition in the present time ('Almighty God, give us grace ...'), thus linking past (the incarnation) and future time (the second coming) in the dynamics of our present life. Furthermore, he encloses the two 'times' of Christ in another antithesis relating to our own condition: 'now, in the time of this mortal life ... we may rise to the life immortal'. It is a perfect example of what I have called a ritual poetics.

Theologically the collect focuses upon the relationship between ourselves and Christ. But Cranmer, though no poet (as he himself admitted), is adapting, in prose of extraordinary clarity and, indeed, simplicity of vocabulary, the form of the collect to increase its power and dramatic impact – a literary process that the most liturgical of medieval English poets, William Langland, would have perfectly understood and applauded.

This chapter has begun to sketch out a still largely unrecognized thesis. Its findings suggest that there is an extraordinary continuity in liturgical vernacularity between the Middle Ages and its literature, and the English *Books of Common Prayer* of the sixteenth century. English prayer books had long been part of lay devotion as well as that of many of the clergy who were not necessarily well educated in Latin, and the liturgical language that came to fruition in the Renaissance genius of Thomas Cranmer and others (as well as in Shakespeare, Marlowe and the English theatre of the late sixteenth century) was deeply embedded in a vibrant literary tradition that was inextricably linked to the Latin liturgy of the Church. In the Hieronymian tradition of translation, the mystery lay behind and beyond words, though for Jerome the very order of words in the biblical text was a mystery. Of its very nature this was not plain language easily to be understood. And if Cranmer certainly does mock the Latin liturgy as 'more like a game and a fond play to be laughed at of all men, to hear the priest speak aloud to the people in Latin, and the people listen with their ears to hear'[90] with a general lack of comprehension, nevertheless he was perfectly well aware of the power of continuity in liturgy (hence his heavy dependence on Sarum) and the power of language to 'speak' beyond mere understanding of the meaning of the words.

Judith Maltby has clearly suggested the nature of the culture of liturgical conformity that quickly impressed itself upon the people of the English Reformation up to the outbreak of the Civil War. When, in 1590, parishioners of a Suffolk church checked, from their own copies of the *Prayer Book*, the tendencies of their nonconformist minister to deviate from the prescribed liturgy, their devotion was complex and deep.[91] For the language of the liturgy which they sought to protect had long been the devotional language of the people, and their defence was not primarily in the interests of sound Protestant doctrine, but rather of a poetic and dramatic tradition, caught by Cranmer and his contemporaries in the midst of their doctrinal and political debates, that had long been the centre of the lives of ordinary men and women. Now, in the time of this mortal life, for the Protestant Suffolk parishioners of 1590, as for earlier medieval folk with their Primers and *Lay Folks Mass Books*, 'within the liturgy birth, copulation, and death, journeying and homecoming, guilt and forgiveness, the blessing of homely things and the call to pass beyond them were all located, tested and sanctioned'.[92]

7

Literature and The Prayer Books of the English Reformation

The poet David Scott, in his poem 'The Book of Common Prayer 1549', celebrates the precision of language in Cranmer's work, 'Words, then, said what they meant; they bit.'[1]

Since the years following the Second Vatican Council, when liturgists have struggled, not least in the Anglican tradition, to find a language of public prayer and worship suited to a modern age, the English *Prayer Books* of 1549, 1552 and 1559 have attracted considerable attention from literary critics who have begun to realize that it was the *Book of Common Prayer* (which reached its more or less final form after the Restoration in 1662[2]), far more than the King James Bible, that made an indelible mark on English language and literature.[3] The two great literary achievements of the reign of Elizabeth I were the plays of William Shakespeare and the 1559 *Book of Common Prayer*, both of them performative, and both Shakespeare and the 'authors' of the *Prayer Book* from Thomas Cranmer onwards were well aware that drama and religion are, in the words of David L. Frost, 'not only a matter of the right words, but the right words said in the right way using the right objects in the right order'.[4] What the debates about liturgical language in England prior to the publication of the *Alternative Service Book* in 1980 (the first new and fully authorized prayer book in the Church of England since 1662) largely failed to recognize was that not only does language change with time, but our attitude towards it and therefore our use of it changes also. We have suggested how in our own time our sense of the English language has become profoundly 'literal' in a way that would have horrified Shakespeare as much as it would have bemused Cranmer.[5] If Eamon Duffy in *The Stripping of the Altars* (1992) firmly demolished the notion that lay people's experience and expression of religion in late medieval and early Renaissance England was naive and simple, then the audiences who attended and appreciated Shakespeare's plays would certainly have not been misled by the dramatic words of Archbishop Cranmer's Prayer of Humble

Access that 'our sinful bodies may be made clean by his body, and our souls washed through his most precious blood', excised from the 1980 Eucharist, Rite A, leaving only the less dramatic (though they are words often quoted by Cranmer) 'that we may evermore dwell in him and he in us', taken directly from John 6.56.[6] Criticism of these words is not new or peculiar to the safety-conscious twentieth century, for as the vigour of Renaissance English decayed towards the eighteenth century it was, as I have already noted,[7] made as early as Gilbert Burnet in his *History of the Reformation* (1679–1714).[8]

But my concern in this chapter is not to take exception to or criticize modern attempts to recover a language of prayer and the sacred. That will be a task for later chapters in this book. It is, rather, to illustrate that a biblical translator like William Tyndale, a liturgical writer like Cranmer, and a playwright like Shakespeare had one thing in common: drawing upon living words of Anglo-Saxon in preference to words of Latin origin, they were all writing, in their different ways, what James Boyd White has called 'constitutive fictions' as ways of both speaking and acting that created public worlds.[9] In the case of Cranmer, these constitutive fictions, within the unique demands of the liturgical context, become a ritual poetics. But Tyndale, Cranmer and Shakespeare all used language to make and change the world, and never was this more the case than with the 1559 *Prayer Book* of Queen Elizabeth I. Much longer lived than its predecessors of 1549 and 1552, the book of 1559 literally shaped a world, its orders of service being enactments, in word and deed, of life from birth to death, experienced within the context of a faith in God's eternal truth. By the 'Act for the Uniformity of Common Prayer and Service in the Church, and the Administration of the Sacraments', with which it begins, the 1559 *Prayer Book* imposes unity, yet in a form and language that has the strength to allow reading between the lines, and a breadth of theological conscience in a manner that is both politically astute and deeply humane. This breadth in uniformity is something with which we struggle today. The 1559 *Book* would brook no rivals, knowing its own strength in an age of theatre and poetry, explicitly forbidding any deviations into the worlds of theatre, poetry or song – good enough reason for Shakespeare's necessarily largely hidden, though still profound, affiliations with the *Prayer Book* to which I will return in due course in this chapter.

In a dramatic moment in the *Prayer Book* of 1559, following directly the order of 1552, after the Sanctus, the great and ancient hymn of praise from Isaiah 6.3, the priest kneels down 'at God's board' and says the Prayer of Humble Access 'in the name of all them that shall receive communion',[10] a direct legacy of Archbishop Cranmer. The glory of God is thus contrasted starkly with our human unworthiness. This prayer, which I have already briefly discussed in Chapter 1, is Cranmer's own composition, first appearing in the 1548 *Order of the Communion* which gives material in English to be inserted into the Mass in Latin.[11] Four years earlier in 1544, when he produced an English Litany at the request of Henry VIII, Cranmer wrote a letter to the king explaining his way of working. He readily admits that he is no poet and that his true medium is prose, heartily wishing that his English verses were not lacking in grace and facility. Essentially Cranmer is a translator and he is well aware, under the unpredictable and theologically conservative eye of his royal master the king, that continuity in liturgical matters was politically wise. Nevertheless, change is sometimes necessary and he felt, at times, 'constrained to use more than the liberty of a translator: for in some processions I have altered divers words; in some I have added part; in some taken part away; some I have left out whole'.[12]

The result of such processes in the Prayer of Humble Access is a triumph of liturgical language.[13] Spoken just before the people's communion, in 1548, the prayer parallels the priest's prayers for 'worthy reception' of the elements, an expression of a Protestant theology in contrast to the theology of the Latin Mass. The position of the prayer is moved in the 1552 (and thus 1559) *Prayer Book* to the centre of the Eucharistic Prayer itself, immediately preceding the so-called narrative of institution, and with only slight changes the prayer survives into the 1662 *Prayer Book*. The reasons for this shift have been much discussed[14] and need not be rehearsed here. But perhaps we need to listen more acutely to the *tone* that Cranmer seeks to convey. If the prayer is penitential, then it is also embedded in the language of the narrative of the Syrophoenician woman in Mark 7.24–30, a biblical text that seems not to have been used in any earlier liturgical texts. It is, indeed, a text in which the woman chastises Jesus who then commends her for her boldness in the use of the image of the dogs under the table. Indeed, the prayer is profoundly rooted, as was Cranmer's liturgical practice, in scriptural sources – the book of Daniel, the Gospels of Mark and John, Romans, Leviticus and Hebrews.[15] In addition, Geoffrey Cuming, who describes the prayer as 'an excellent example of Cranmer's method of composition', suggests that it

> reflects the range of Cranmer's reading: possible sources of its language include the Liturgy of St Basil ... the Hereford Missal, the Litany, St Thomas Aquinas, Florus of Lyons, and Paschasius Radbert. With the exception of the gospel references, none is so literally reproduced as to be definitely identifiable as a source; but each, filtered through Cranmer's

retentive memory, may have contributed something to the general sense, and a word or two of the actual phrasing.[16]

Setting aside the arguments over Cranmer's eucharistic theology (Gregory Dix finally qualified Cranmer's theology as Zwinglian[17]), we should pay closer attention to the nature of our modern sensitivity to the powerful words 'that our sinful bodies may be made clean by his body and our souls washed through his most precious blood'.

Typically Cranmer is also echoing earlier liturgical texts. F. E. Brightman notes that the words 'made clean' and 'washed' probably derived from the Westminster and Hereford Missals.[18] Katie Badie has also noted the probable presence of Hebrews 10.22 (part of the Epistle reading for Good Friday), which reads, 'Let us draw nigh with a true heart in a full faith, sprinkled in our hearts from an evil conscience, and washed in our bodies with pure water' (Tyndale, 1534).[19] The doubling is clear, and leaves the most shocking image until the last: bodies/body; souls/blood, in each case connected by the active verbs 'clean' and 'washed'. In every respect it is a moment of drama in language worthy of Shakespeare himself, the words carrying energy and a physicality into the very heart of the eucharistic action. Indeed, we may place this moment in the liturgy alongside a moment in Shakespeare's *Macbeth*, the scene of Lady Macbeth and, in the words of her Gentlewoman to the Doctor, her 'accustomed action with her to seem thus washing her hands'. Lady Macbeth seeks to wash away her sins, yet there is 'the smell of blood still. All the perfumes of Arabia will not sweeten this little hand.'[20] The irony is deepened by the absence in the play of Christ's healing blood in the presence on her hands, rather, of the blood of murder which no human application can cleanse. It is usually supposed that *Macbeth* was first performed before James I and his royal guest, King Christian IV of Denmark, at Hampton Court in August 1606. By then Shakespeare was no stranger to Hampton Court, having played with the King's Men before King James at Christmas 1603, just prior to the Hampton Court Conference of January 1604 which is best known for its promotion of what would become known as the King James Bible but, perhaps more importantly, was called in response to a Puritan demand for the reformation of the English Church and above all the *Book of Common Prayer*.[21] The link between Shakespeare, then at the height of his creative powers, and the Church's preoccupation with the *Prayer Book* is strong indeed.

Or again, there is the ending of Christopher Marlowe's *The Tragical History of Doctor Faustus*, probably written in 1588. As Faustus, at the end of the play, is dragged into hell he seeks to leap up to God for salvation:

See, see, where Christ's blood streams in the firmament
One drop would save my soul, half a drop. Ah, my Christ!
Ah, rend not my heart for naming of my Christ!
...
Oh God, if thou wilt not have mercy on my soul,
Yet, for Christ's sake, whose blood had ransomed me,
Impose some end to my incessant pain.
Let Faustus live in hell a thousand years,
A hundred thousand, and at last be saved.[22]

But there is not one drop of Christ's blood, no Eucharist, to wash Faustus' soul. Not even the idea of Purgatory with its final promise of salvation is offered to him. The issue of Purgatory had been for a long time on the political agenda and was a matter of parliamentary measure when, as early as 1536 in the reign of Henry VIII, the Imperial Ambassador, Eustace Chapuys, noted amid Parliamentary business 'the suppression of all Church ceremonials concerning images and the worship of saints, and likewise against those who affirm that there is a Purgatory'.[23] In 1563, Convocation, under Queen Elizabeth, issued the first text of the Thirty-Nine Articles of Religion, 'for the establishing of consent touching true religion', later to be included in the *Book of Common Prayer*, of which Article 22 expressly rejects the 'Romish Doctrine' of Purgatory. For Faustus, whose soul is still immortal, then, there can be no salvation for 'no end is limited to damnèd souls'.[24]

It is not difficult to see why Shakespeare and Marlowe could not but be profoundly familiar with both the language and the theology of the *Book of Common Prayer*, but also why they could assume that their theatre audiences were similarly instructed. For the 1559 Act for the Uniformity of Common Prayer makes it perfectly clear that failure to attend church where the *Prayer Book* was faithfully followed attracted severe penalties for the laity as for the clergy:

> ... all and every person and persons inhabiting within this realm, or any other the Queen's Majesty's dominions, shall diligently and faithfully, having no lawful or reasonable excuse to be absent, endeavor themselves to resort to their parish church or chapel accustomed, or upon reasonable let thereof to some usual place where common prayer and such service of God shall be used in such time of let upon every Sunday and other days ordained and used to be kept as holy days. And then and there to abide orderly and soberly during the time of the common prayer, preachings, or other service of God there to be used and ministered,

> upon pain of punishment by the censures of the Church. And also upon pain that every person so offending shall forfeit for every such offense twelve pence to be levied by the churchwardens of the parish where such offense shall be done ...[25]

Such required attendance at church, furthermore, seems to have been, for many at least, not a burden but a matter for considerable enthusiasm. Judith Maltby's studies of churches in Cheshire and the diocese of Lincoln during the Elizabethan and early Stuart periods suggest that some lay-people at least wanted not only Sunday services but worship on weekdays, saints' days, and holy days as well, and woe betide the parson who failed them.[26] Such regular absorption of the rhythm and scriptural calendar of the 1559 *Prayer Book*, not to speak of its presence at the most significant moments in life – baptism and childbirth, marriage, times of sickness and death – promotes a dramatic and memorable pattern to the year, built around the salvation in Christ offered to sinful yet devout worshippers. Deeply embedded in such worship was the dramatic rendering of the Litany which, according to the rubric, was 'to be used upon Sundays, Wednesdays, and Fridays, and at other times, when it shall be commanded by the ordinary'.[27] It quickly became the practice to use the Litany on Sundays between Morning Prayer and Holy Communion as, for example, directed by Archbishop Grindal of York in his visitation of 1571 when the three services were to be said together without any intermission.[28] As the first vernacular service to be authorized in England (on 27 May 1544), the Litany, a processional service of intercession, is the earliest surviving example of Cranmer's liturgical skill.[29] It is a spectacular and dramatic form of words – the parson intoning and the people responding with repeated phrases: 'Good Lord deliver us', 'We beseech thee to hear us good Lord.'

> From all evil and mischief, from sin, from the crafts and assaults of the devil, from thy wrath, and from everlasting damnation.
>
> From all blindness of heart, from pride, vainglory, and hypocrisy, from envy, hatred and malice, and all uncharitablness.
>
> From fornication and all other deadly sin, and from all the deceits of the world, the flesh, and the devil.
>
> From lightning and tempest, from plague, pestilence, and famine, from battle and murder, and from sudden death.
>
> From all sedition and privy conspiracy, from all false doctrine and heresy, from hardness of heart, and contempt of thy Word and commandment.[30]

It goes on at great length. The solemn and haunting drama of such a Processional, its sources drawn by Cranmer from the Sarum rite of medieval England, as well as back to John Chrysostom (*c.* 347–407), in a Latin translation from Chrysostom's Greek, up to Martin Luther, would not have been lost on Shakespeare. Its phrases and vocabulary lie behind and fuel the distorted imagination of Edmund in *King Lear* as he reflects to Edgar on the disintegration of Lear's household and court:

> I promise you the effects he writes of succeed unhappily; as of unnaturalness between the child and the parent; death, dearth, dissolutions of ancient amities; divisions in state, menaces and maledictions against King and nobles, needless diffidences, banishment of friends, dissipation of cohorts, nuptial breaches, and I know not what.[31]

As John D. Cox has suggested, with particular reference to the influence of the *Book of Common Prayer* even upon a 'desultory Elizabethan churchgoer' (but also looking forward to Richard Hooker, to whom we shall return in due course), 'the religious narratives in Shakespeare's culture offered for suspecting human motives and actions were more pervasive, incisive, and compelling than contemporary skepticism'.[32] A culture that was bound by ritual and steeped in religious imaginings, the England of the late sixteenth and early seventeenth centuries was ordered, and its sense of time shaped, by the language and faith of the *Book of Common Prayer*.

And as the poet David Scott has observed, words then said what they meant – they bit, freed from all dry literalisms and rational equivalences. Geoffrey Cuming has noted that Cranmer's preference was for Anglo-Saxon rather than words of Latin derivation, as for example in the Collect for Whit-Sunday when he replaces (from the version in *The King's Primer*) 'instructed' with 'taught' and 'information' with 'sending light':[33]

> O God, which by the information of the Holy Ghost, hast instructed the hearts of thy faithful ... (*The King's Primer*)

> God, which as upon this day hast taught the hearts of thy faithful people by the sending to them the light of thy holy Spirit ... (Cranmer)

English was in the sixteenth century, of course, a language in transition. As Stella Brook, in her seminal work *The Language of the Book of Common Prayer* (1965), remarked, it is difficult to distinguish clearly between French and Latin loan words in English, and this, together with the use of words centred on Old English (*hālig* [holy] as opposed to the Latin *sanctus*), results in the frequent use of two words when one might have seemed adequate as a characteristic of Cranmer's liturgical English.[34] Familiar examples from the *Prayer Book*, all taken from the office of Evening Prayer, are 'perils and dangers', 'rest and quietness', 'sins and wickedness', 'devices and desires', and so on. Such doublings set an internal structure for the language of prayer which continued into the seventeenth century in such works as Lancelot Andrewes' *Preces Privatae*, originally written as personal devotions in Hebrew, Greek and Latin, though quickly translated into English from 1630 onwards,[35] a feature which was noted by Brightman in his 1903 edition of the *Preces* and later acknowledged by T. S. Eliot.[36] Such language moves forward by accumulation in a poetic structure that was analysed by James Mozley as long ago as 1842 in the high church journal the *British Critic*. I will return to this in more detail in due course.

Cranmer's preference for Anglo-Saxon words (which he shared with the biblical translator William Tyndale) suggests, as we saw in the last chapter[37] and as C. S. Lewis long ago observed, that the presence of the *cursus* of medieval Latin in the *Prayer Book* has been much overestimated.[38] Rather, as Lewis put it, the *Prayer Book* compilers and translators 'were fond of clashing strong syllables together in a manner that is purely native', and Lewis gives as examples 'borne of a pure virgin', and 'all desires known'.[39] If we extend Lewis' observations with regard to the development of the *Prayer Book* from sources such as Sarum and the late medieval English lay prayer books, the Primers, it is clear that it provides a worthy match for the prose and poetry of Shakespeare, a dramatic language that is at once elastic and exact, rooted in the imagination yet avoiding excess, adapted to public speaking and yet also deeply intimate and private.

I turn now to a moment in Shakespeare's dramas which suggests both his saturation in the *Prayer Book* and his theatrical appropriation of it despite the warnings in the Act of Uniformity against 'interludes, plays, songs, rhymes, or ... other open words', thus disallowing any direct quotation or reference to the *Prayer Book* on the stage. Older literary critics such as Roy W. Battenhouse and O. B. Hardison Jr as well as, more recently, Daniel Swift, have said something concerning Shakespeare's theatrical appropriation of the Eucharist, but so far there has only been one major study by Stephen Greenblatt of the 'afterlife' of Purgatory in Shakespeare's dramas.[40] Purgatory, described in the 22nd of the Thirty-Nine Articles of Religion as that 'Romish Doctrine' that is 'repugnant to the Word of God', stalks the pages of *Hamlet* from Hamlet's ghostly father's injunction to his son to 'remember me',[41] to Hamlet's agonized nightmare of revenge as scourge and minister. This is turned to a purgatorial laying bare of his own soul – 'to be or not to be' – until the final silence and the end of Hamlet's purgatory when the flights of angels (in Horatio's prayer, which is a jumbled translation of the '*In Paradisum*' from the Sarum rite[42]) sing him to his rest before the drum of Prince Fortinbras brings the audience back into harsh political reality.[43] The Ghost's demand that Hamlet 'remember me' is freighted with liturgical and theological complexities. As Daniel Swift has reminded us in his discussion of *Hamlet*, a liturgical 'remembrance' is far from something simply passive; it is 'the liturgical term [in the late medieval period] for the set of intercessory prayers given for a departed soul at regular intervals after death'.[44] Furthermore, the theological debates over 'remembrance' were at the very heart of Protestant controversies over the Eucharist. They were nothing short of a matter of life and death. The Ghost's command to remember is indeed enough to drive anyone to the brink of madness.

And what of that strange, mad scene in the graveyard at the beginning of Act 5, with Hamlet and Horatio's entrance being preceded by two clowns – a sexton and his mate? As the clowns prepare to dig Ophelia's grave they begin with a theological question regarding Ophelia's suicide and thus the propriety of Christian burial: 'Is she to be buried in Christian burial when she willfully seeks her own salvation?'[45] It was, of course, illegal to perform church rites on the stage[46] and so, before the procession with the corpse of Ophelia enters, including a 'Doctor of Divinity in cassock and gown', who offers advice for their 'maiméd rites' lest they 'should profane the service of the dead' with a requiem inappropriate for a suicide, Hamlet meditates upon the funeral liturgy with the skull of Yorick, the erstwhile king's jester.[47] As merely a stage rite this is necessarily 'maimed', at one level a far from exceptional scene in Renaissance drama (or, indeed, Counter-Reformation imagery[48]) employing a skull as a reminder of mortality, a *memento mori*, at another an ironic echo of the words of committal from the *Book of Common Prayer*, intoned by the priest as the body is lowered into the grave. In the 1549 *Prayer Book* the words are spoken *to* the deceased, but in 1552, and in subsequent *Prayer Books*, including that of 1559, there is a shift into the third person and the dead is spoken not *to*, but *about*. The dead, like Purgatory itself, are becoming more remote, a theme that underlies Hamlet's meditations. As Eamon Duffy has observed:

> If in the rites of the dying the prayer-book of 1552 seems to come from a different world not only from the medieval church, but even from the 1549 book, that gulf [between the living and the dead] is displayed even more starkly in the rites of the dead.[49]

Thus the priest intones, in words that would have been all too familiar to Shakespeare and his audiences as they watched and listened to *Hamlet*, 'we therefore commit his body to the ground, earth to earth, ashes to ashes, dust to dust, in sure and certain hope of resurrection to eternal life, through our Lord Jesus Christ, who shall change our vile body that it may be like to his glorious body ...'.[50]

Other uses of skulls on the Jacobean stage to remind us of the brevity and vanity of human life differ from *Hamlet*'s absorption with the liturgy of the *Book of Common Prayer*. Almost contemporary with Shakespeare's play is *The Revenger's Tragedy* (1607), normally attributed to Cyril Tourneur, in which the revenger Vindice holds aloft the skull of his erstwhile lady and utters the grim words:

> Does every proud and self-affecting dame
> Camphor her face for this, and grieve her maker
> In sinful baths of milk ...[51]

Hamlet, however, placing the skull of Yorick on the ground, reflects on the 'noble dust of Alexander', which is changed not into a glorious, Christ-like body in the resurrection, but is rather traced in the imagination 'till a' find it stopping a bung hole'. Hamlet follows, and then distorts, the logic and narrative of the Church's liturgy of the burial of the dead

> as thus – Alexander died, Alexander was buried, Alexander returneth to dust, the dust is earth, of earth we make loam, and why of that loam whereto he was converted might they not stop a beer-barrel?[52]

Shakespeare is here deliberately unpicking the logic of the shifting theological emphases in the funeral liturgy from the *Prayer Books* of 1549, to 1552 and then 1559. In Duffy's words:

> The dead could be spoken to directly, even in 1549, because in some sense they still belonged within the human community. But in the world of the 1552 book the dead were no longer with us. They could neither be spoken to nor even about, in any way that affected their well-being ... The service was no longer a rite of intercession on behalf of the dead, but an exhortation to faith on the part of the living.[53]

And so, as Hamlet, still among the living, muses upon the fate of the great Alexander, he is disturbed by the arrival of the royal party with the Doctor of Divinity and the body of Ophelia 'with such maiméd rites'. As

Hamlet and Laertes leap, one after the other, into Ophelia's grave they, with Claudius and Gertrude, are in effect by now not with the living but already among the dead, even now beyond the boundaries of the human community.

As has often been noted, the reformation of burial rites within the tradition of the English *Prayer Books* was both compromised and contentious. There were even protests from those who regarded burial as a merely secular matter.[54] In *Hamlet* Shakespeare is exploring both these anxieties and also, despite the prohibition in the Thirty-Nine Articles, the persistent ghostly afterlife of medieval beliefs in Purgatory and other 'Romish doctrines' in the context of the dramatic culture of Renaissance revenge tragedy, unpicking in dramatic verse the theological world that was at the same time bound by the *Book of Common Prayer*. As Robert Ornstein well expressed it, writing of an age of imposed liturgical uniformity, 'Because he sees the world feelingly, Shakespeare performs the immemorial service of the artist to society: he humanizes the categorical imperatives which the stern didacticist offers as the sum of ethical truth.'[55] Yet, it might be said, the 1559 *Book of Common Prayer* was a worthy opponent for Shakespeare, wrought from the same rich tradition of language expressed through its ritual poetics.

The culture and manner of learning of the *English Prayer Books*, so much of which began in the mind and spirit of Archbishop Thomas Cranmer, was continued in the patterns of prayer and devotion in the seventeenth century and provided a poetic framework and diction that defined Anglicanism and saturated English literature. Bishop Lancelot Andrewes' *Preces Privatae* were compiled for his personal use, for private rather than public prayer. The first comprehensive edition, in Greek and Latin, with some Hebrew, was published in 1675, but numerous English, at first partial, translations and selections were published from 1630 onwards, including, much later, a text translated by John Henry Newman as the 78th of the *Tracts for the Times* in 1840. It was upon this version, together with the 1844 translation by John Mason Neale, that the liturgical scholar F. E. Brightman, the author and editor of *The English Rite* (1915), depended heavily for his critical edition of the *Preces Privatae* of 1903. Of the original manuscript of the prayers used by Bishop Andrewes, Richard Drake, their first translator, wrote:

> Had you seen the original manuscript, happy in the glorious deformity thereof, being slubbered with his pious hands, and watered with his penitential tears, you would have been forced to confess, that book belonged to no other than pure and primitive devotion.

Like all good working prayer books and Bibles, Bishop Andrewes' book of devotion was worn by much use and handling.[56] Penitential, like the *Book of Common Prayer* itself, the *Preces Privatae* provide a confessional and devotional framework within Anglicanism for the whole Christian life, both personal and national. As with Cranmer's liturgical compositions, they are woven from Scripture and Bishop Andrewes' own wide reading in ancient Christian liturgies both Eastern and Western, the Primers and medieval rites, the prayers of the synagogues and rabbinical writers, the early Church Fathers, above all John Chrysostom, the thirteenth-century *Golden Legend* of Jacobus de Voragine, and classical authors. In Dean R. W. Church's words, the *Preces* bring the spirit of the *Prayer Book* 'from the Church to the closet'.[57] They are both private and communal.

But Bishop Andrewes differs from Archbishop Cranmer in one important respect. If Cranmer admitted that he lacked both grace and facility in verse, then Andrewes, in both his private prayers and his sermons, brings the *Prayer Book* firmly into the realm of a ritual poetics. James Mozley expands upon this at length in his article 'Bishop Andrewes' Sermons' in the *British Critic* for January 1842. To begin with, Mozley affirms, Andrewes' prayers embrace a holistic vision which connects each day with a sense of the unity of all creation under God and 'which realizes the facts of Scripture, sees mysteries in common things, and feels itself still living amid visible traces of a divine dispensation'.[58] Andrewes' grammar progresses by a process of accumulation, like that of the *Prayer Book*, words building precisely upon words in a manner to be explored theologically by Newman in his *Grammar of Assent* (1870) until the moment of assent, or faith, is realized rather than arrived at by the processes of logic. T. S. Eliot, who as a poet learnt much from Andrewes, expresses this dramatically.

> Andrewes takes a word and derives the world from it; squeezing and squeezing the word until it yields a full juice of meaning which we should never have supposed any word to possess. In this process the qualities which we have mentioned, of ordonnance and precision, are exercised.[59]

In Andrewes' 'poetry', as in the verses of George Herbert, the sense of words multiplies by growing combinations, constructing what we have called constitutive fictions whereby a public world is created.[60]

Here is one example, using Brightman's translation. It is a prayer to be used 'On Waking', prior to the recital of the morning hymn, the *Gloria in Excelsis*.[61] This brief prayer of Bishop Andrewes draws almost entirely upon Psalms 43, 4, 36 and the book of Numbers, and also has a passing reference to Matthew 5.45, from the Vulgate version:

Thou who sendest forth the light, createst the morning,
makest the sun to rise on the good and on the evil:
enlighten the blindness of our minds with the
knowledge of the truth:
lift Thou up the light of thy countenance upon us
that in thy light we may see light,
and, at the last, in the light of grace the light
of glory.[62]

Apart from the obvious references to the psalms, there is also the echo of the Third Collect for Evensong from the *Prayer Book*, 'for Aid against all Perils', with its double meaning in the words 'lighten our darkness we beseech thee, O Lord'. This is now revisited in the light of morning which comes also with the 'knowledge of the truth'[63] to the darkness of our minds. The theme of light is developed further with a reference in the next line to the great priestly prayer from Numbers 6.24–26 which reads (in the King James Version):

The Lord bless thee and keep thee:
The Lord make his face shine upon thee, and be gracious unto thee:
The Lord lift up his countenance upon thee, and give thee peace.

The word 'light' is finally used four times in the last two lines of the prayer, reminding us of Eliot's image of 'squeezing and squeezing the word until it yields a full juice of meaning'. In the light of God, which he sends each morning as he creates the world anew, we 'see light'. (Compare Psalm 36.9 in the Coverdale translation as used, after Andrewes' time, in the 1662 *Book of Common Prayer*: 'For with thee is the well of life: and in thy light shall we see light.') Eventually, in an eschatological image 'at the last', by the light of grace we enter the light of glory. The day begins, then, for Bishop Andrewes with a meditation upon the new light created by God, through an accumulation of reflection as the word 'light' bears, little by little, a growing theological burden of meaning. The prayer is a perfect example of Brightman's description of Andrewes' liturgical poetic processes, and he has learnt this from his absorption in the *Prayer Book*. In Brightman's words:

... the structure is not merely an external scheme or framework: the internal structure is as close as the external. Andrewes develops an idea he has in his mind: every line tells and adds something. He does not expatiate, but moves forward; if he repeats, it is because the repetition has

> a real force of expression; if he accumulates, each new word or phrase represents a new development, a substantive addition to what he is saying ... His quotation is not decoration or irrelevance, but the matter in which he expresses what he wants to say.[64]

It was precisely this process that gained the approval of T. S. Eliot and which Eliot built into his own poetry written after his conversion to Anglicanism in 1927, and increasingly under the shadowing wings of the *Book of Common Prayer*. A perfect example of Eliot's poetics within this tradition is the opening of his poem 'Journey of the Magi' which is drawn directly from a sermon of Bishop Andrewes on the journey of the wise men from the East. In the end, are the words Andrewes' or Eliot's – or are they drawn together in a new unity that is 'common' (a word, we may recall, used to effect in *Hamlet*) to both, held somewhere between what I have termed in Chapter 3 a fictional poetic and a ritual poetic? Here is Andrewes' sermon:

> It was no summer progress. A cold coming they had of it at this time of the year, just the worst time of the year to take a journey, and specially a long journey in. The ways deep, the weather sharp, the days short, the sun farthest off, *in solstitio brumali*, 'the very dead of winter.'[65]

And now Eliot's poem:

> 'A cold coming we had of it,
> Just the worst time of the year
> For a journey, and such a long journey:
> The ways deep and the weather sharp,
> The very dead of winter.'[66]

The uniformity demanded by the *Book of Common Prayer* of 1559 is somehow built into the very language of the prayers. It is a commonality approved and explored by Richard Hooker in Book V of *Of the Laws of Ecclesiastical Polity* (1597), his most extended discussion of Anglican worship. As in the *Prayer Book* and the work of Bishop Andrewes, Hooker writes from within a network of biblical allusion, combined with references to the Church Fathers – Ambrose, Basil, Chrysostom (of course) and so on. Public prayer, Hooker affirms, lies at the very heart of the community and our commonality.

> When we publicly make our prayers, it cannot be but that we do it with much more comfort than in private, for that the things we ask publicly

> are approved as needful and good in the judgment of all, we hear them sought for and desired with common consent.[67]

For Hooker, prayer is nothing less than a duty to our neighbour, maintained by 'the zeal and fervency' of the priest, for:

> If he praise not God with all his might; if he pour not out his soul in prayer; if he take not their causes to heart, or speak not as Moses, Daniel, and Ezra did for their people: how should there be but in them frozen coldness, when his affections seem benumbed from whom theirs should take fire?[68]

Hooker's parson is clearly akin to the Country Parson of George Herbert's prose manual *A Priest to the Temple* (published posthumously, 1652), written 35 years after Hooker's work was published. His very prose resonates with the insistences of the language of the *Prayer Book*. It is hardly surprising then that Hooker's editor in 1865 was John Keble, another Anglican divine whose poetry and prose, in prayer, theology and sermon, was also utterly embraced by the *Prayer Book* and its cadences.

We have seen how the constitutive fiction and ritual poetics of such cadences, a description that does not seek for one moment to deny its claims to truth under God, even as lived under the imperfections of theological debate and argument, spread deeply into the fabric of English language, literature and culture. Without the *Book of Common Prayer* of 1559 there would be no Shakespeare as we know him, its particular rhythms, ceremonials and processions running deep within the fabric of society even as faith itself began to wane and language became more literal and less imaginative. To return to it is to be reminded of a truth at once simple and profound: that we have been, are and continue to be built upon language, not least in the life of our liturgy, and to lose the sense of its care for us by our failures of attention is perilous indeed.

> We needed only the help which
> the right placing of a relative pronoun
> could manage. Words, then, said what they meant;
> they bit.[69]

PART IV

The *Alternative Service Book* and *Common Worship*

8

Language and Liturgical Revision in the Church of England

Εοἰκε δε ... Περι ταυτα και ἐν τοις αὐτοις εἰναι ἡ τε φιλια και το δικαιον

(Aristotle, *Nichomachaean Ethics*)

I turn now to the processes of liturgical revision that took place in the Church of England in the later part of the twentieth century and the early twenty-first century. This is not intended in any sense to be a comprehensive review either historically or theologically. Rather, I will seek to build upon what I have so far said about the language of ritual poetics in both the early Church and the English Reformation in the earlier parts of this book. I begin by referring to an essay written by an Australian professor of English literature and a conservative opponent of the revision of liturgical language that led in the Church of England, eventually, to the publication of *The Alternative Service Book*[1] in 1980.

I first encountered Professor Barry Spurr long before I actually met him in person in the University of Sydney, as is often the way with academics, through reading one of his essays on the 1978 *An Australian Prayer Book* which he contributed to a book entitled *No Alternative: The Prayer Book Controversy* (1981).[2] Spurr described the *Australian Prayer Book* of 1978 as 'a testament to disunity' and 'a theological patchwork and a linguistic potpourri'.[3] Spurr's essay was written at a time of immense liturgical revisionary activity within the Anglican Communion world-wide which in England culminated, for a time at least, in 1980 and the *ASB*, the first authorized book of worship in the Church of England for over 300 years since the *Book of Common Prayer* of 1662. My father Ronald Jasper, as Chairman of the Church of England Liturgical Commission between 1964 and 1980, was perceived by many people as one of the 'well-intentioned wreckers'[4] of the glories of the *Prayer Book*, scholars and church-people who were robbing the Church of England of its liturgical strengths and above all the glories of its language.

In the passage of time the *ASB* itself has passed into history, and many of the debates in the Church up to 1980 that focused upon the impoverishment of language in contemporary forms of worship have been largely forgotten and would seem now rather old-fashioned. But they did address real issues and they may be worth returning to and their underlying significance re-examined in a more contemporary context. It was indubitably the case that the English language of the later part of the twentieth century was more prosaic, literal and utilitarian than the prose and verse of the sixteenth century that was to reach its finest flowering in the English of Shakespeare and his contemporaries. But equally it would be absurd to maintain that a century that gave us in the field of literature and poetry James Joyce, T. S. Eliot, W. H. Auden and Seamus Heaney, among many others, was bereft of a linguistic instrument that could sound within a liturgical and ritual poetics with subtlety and extraordinary beauty. It is true that some of the reasons for the difficulties felt within the sphere of liturgical language may lie within the nature of the contemporary Church itself which has rendered it peculiarly difficult to speak with proper resonance in the particular language and poetics demanded by liturgical utterance and practice. For on the whole theology has not flourished in the Church of England, with some memorable exceptions among its archbishops from Michael Ramsey to Rowan Williams, and as it forgets its theological and spiritual richness, both historically and culturally, the Church begins to speak in the language of its own marginalized nature and gets the dull liturgy it deserves. Archbishop Cranmer, as he knew to the ultimate cost of his life, lived in stirring times, not least theologically, and thus language really *mattered* and words bit. But, still, it was never simply the case that when we ceased to speak in the language of Archbishop Cranmer we lost touch in church with the 'markers of transcendence', as David Martin once suggested.[5] There was far more to it than that.

It is a deep irony that those who have most vigorously defended the Anglican *Book of Common Prayer* – a seventeenth-century book that is deeply rooted in the sixteenth century – on the bases of beauty, mystery and antiquity have often done so in terms that Thomas Cranmer himself would have profoundly rejected.[6] Writing to Queen Mary during his imprisonment and awaiting death, Cranmer insisted upon the use of language in the liturgy in all its aspects that must be contemporary and clear, qualities that need not rob it of the sense of mystery beyond our understanding. Cranmer writes:

> ... that whether the priests rehearse the wonderful works of God, or the great benefits of God unto mankind above all other creatures, or give

> thanks unto God, or make open confession of their faith, or humble confession of their sins, with earnest request of mercy and forgiveness, or make suit unto God for anything; then all the people, understanding what the priests say, might give their minds and voices with them and say Amen ...[7]

This was the principle upon which William Tyndale produced his English translation of the Scriptures, as expressed in his rendition of Erasmus' *Exhortations to the Diligent Study of Scripture* (1529), recalling, somewhat idealistically, the spiritual needs of the ploughman and the weaver, and further stating, 'I would desire that all women should reade the Gospell and Paule's epistles, and I wold to god they were translated in to the tonges of all men.'[8] Tyndale's point is that the words should be clear that the mystery may, through them, sink in. As in Shakespeare's greatest plays, the language of Scripture must combine a naturally accessible sense and rhythm with, as we saw in Chapter 1,[9] a subtle employment of grammar and rhetoric. Not only is the scholarly Tyndale wholly alert to the expressive word-play in *koine* Greek, as opposed to the heavy Latinate tendencies of more recent twentieth-century translations such as the *New English Bible*, but he combines this with what David Daniell has called his 'conscious use of everyday words without inversions, a neutral word-order, and a wonderful ear'.[10] Tyndale's language is rarely less than natural, but nonetheless poetic for that.

Cranmer was also well aware of the way in which language continually changes, and that therefore both Scripture and the liturgy must regularly be re-translated and revised, writing of the English of the Saxon Bible that when it 'waxed old and out of common usage, because folk should not lack the fruit of common reading, it was again translated into the new language'.[11] His observation is far from unique: it was made long ago by Thucydides writing of the Peloponnesian War at a time in Greece when words were losing their meaning; Proust writes of such linguistic deterioration in France at the end of his life in the early twentieth century. Yet change is not always a matter of decay, but may also be deeply creative. Henry David Thoreau, for example, moving to live in solitary splendour by Walden Pond in the woods in 1845, writes of creating a new life and new language.[12]

It is one thing to delight in a glorious performance of Shakespeare on the stage, and quite another to imagine what it would be like to employ the rich and complex language of a Hamlet or a Lear in daily life today. The language of the liturgy, on the other hand, makes different and unique demands upon us, and the glory of the *Book of Common Prayer* lies to a large extent in its capacity to address the common joys and sorrows of human life, of marriage and death, of sun and rain, living in a subtle language that sustains for us at the same time the mystery of God. For its words and grammar speak of heaven and they do so with a necessary theological delicacy and precision, a discipline by which Shakespeare was never so constrained. The pressure for liturgical reform in the Church of England was far from new in the twentieth century though its earlier obsession, most particularly in the nineteenth century, was almost entirely with theological questions and rarely with matters of language.[13] But care for both theology and its language in worship and praise cannot be separated. It was the twentieth century, after the reforms of the Second Vatican Council and with its broader philosophical and cultural anxieties about the crisis in language after Ferdinand de Saussure and Heidegger and up to Michel Foucault and Derrida,[14] that brought the dilemma of the Anglican liturgy to a head. It was not just a crisis in language, it was an issue of *liturgical language*.

Bishop Stephen Neill once wrote that the Church of England in the twentieth century had only two great 'liturgiologists', as he termed them: F. E. Brightman, the author and editor of the still standard work *The English Rite* (1915), and F. C. Burkitt, Norris Professor of Divinity at Cambridge from 1905 until shortly before his death in 1935, who once stated that he wished for only one change in the 1662 liturgy – the substitution of 'and' for 'or' between the prayer of oblation and the prayer of thanksgiving.[15] The only recent competitor to Brightman's work, now more than a century old, is the edition of the *Prayer Books* of 1549, 1559 and 1662 by a professor of English Literature, Brian Cummings, who, despite a fine sense of the theological, tends to present the sixteenth-century *Prayer Books* as examples of 'literary revivalism' as much as or even more than 'liturgical reform'.[16] The problem is, of course, that no one in the present time in the Church of England has ever quite decided what a 'liturgiologist' exactly is. To put this another way, and as is the case with most academic disciplines, is it safe to leave the liturgy of the Church and its reform entirely in the hands of the 'liturgists'? Most serious scholars of liturgy (and those most responsible for its reform in various churches and denominations after Vatican II) have been historians, with an entirely proper sense of historical continuity not simply from the Reformation, but from the earliest times of the Christian Church until the present day. By far the most popular, and perhaps the most influential, work in English liturgical studies in the twentieth century remains Dom Gregory Dix's *The Shape of the Liturgy* (1945), written by a man who had not the slightest interest in the problems of liturgical revision, who harboured an almost pathological hatred of Archbishop Cranmer and the Reformation, held a particular, if not peculiar, sense of theology and was, as Neill puts it, 'highly skilled in making the worse appear the better reason'.[17] He took no interest whatever in the problems of a contemporary liturgical language.

Now, at a time when the study of liturgy is barely given any space in serious theological study or ministerial training and many clergy are, as a result, broadly liturgically illiterate, neither theologians nor literary critics properly participate in discussions that require a delicate balance between the two fields of theology and the study of language in literature. Without this careful exchange, how is the proper practice of liturgy in the midst of life, when people require meaningful words when they are married, die, seek forgiveness or celebrate things of most importance, to be sustained by a careful articulation of profound truths that can become sour and toxic unless carefully tended by the right words said in the right way? The study, writing and practice of liturgical language may be one of the few genuine examples of the enterprise of 'interdisciplinarity' about which so much is spoken in our universities – and so little actually done. For interdisciplinary study is caught within a dilemma, as Stanley Fish, a professor of English and of Law, once described it in an essay entitled 'Being Interdisciplinary Is So Very Hard to Do', where he points out that it usually involves the annexation of one or more fields by another, and students of literature, in particular, have become very adept at colonizing philosophy, psychology, and even theology, frequently with strange results. Fish, however, with typical irony, celebrates the imperialistic success of literary studies inasmuch as 'from a certain point of view, the traditional disciplines have played themselves out and it is time to fashion a new one'. But the sting is in the tail as Fish concludes:

> ... my pleasure at these developments has nothing to do with the larger claims – claims of liberation, freedom, openness – often made for them. The American mind, like any other, will always be closed, and the only question is whether we find the form of closure it currently assumes answerable to our present urgencies.[18]

And so, in this culture of the closed mind, what of the liturgy and its theological claims for liberation, freedom, salvation? Or does it also rejoice in closure and isolation? In fact, the seeming divorce between liturgy and theology relentlessly takes us to Fish's position – celebrating the new 'field' of cultural studies while neglecting the larger claims with a dangerously closed mind. The dilemma is exposed in the forms of language we are content to use, and within that the fundamental theological debates that examine how we express and find God: whether we pursue theo*logy*, beginning from human thought and speech about God, or *theo*logy, which responds to God's revelation to us through words with bite.[19] Bridget Nichols, in a sadly neglected book, *Liturgical Hermeneutics* (1996), has pointed out that 'in structural terms, liturgical language and secular language share fundamental grammatical conventions, as well as the characteristic of ritual or iterability'.[20] Of course the overlap and commonalities are crucial if liturgical language is to remain meaningful and effective, the same as yet different from the language of everyday life. Words in liturgy *do* things, though not in the sense of the performative utterance of J. L. Austin[21] – as the poet says, they bite. Nichols goes on to suggest what lies at the heart of the concerns of all those who expressed anxiety about what was felt to be the rather dull, prosaic language of twentieth-century liturgical reformers.

> The real risk in liturgical language is not that it is different, but that it is reassuringly the same. Only, it engages its user in *qualitatively more profound commitments* than they will have experienced when making similar verbal contracts in the extra-liturgical context.[22]

Liturgical language and its poetics, then, is different, it is odd and risky, actually *doing* that which theologians just talk about. It may be that the genius of a Tyndale or a Cranmer got it just right in their day, under the pressures of acute political and theological anxieties but today, as formal religion fades, liturgy has to engage fully with the hermeneutical issue of horizons, and to express a faith that is eschatological and forward looking. It has to perform the task of being a vehicle that retains its living continuity with the past but also promises a future within the frequently mundane realities of the present. What Nichols finally urges us to seek in liturgy and its language is the capacity to preserve 'the traces of the sense of the sacred origin of humanity, and the notion of ultimate worth defined by something beyond the human sphere'.[23] This is a hard task in today's world.

There are, of course, no simple answers to this challenge to recover a ritual poetics in our words of worship. When, in 1990, in the last year of his life, I edited with my father a volume of essays entitled *Language and the Worship of the Church*, we tried to cover the outfield, but in the end, I think, we missed the heart of the matter. Essays in that book on early Christian rhetoric, Cranmer as creative writer, sociolinguistics and music all finally shied away from the essential task of rethinking theologically the very foundations of the form of liturgical language. Perhaps the most important essay in the book was by the philosopher Martin Warner with its careful introduction to the distinction between 'implicate' and 'implicature', the latter stretching 'wider than mere implications, for they [implicatures] are context-dependent, often in non-conventional ways; even if the implications of what is said are entirely innocent it does not follow that the implicatures are'.[24] We have been warned – we are in dangerous territory, not entirely innocent, or rather, we stand fearfully on holy ground. With such a warning we are wise to have our wits and intelligence about us in the matter of language, and with our spiritual awareness at full stretch. When, in the early 1980s, I began in Durham University the series of academic conferences on theology and literature that continue to the present day, we were wisely advised to have a philosopher at hand for the sake of just such precision in language and thought. Thus D. Z. Phillips warned us of the importance of good grammar, for 'if we infringe these grammatical requirements we shall soon find ourselves engaged in trivialities or nonsense. The most common infringements come about by trying to sever a concept from the conditions of its application.'[25] And philosophers can, at times, in their careful thinking, be more spiritually conscious than they are aware themselves.

This return to the theme of grammar is deliberate and takes me back to John Henry Newman's key work, the *Essay in Aid of a Grammar of Assent* (1870). For it was Cardinal Newman who learnt from the poet Samuel Taylor Coleridge that notion of verbal tradition and the sense of language as, in John Coulson's words, 'a living organism whose function is to reconcile the past and present experiences of a community'.[26] Such language we might describe as 'fiduciary' – a term that I have already briefly discussed at the beginning of Chapter 1.[27] It is by such language that, in both poetry and religion, we are drawn by inference to make an act of assent, a process that necessarily begins with trust (what S. T. Coleridge in his *Biographia Literaria* [1817] described as the willing suspension of disbelief[28]) in expressions that are often highly elusive, symbolic or metaphorical. Thus, as John Coulson remarks, without forgetting the distinction between them, 'understanding religious [and, we may add, liturgical] language is a function of understanding poetic language'.[29] Cardinal Newman (himself a poet), however, takes a further step that is not to be found in Coleridge. He returns us to the theological. Coulson acknowledges that Coleridge seeks to describes *how* we respond to what we might call the language of ultimate concern, but he fails to make the next move which is concerned with *what* that language is about. In short, is such language, unlike Austin's performative utterance, finally true or false and is it capable of sustaining an enquiry into such a distinction?[30]

It is precisely this enquiry that Newman embarks upon in the *Grammar of Assent*, and it is why this book is such a key text for our present concerns with liturgical language. In many ways the *Grammar* has its origins in Newman's *University Sermons*, delivered in Oxford between 1826 and 1843, which focused upon the theological issue of the relations between faith and reason. At the heart of Newman's careful epistemology of assent is the sense of living language that he had first encountered in the writings of Coleridge. As Newman moves towards his crucial notion of the Illative Sense, that is, the faculty of judging from given facts by processes that are beyond logic, it is just such fiduciary language that underlies it. In the matter of religious assent, Newman carefully distinguishes between 'certainty' and 'certitude'. He writes:

> Certitude is not a passive impression made upon the mind from without, by argumentative compulsion, but in all concrete questions (nay, even in abstract, for though the reasoning is abstract, the mind which judges of it is concrete) it is an active recognition of propositions as true, such as it is the duty of each individual himself to exercise at the bidding of reason, and, when reason forbids, to withhold. And reason never bids us be certain except on an absolute proof; and such a proof can never be furnished to us by the logic of words, for as certitude is of the mind, so is the act of inference which leads to it.[31]

The context for such a careful description of religious certitude can be nothing less than a form of language that is both theologically and poetically embraced by the act of worship – in short, liturgical language and its ritual poetics.

Such language, by virtue of its very energy that runs beyond mere logic, can never be 'normal' as it stretches at once both from and towards the divine mystery, yet it lives and breathes through the cadences of living, everyday (in Newman's word 'concrete') speech. Open to change, it yet develops in range and subtlety precisely by a *resistance* to new words and ideas (an adherence to the tradition), whereby it comes to adapt and to accommodate new patterns of thought.[32] The characteristics of such language are creativity and poetic allusiveness: as the poet Emily Dickinson teaches, 'Tell all the Truth but tell it slant.' For truth, she goes on, must 'dazzle gradually' lest it blind us.[33] This is also the nature of the language of transcendence – that of theo*logy* rather than *theo*logy, though utterly embraced by the careful processes of theological thinking. It recognizes the necessity of continuity while at the same time it is open to the radically new, facing the future in God. It might best be described in the words of the French phenomenologist and philosopher Jean-Luc Marion as the 'prolegomena to charity' within which, in the final analysis we live, breathe and have our being.[34]

And so, as I draw this short chapter to a conclusion, and before I move on to the issue of modern liturgical revision in the Church of England, I have sought here to revisit an old argument and to add a few new thoughts to the finally elusive issue of the nature of liturgical language – a language close to that of the poet but always and of necessity more, and more strange. And we find now, as the churches of the West decline, that their liturgical context grows, paradoxically, wider. In a post-Heideggarian world, liturgy becomes a form of dwelling in the presence of God (*coram Dei*) and, as the Christian asks what it is to exist liturgically in the 'place' of prayer, so the ancient, transgressive, sacred language of the liturgy contains the most dynamic of all words meeting the unthinkable which has given them life. Liturgy and its practice is not simply about going to church and what we do there (though that, and its particular language, does remain profoundly important). But finally, liturgy, and through it theology, becomes a whole way of living, its language less an affirmation or attempt at bold statement, than words that express an existence that is known as genuinely *kenotic*. In the words of Jean-Yves Lacoste, we then begin to approach, in the attempt to 'live' liturgically, 'the paradoxical joy that is born of humiliation [which] may be the *fundamental mood* of pre-eschatological experience'.[35] It is, perhaps, only then that we can enter, in time and in eternity, into the joy of the Sanctus within the great Eucharistic Prayer of thanksgiving, when finally all human words are lost in wonder and praise.[36] Perhaps only then can we begin again to regain that faith in language that has so often in recent years seemed thin and uncreative. A poet like R. S. Thomas might express his despair in the face of the contemporary Augean stable of utilitarian newsprint, pompous bureaucrats and drab business style so that 'when so much of that language is either vile or without flavour, the poet has no sound basis from which to work'.[37] Yet, dare we say, is this not to look in the wrong place for the words of worship? We look out and live in the real world of cities and economies and we look back to the wisdom of the tradition of prayer and praise that continues to teach and inspire us, but finally we look up for the word that will be given to us.

And so I turn now to the more immediate matter of liturgical revision in the Church of England during the two decades before the publication of the *ASB*.

9

The Background to *The Alternative Service Book*

Some things, it seems, never change. It was over a hundred years ago in 1903 that the liturgical scholar Percy Dearmer began the fourth edition of his influential book *The Parson's Handbook* with these words.

> The object of this Handbook is to help, in however humble a way, towards remedying the lamentable confusion, lawlessness, and vulgarity which are conspicuous in the Church at this time.
>
> The confusion is due to the want of liturgical knowledge among the clergy, and of consistent example among those in authority.[1]

The words, sadly, seem as relevant today in the early twenty-first century. But we must begin by going back some fifty years or so. This chapter will examine the debates on liturgical language that accompanied the processes of liturgical revision that took place in the Church of England in the later years of the twentieth century, primarily between 1960 and 1980, and in the ecumenical aftermath of the Second Vatican Council, debates in which, if there was considerable liturgical scholarship employed, there was also certainly a disjunct between the arguments regarding the language of the liturgy and the wider cultural and philosophical concerns with the nature of, and sense of crisis in, language within culture and society. No one seems to have been aware of issues in language since Ferdinand de Saussure or Wittgenstein.

In 1974, a collection of essays edited by my father, R. C. D. Jasper, when he was Chair of the Church of England Liturgical Commission, most of them written by fellow members of the Commission, was published under the title *The Eucharist Today: Studies on Series 3*. Six years later it was this same Commission that produced, under the authority of the General Synod of the Church of England, *The Alternative Service Book* (1980), the first new authorized liturgical book for public worship in the Church of England since the *Book of Common Prayer* of 1662. The last essay in the collection, by J. L. Houlden, a member of the Commission, is a curious exercise in criticism which raised questions that were, it seems, as quickly forgotten as they were asked. Houlden, a notable New Testament scholar and an Anglican clergyman who was at that time Principal of Cuddesdon Theological College, laments the isolation of liturgical study both within the broader realm of theology and beyond its boundaries. In reflecting upon the hugely significant exercise of liturgical reform in the Church of England, and in other denominations also, Houlden remarks:

> You discover that the principles of liturgy have become a discipline in their own right, quite apart from other aspects of Christian thought. It is a fact that is worth contemplating, for it is surely quite new in Christian life, that liturgy can be constructed without significant reference to the total theological scene and seeing itself as an independent skill. Is this not disturbing?[2]

Houlden suggests that the main achievements of liturgical reform in his time have been twofold: to make it easier to understand and to modernize the language 'though with haziness about the criteria'.[3] Whether liturgy should be easy to understand and clearly comprehensible is indeed a serious question, as I have suggested throughout this book, but my concern in this chapter will be largely with the related issue and particular problem of the attempt to modernize liturgical language for use in the twentieth century. One should note in passing, however, that in the passage of time words both lose and change their meanings, so that, for example, 'incomprehensible' as used in the Athanasian Creed of the 1662 *Prayer Book* meant then not 'unintelligible' but 'without limits'.[4] At the same time, it is important to recognize that, as Ferdinand de Saussure acknowledged in his studies upon the consequences of the arbitrary nature of the sign, the development of meaning in language is both synchronic and diachronic, with priority clearly ascribed to the former so that forms and meanings in words 'constitute an unbroken chain of synchronic identities'.[5] Language changes within a certain consistency. The consequences of such synchronicity have very infrequently been acknowledged in debates on liturgical language (by liturgists, theologians, sociologists and others, all of them but rarely if ever students of linguistics) that simply assume a diachronicity in language through the processes of history that Saussure, for one, would have questioned. The study and reform of liturgy has been almost exclusively a matter for historians or at least those historically trained. But I run ahead of myself.

To return to Houlden's essay, I would expand, therefore, his criticism even further, and enquire as to the consequences of liturgical isolation not only from the development of theology, but also from far wider issues in thinking and scholarship concerning language within the sphere of the humanities and social sciences. In the volume entitled *Language and the Worship of the Church*, which my father and I edited in 1990, there were only two essays that seriously extended the discussion beyond ecclesial boundaries. This, as I reflect back, was a considerable weakness in the book. The first, by David Crystal, a professor of linguistics who, as more or less a lone voice, has published widely on liturgy and linguistics as well as on the English language since the King James Bible,[6] notes at the outset that 'the changes which have taken place in religious language since the 1960s require a ... broadening of perspective if the distinctiveness of contemporary liturgical language is to be appreciated'.[7] The second, which I have already mentioned briefly in the last chapter,[8] by a philosopher, Martin Warner, suggests a philosophical issue that has never, as far as I am aware, been further pursued in attentions given to liturgical language. It concerns the distinction between 'implicate' and 'implicature', fully recognizing the difficult, and by no means entirely innocent, nature of the language of worship.

> The terms 'implicate' and 'implicature' are constructed after the analogy of 'imply' and 'implication'; the latter are truth-functional notions to be analysed according to standard logical principles, but implicatures stretch wider than mere implications, for they are context-dependent, often in non-conventional ways; even if the implications of what is said are entirely innocent it does not follow that the implicatures are.[9]

Clearly this is of importance for what I have been suggesting is the 'odd' nature of liturgical language and its ritual poetics as 'context-dependent' and 'non-conventional'. Thus, in the light of this unheeded warning from Warner it behoves us, I think, to return, briefly, to broader issues in religious language and theology that were kept well in the background during the arguments on language and worship in the Church of England up to the publication of the *ASB* in 1980. Bishop Ian Ramsey's widely read book *Religious Language* was published in 1957 and remains useful today, though largely forgotten. Beginning in the eighteenth century with Bishop Butler and 'religious situations' Ramsey stressed the 'oddity' of religious language drawn, ultimately, from the literature of the Bible and regarded in clear distinction from John Locke's claim for a 'plain and intelligible' account of biblical history. A 'characteristically religious situation' is evoked, Ramsey suggested, 'when the explorer steps into hitherto unknown and untrodden land. For here is mystery and awe in large measure.'[10] The sense in such a situation, however, must always be eschatological and forward-looking rather than retrospective. At the same time, such language is not imprecise but, quite to the contrary, demands careful logical mapping as a preliminary to any controversy or doctrinal debate. In the distinctive context of Christian language there is necessarily both 'impropriety' *and* 'intelligibility' (what one might call a disciplined oddity), and in this context, although Ramsey does not address specifically the language of worship and liturgy, he states quite clearly that 'a theology which cannot be preached is about as objectionable as preaching which cannot be theologically defended'.[11] The shadows of Percy Dearmer's warnings on the dangers of ignorance among the clergy in 1903 are coldly felt.

At the same time, theology and its practice in the Church was failing to acknowledge the broad shadow of Ludwig Wittgenstein and his philosophy of language. In the work of Fergus Kerr in *Theology after Wittgenstein* (1986), and behind Kerr the even larger philosophical shade of Stanley Cavell in *The Claim of Reason* (1979), we perceive how the Wittgenstein of the *Philosophical Investigations* (English edition 1953) was eroding the 'metaphysical load that Christian practice and discourse carry'.[12] Kerr's argument is that theology in the twentieth century was unable to free itself of 'versions of the mental ego of Cartesianism' in its understanding of the self, and more often than not was even unaware of this.[13] At the heart of this discussion is a sense of language that in Wittgenstein becomes an invitation 'to renew and expand our sense of wonder'[14] in and beyond the immediacy of words. Kerr's summary of Wittgenstein's achievement might be read as an invitation to liturgical reflection, utterance and practice – an invitation that went unheeded inasmuch as the Cartesian ego remained trapped (entirely unselfconsciously) in its own ultimate isolation. Kerr puts it clearly in this way.

> Wittgenstein's critique is directed at much less blatant varieties of the Gnosticism that is disseminated throughout our culture ... His emphasis on 'our life', on 'action' and on the human being as the best model of the mind, certainly puts an end to the picture of the solitary disembodied consciousness that the metaphysical tradition favours. The metaphysical tradition just *is* the disavowal of the mundane world of conversation and collaboration in which human life consists. In countless, often almost invisible, ways, the metaphysically generated fantasy of the human estranges us from ourselves.[15]

The substance of this estrangement lies in the language we use, and it is an issue that is far more profound than liturgical debate in the twentieth century ever acknowledged or even realized. One final remark on Wittgenstein's text is necessary before we move on. Stanley Cavell wrote of his own first serious study of the *Philosophical Investigations*,

> in which the recurrence of skeptical voices, and answering voices, struck me as sometimes strangely casual and sometimes strangely conclusive, as sometimes devious and sometimes definitive. I knew reasonably soon thereafter and reasonably well that my fascination with the *Investigations* had to do with my response to it as *a feat of writing*.[16]

Such a fascination and response to this 'feat of writing' might be understood as, in some sense, an honest acknowledgement of the crisis of language in the twentieth century, felt first as the consequence of realizing the most elementary principle of Saussure's theory as to the arbitrary nature of the linguistic sign and from this, in English theology, to Ian Ramsey's attempt to rescue religious language from the dry world of positivism and the philosophy of Bertrand Russell. More broadly it is a crisis that provoked the broad modernist response in literature and art and eventually leads us, by circuitous pathways, to the wide spaces of deconstruction and post-modernism. In this, best expressed by Jacques Derrida in his own texts that exist somewhere between literature and philosophy, language exists in 'free play' in spite of, in Christopher Norris' words, 'the rooted Western prejudice which tries to reduce writing – or the "free play" of language – to a stable meaning equated with the character of *speech*'.[17]

The implication of Derrida's observation is that the spoken word is stabilized and is 'present' to the speaker by an intuitive co-operation between intention, utterance and reception, a 'fit' that is absent from the written word deriving, according to Derrida and rooted ultimately in Plato's *Phaedrus*, from the deep mistrust of textuality that pervades the Western tradition. But how does all of this relate to the problems of liturgical language inasmuch as it is both textual and performative? First, it is precisely clear that liturgy and its words are uncomfortably – or perhaps, more positively, creatively and oddly – suspended between the written text and oral utterance. The earliest liturgical records, such as Hippolytus' *Apostolic Tradition*, provide models or guidelines for liturgy that are no more than that and the celebrant 'shall not say word for word <*the same prayer*> but with similar effect':[18] texts are provided that allow for freedom of utterance by the celebrant. What does this say about the language of the liturgical text? Second, contemporary debates concerning the preservation or revision of the language of the 1662 *Prayer Book* and its predecessors in the sixteenth century in England fail to appreciate the massive shift in the intervening centuries from a predominantly oral culture to a predominantly written one (now governed by ever more controlling technologies) and the concomitant effect of the desacralizing of the word. Walter Ong, SJ has precisely described this erasure of orality in the English tradition:

> Oral habits of thought and expression, including massive use of formulaic elements, sustained in use largely by the teaching of the old classical rhetoric, still marked prose styles of almost every sort in Tudor England some two thousand years after Plato's campaign against oral poets ... They were effectively obliterated in English, for the most part, only with the Romantic Movement two centuries later.[19]

This is exactly why I have spent so much time in this book (Chapter 6) in emphasizing Archbishop Cranmer's character as a late medieval as well as a Renaissance liturgical scholar. We now are quite different creatures of the printed book.

My point here is not to offer any solutions, but merely to observe the remoteness of the arguments over liturgical language in the twentieth century from any acknowledgement that post-Saussurean linguistics in the early years of that century had heralded a crisis for language that demanded both technical sensitivity to and awareness of the deep cultural shifts and understanding of the very nature of language itself that, quite apart from the use and meaning of words, liturgists have almost entirely failed to address. They have also failed to acknowledge at once the differences as well as the continuities with Cranmer's liturgical English. One is led to wonder, therefore, this being taken together with Leslie Houlden's observations about the theological sterility of liturgical discussion, about the very nature of the utterances we make in church and their isolated place in our modern and post-modern world. Might this, perhaps, be another factor in the almost universal decline in church membership in the West outside the charismatic movement, certainly in churches and denominations that adhere closely to a fixed and formal liturgy?

Very occasionally one finds exceptions to the theoretical sterility, not to say philosophical incomprehension, in the recent discussions of liturgical language. Gail Ramshaw's short book *Liturgical Language* (1996) contains some acute observations on metaphor that at least acknowledge the importance of major theoretical works like Paul Ricoeur's *The Rule of Metaphor: Multi-Disciplinary Studies of the Creation of Meaning in Language* (1977), though her brief statement that 'Paul Ricoeur has helped liturgists see why liturgical language is and must be metaphoric'[20] would not be easy to confirm in fact. I have not encountered any other liturgical scholar who appears to have actually read Ricoeur seriously. But I shall return to Ramshaw's work in due course. Or again, in his major work *New Horizons in Hermeneutics* (1992), Anthony Thiselton has a short discussion of Austin's speech-act theory, provocatively suggesting that 'in liturgical texts, for example in the Psalms, *readers* are invited to perform illocutionary acts which carry commitments and responsibilities beyond the saying of the words themselves'.[21] Unfortunately he does not expand upon this brief reference, suggestive of an outward-looking perspective on language that stands in stark contrast to the largely inward, historically governed, gaze of most liturgical debate.

It was in India and the Church of South India that the first steps were taken to move outside the Anglican tradition of the 1662 *Book of Common Prayer* in the last century. As long ago as the First World War a *Liturgy for India* was prepared jointly by J. C. Winslow, the founder of the Christa Seva Sangh at Poona, and the Cambridge liturgical scholar E. C. Ratcliff.[22] The issue in India, according to Bishop Stephen Neill, later secretary of the General Council of the Church of India, Burma and Ceylon, was the balance to be maintained in liturgy between continuity and change, Neill's emphasis being firmly upon the former. But it was the ecumenical activity that followed the Second Vatican Council (1962–5) that provided the immediate context for liturgical revision and, in the Church of England, through a complex process in the General Synod, led finally to the publication of the *ASB* in 1980.[23] It is the debates that took place during and shortly after this period to which we will now give some attention.

There is indeed an irony that this period of liturgical reform coincided with those dry forms of theology best characterized in England by Bishop John Robinson's *Honest to God* (1963) which, in the blurb produced for its first edition, seeks to speak 'for those who find their integrity strained by the thinking, piety and moral attitudes of the conventional Church'. (A leading Anglican scholar of the day, and one acutely tuned to the power of words, Ulrich Simon, described *Honest to God* as 'a mean little book'.[24]) A few years later, the American scholar Daniel B. Stevick, in his book *Language in Worship: Reflections on a Crisis* (1970) addressed the question of liturgical language in an age of what Dietrich Bonhoeffer had famously called 'religionless Christianity'. The Christian churches and their liturgy must start to look outwards, Stevick suggests, for 'the old inward attitudes and with them the old external supports begin to look like abandoned dwelling places'.[25] As the theology of Bishop Robinson and others seemed to be demanding that we should be trying to articulate, in Bonhoeffer's phrase, a 'living before God as though he did not exist',[26] so liturgy and its language should be meeting this challenge with a far more complex response than the simple appeal to historical continuity, on the one hand, and the assumed imperatives of linguistic clarity (or perhaps more precisely simplicity) and comprehensibility, on the other. Liturgy (and it was *this*, perhaps above all, rather than verbal virtuosity, that was the genius of Cranmer) should take its own age and the forms of expression used in it with the utmost seriousness. And, like Cranmer, we live in an age of change. As Stevick well put it, saying perhaps more than he was actually aware of in his call to meet the challenge of a 'godless' age:

> ... a discussion of so 'religious' an activity as liturgy ought to take more account than we have taken so far of the contention that religion is through.[27]

Now to return to Walter Ong's contention that, until the Romantic Movement (which means until the early nineteenth century), the primarily oral habits of the English of the Tudor period remained substantially in place, sustained by the teaching of classical rhetoric. What, according to Ong, are the primary characteristics of such oral habits of thought and expression? In them, a word is an event – the Hebrew term *dabar* means both of these things, word/event – and as such *sound* is crucial, the very utterance of words having something like a magical potency. Furthermore there is a tendency in orality to what in a more literal phase of language might be taken as redundancy, that is towards what Ong calls the aggregative rather than the analytic.[28] Such a form of language actually persists, sustained by the style of classical rhetoric, in cultured English even into the nineteenth century, the forms of orality maintained in the precise pilings up of a language that is felt as spoken even as it is read. Here is an example of what I mean. In his revisionary Preface to the *Revised Latin Primer*, a textbook used in schools well into the twentieth century but written at the end of the long nineteenth century, B. H. Kennedy, who was Regius Professor of Greek at Cambridge, wrote:

> When, however, I found that a revision of the Primer was generally desired, and when, after communication with the Conference of Head Masters, I found myself in a position to act in the matter of revision upon my own responsibility, I gladly entered upon the work of which the present Revised Primer is the result. My first step was to collect as widely as possible from Masters of Public and Private Schools opinions with regard to the objections to the Primer as it stood, and the nature and extent of the changes which teachers of experience deemed to be desirable.[29]

Nobody would write like this today. We, to the contrary, are firmly the products of a 'sparsely linear or analytic thought and speech [which] is an artificial creation, structured by the technology of writing'.[30] Kennedy's prose does, however, have much in common with the structure of the language of the 1662 *Prayer Book* and that form of English that is championed in one of the key texts for the defenders of the language of Cranmer and 1662, Ian Robinson's much-quoted essay of 1973 'Religious English'.[31] There is in Kennedy's English a density, the use of couplet, a precision achieved by careful employment of subordinate clauses, and a sense of spoken English and words as heard in the head even as they are being read – the resonance, in short, of the schoolmaster or the cleric. The words are to be read slowly and deliberately if they are properly to be received and understood. In brief, this is language that is nicely balanced between the oral and the literary, having what Ong describes as a 'lingering orality'[32] – an art that has now been largely lost, or perhaps needs to be discovered anew in our own time.

There is one further quality in liturgical language that Kennedy's prose does not illustrate. It is the language of ritual, or ritual poetics. We have already noted more than once that Hippolytus' *Apostolic Tradition* provides a model or pattern of language for liturgical celebration without regarding the actual words of his text as mandatory. Following the Gospels and St Paul it is clear that certain words and phrases in the early Church were, almost from the beginning, ritually repeated – 'This is my body', 'This is my blood', 'Do this in remembrance of me' – being preserved in oral memory but never cited in exactly the same way when found in different books of the New Testament.[33] This is typical of ritual language, as discussed at length in Roger Grainger's *The Language of the Rite* (1974). In ritual utterances religion and language take on the same qualities. As Grainger puts it:

> ... a religion is a kind of language. It is built up out of similarities and oppositions, as human thought, and consequently human communication, expresses itself dialectically and analogically. It obeys its own rules, as language does, and can be translated only as a whole if it is to make complete sense.[34]

Such language, like religion itself, flourishes in the presence of the unlikely and the odd, using 'homogeneity and sameness to demonstrate *difference*'.[35] In such words there is the joining of outer and inner, or perhaps the transcendent and the immanent, in the language of the unthinkable of which the prime agency, in the Christian tradition, is the God who 'speaks':

in Grainger's words, 'it is God who uses the ritual forms and techniques to change the situation for men'.[36] This is precisely why the language and theology of John Robinson does not work liturgically. The language of ritual, analogously to the poetic, contracts the difference between time and eternity and thus 'acts' theologically through the 'historical' event of Christ that is thus participated in, sacramentally, 'outside time'.[37] Time and place are both precise and universal.

Very occasionally in the literature of liturgical revision exactly this sense of language and its biblical roots is acknowledged and felt. For example, R. C. D. Jasper and Paul F. Bradshaw in their *Companion to the Alternative Service Book* (1986), writing on the psalms in the daily offices of Morning and Evening Prayer, suggest that:

> ... in the course of time the psalms came to be thought of not so much as God's word to human beings to which they responded, but as their praise and prayer to God.[38]

The point is, of course, that *both* senses are true.

The difficulty as regards the actual debates that took place prior to and just after the publication of the *ASB* in 1980 is that they lost track of the essential issues in language involved, the profoundly delicate issues of liturgical language being sought at a time when language itself in the West was in crisis and, like the absorption of knowledge and culture as a whole at a time of overheated development in the field of the technology of information (too much information and too little knowledge), was unable in either form or vocabulary to keep up with the speed of change. For the reformers, clarity and ease of understanding became obsessions, while the conservatives were trapped in a time-warp, unable to move beyond the seventeenth century.

On the publication of the *ASB* two highly critical volumes of essays were quickly produced, Brian Morris' *Ritual Murder* (1980) and David Martin and Peter Mullen's *No Alternative* (1981). There were later more considered books such as the single-authored *The Word in the Desert* (1995) by Barry Spurr, as well as a plethora of pamphlets and essays. The politics of these within the Church of England do not concern me here. They range from the scurrilous to the more considered. The literary scholar Ian Robinson, in his influential book *The Survival of English: Essays in Criticism of Language* (1973), which has already been mentioned, at least establishes his central question as what it is to be human in our time and place in the context of the Wittgensteinian 'grammar' of words,[39] but he, like the majority of the more conservative haters of 'modern' attempts at liturgical language, suffers from being caught in the Cranmerian time-warp. In the context of the theatre no one would question the statement that we cannot write like Shakespeare today, but this should not necessarily discount all contemporary theatre as trivial or worse and all modern playwrights as virtually illiterate. The point is valid, that the language of the liturgy is the means of communicating, and perhaps even communicating with, the mystery of God, but this must be seen in its time and within the presently available resources of language – metaphor, metonymy, grammar, and so on. Poets like T. S. Eliot have written subtly on continuities and discontinuities in tradition and the individual talent, while critics like Harold Bloom acknowledge in the theory of poetry the complexities of the anxiety of influence.[40] So ought it to be with liturgists.

Barry Spurr, a distinguished Australian literary critic, rightly subscribes to liturgy as the place of the language of mystery and communality, being himself utterly convinced that the liturgical reformers' concern for familiarity and clarity sets them in opposition to that mystery. The difficulty with his book *The Word in the Desert* is that it is both backward looking to the Cranmerian paradigm and conveys an overall sense that the Anglican tradition is in a state of final decay, not least in its forms of worship. This may or may not be the case, but it is hardly a helpful starting point. Instead of pursuing the possibility of an authentic contemporary language and poetics for worship, Spurr diverges from an author whom he otherwise quotes with some approval, Edward Robinson and his book *The Language of Mystery* (1987), which recalls us to our own responsibilities for expressing the holy in our lives. As Robinson puts it:

> ... we need museums and archives, to see that nothing is permanently lost, to be a resource that future generations may go back to. But nobody wants to live in a museum. It is only a living tradition, not an embalmed one, that can give the creative imagination the support it needs. And that support is mutual.[41]

And so what of the revisionists themselves? A general observation begs a number of questions to which there are no simple answers. Liturgists have tended to be, as I have already suggested, in the main, very historically minded (and often historically trained) scholars and churchpeople. There is good reason for this, given the nature of liturgy and its continuances through history. Poets have, by and large, not contributed a great deal to the process of liturgical revision, though occasionally invited to, and some of the best new prayers within Anglican worship have been the work of

David L. Frost, a literary don with a background in Renaissance literature and a solid technical sense of how language actually works. I have already suggested in Chapter 1 how Frost's now-familiar post-communion prayer in the *ASB*, 'Father of all, we give you thanks and praise ...' has all the rhetorical qualities of a good 'Cranmer' prayer.[42] Practising clerics who actually utter the words of the liturgy in public sometimes have good practical advice to offer, though all too often in this context, and sadly, we are led back to the words of Percy Dearmer with which this chapter began. So – from whence comes the language of mystery within the services of the Church for our own time?

Certainly we cannot ignore the riches of the past, any more than a student of English literature can ignore Chaucer, Shakespeare or Wordsworth, even though she lives in the time of Ian McEwan or Geoffrey Hill. The obverse, of course, is also true. There is no denying that contemporary liturgy has been over-concerned with comprehensibility to the point of simplicity, and literalism to the extinction of metaphor. Issues in gender-inclusive language have been given understandable attention (at least since the publication of the *ASB* in 1980) though I fear that, with all their laudable political correctness, they have been more of a distraction and hindrance than a help. (I will return to this point later.) The claimed popularity of the new liturgies (and there are complex reasons for this) is sometimes in danger of dismissing the arguments, seeking solutions by the route of the lowest common denominator – a line taken, it may be observed, by recent British politicians with disastrous results. In short, it is always dangerous to reach for simple conclusions in matters of extreme delicacy and complexity, and this is as true of language as anything else. Thus Michael Perham begins his essay entitled 'The Language of Worship' in his volume *Towards Liturgy 2000* (1989) with the rather crass statement:

> It is part of the success of *ASB 1980* that there can be no real doubt that the main texts of any future service book will be in modern English, not unlike the style of the present book ... The sheer success of the *ASB*, its sweeping introduction across the Church, far from being an episcopal plot, surprised bishops, Synod and publishers alike. The Church took to it like a duck to water. A series of essays that have examined its deficiencies needs to bear that in mind![43]

There are many comments that might be made about this, not the least that one would not wish to see such language and analogies in any service book, at any time! But liturgical language, which is, like all 'religious' language, strange, cannot be judged in terms of any success ethic or popularity. Certainly some of the most considered defences of the modern liturgies of the Church of England have been by David L. Frost in his careful linking of them, rather than contrasting them, with the language of 1662 and in his comments, sometimes quite technical, on the place of rhetoric and drama. We have seen what he says about the Prayer of Humble Access and the desperate literalism of an age that can produce *Honest to God*, lacking in metaphorical sensitivities.[44] But Frost's argument for the reception of metaphor opens up a route towards liturgical language that remains largely unexplored in any serious sense. The *ASB* and its successor in *Common Worship* (2000) are not half as bad as their detractors have often claimed but, in the end, perhaps, they are too apologetic, even beginning with one false assumption that is born of modesty. The Preface to the *ASB* suggests the following.

> But words, even agreed words, are only the beginning of worship. Those who use them do well to recognize their transience and imperfection; to treat them as a ladder, not a goal; to acknowledge their power in shaping faith and kindling devotion, without claiming that they are fully adequate to the task. Only the grace of God can make up what is lacking in the faltering words of men.[45]

Ignoring the final gender specificity, which was, no doubt, of its age, there is a profound misjudgement in this statement. Words are *not* the beginning of the worship; they are, in their performance, the very heart of worship, the very wheels of Ezekiel's 'living chariot that bears up (for *us*) the throne of the Divine Humanity'.[46] Perhaps the failing of liturgical revision is, finally, its lack of confidence and its anxiety to be understood – that in all true worship the grace of God *is* present, even in our human language, as in the language of the Bible in which God's words to which we respond become the very vehicles of our praise and prayer.

To explore this in a rather different way let us return to Gail Ramshaw's essay *Liturgical Language*. Ramshaw's concern at the outset is to tease out the nature and power of metaphor, beginning with the clear statement that 'in order for human language to talk about God, it requires metaphor'.[47] (I am not quite sure that the purpose of liturgical language is 'to talk about God', but I will leave that for the present.) To clarify what we mean by the term 'metaphor', Ramshaw takes us back both to the philosopher and theoretician Paul Ricoeur and to the poets Wallace Stevens and Emily Dickinson. Metaphor's relationship with 'realism' (or 'literalism') is odd, inextricable and endlessly puzzling. Above all it provides an access to 'truth' that is endlessly malleable and provocative. In Ramshaw's words:

> Metaphor bends reality into odd twists and turns. Metaphor is not only a new look at reality, a slight of the mind: it is also multivalent. One reason that metaphor can be more true than fact is that it contains many layers of meaning simultaneously.[48]

Her reference to truth and fact is a literary one, though, in passing, Aristotle would also have approved of it. It is also true within a ritual poetics. The novelist William Faulkner, whose work on the American South is soaked in metaphor and therefore conveys to the reader profound truths, once famously quipped, 'I tell the truth. When I need a fact, I make it up.'[49] But Ramshaw rightly insists on keeping a clear distinction between liturgy and poetry. For the former, she suggests, involves the pronunciation of the 'central metaphors of the faith' that are grounded in the assembly of the people of God, all of whose voices are to be heard.[50] Thus we encounter the issue of inclusivity, not by the route of political correctness, but by a theological one. We are reminded also of the need for precision in words. The word 'man', for example, as Ricoeur himself once observed, has 'no unequivocal meaning outside a specific context'.[51] (It is, like Warner's implicature, 'context-dependent'.[52]) Thus, in our liturgy we now should adjust a phrase, in the Nicene Creed in *ASB* Rite A, like 'for us men and for our salvation', which once *may* have been understood as non-gender specific, but which now sounds exclusive; but at the same time we must not forget that a statement like 'All men have the vote' was *always* exclusive and gender specific. Words are slippery items and need to be treated with infinite care. Ramshaw points out that a great deal of what we say in the normal course of events is actually shoddy and even plain wrong. For example, when we say 'I don't think so,' we do not really mean that. What we should have said was, 'I think it is not so,' rather than actually admitting that we 'do *not* think'.[53]

Ramshaw's point is that liturgical language is *not*, whatever Michael Perham might say, the language of common parlance and conventional, sloppy conversation. It is tensed by the metaphorical and as sharp and grammatically precise as it is possible to be. We have learnt from Ricoeur the implicit negativity of all metaphorical language. Every metaphor both is and is not appropriate – and that is its power, its living quality and mystery which seeks to provoke and energize as part of the process of illumination; that which Ian Ramsey would have called the moment when the penny drops. Then language *works*. In liturgy, as in all poetics, far from being dormant, we should be alive to the power of metaphor in its affirmation and its negation, so that, for example, as Ramshaw reminds us, it strips the dangers of unquestioned authoritarianism from the 'myths' of religion:

> ... 'the kingdom of God' is imaginally captivating enough that the Church forgets the 'No' required of all metaphoric speech. The totalitarianism implied by the myth works against mature political responsibility: neither in the political sphere nor in the spiritual life are answers readily available through helpless appeal to authority.[54]

In a sense the Church is at risk every time the liturgy is celebrated, both affirming and challenging in the 'yes' and 'no' of metaphor the very truths upon which it is founded. This is something of which Cranmer was acutely aware.

Such a careful and lively response to the tropes and metaphors of religious and liturgical language is also, it should be noted, a return to the life of theology. One of the best commentaries on Ramshaw's observation on the metaphor of the kingdom is in the theologian Robert P. Scharlemann's essay 'The Being of God When God Is Not Being God', which explores carefully the issue of theological reference in our post-Heideggerian world.[55] Thus in the celebration of the liturgy we are in action at the heart of the theological mystery of the Church's life, whether we are aware of it or not, and it will work upon us as God's word to us. The family of metaphor, to use Ricoeur's phrase, is close knit though various, and includes the wealth of metonymy, synecdoche and irony, among other tropes, each engaged in the wit of persuasion and expression. Each allows us that moment of negation that is inevitable but necessary in our discourse with God. Rhetoricians use the term *catachresis* when an inappropriate term is employed because an appropriate word is not available. Indeed, as Ramshaw reminds us:

> To speak of divinity with human speech, words will of necessity be misused or reused for specific religious meaning. Thus just as the Christian mystics free liturgy for circumlocution, systematicians offer liturgy catachresis, words not quite right, some actually quite wrong, but baptized to filled the semantic lacunae in human speech.[56]

All of this may seem a long way from the politics and immediate practicalities of liturgical revision and the production of the *ASB*, but those engaged in such matters simply cannot divorce themselves from such linguistic and theological precision without great peril. Archbishop Cranmer knew that in his own time, and in many ways that is his greatest lesson to us. But it has to be confessed that the course of liturgical revision in the later twentieth century was too quickly absorbed into the politics of ecumenism after the Second Vatican Council which, while they undeniably promoted the cause of Christian unity, probably impeded serious liturgical advancement by distracting it in different directions.[57] The cracks just beneath the surface may be discerned in the statement from the Report of the Fourth Section of the Faith and Order Conference at Montreal in 1963.

> Among the many recent blessings of the ecumenical movement, one in particular is of decisive importance for the common mission of the churches in our time. It is the current 'rediscovery' of Christian worship – of that twofold 'service' to God and to the world which is expressed in the biblical term *leitourgeia* (liturgy) – as the central, determinative act of the Church's life.[58]

Such ecumenical co-operation, and its outcomes in the work of groups like the International Consultation on English Texts (ICET) and their common English forms of universal prayers of the Christian Church such as the Lord's Prayer and the *Gloria in Excelsis*[59] served an invaluable end at the expense, to a degree, of serious theological reflection and a critical awareness of the wider cultural context of the later part of the century. The process was, in the end, too inward looking. In short, it was a process too narrowly focused on the affairs of the churches themselves, and thus lost the broad edge of language and expression that is finally vital for all liturgy and indeed theology. Although I deplore the dissatisfied, unkind, and rather unhealthily backward-looking tone in the writings of the conservative Roman Catholic Michael Davies in his books *The New Mass* (1977) and *The Roman Rite Destroyed* (1978), I have to admit a certain truth in his recognition of ecumenism as carrying with it a cost to the development of a liturgical language and ritual poetics that are open to all the heavy demands made upon the words in worship and their theological burden during the past century. Sadly there is some truth, though overstated, in the words of the Australian poet James McAuley when he remarked that the desire for 'a sentimental and specious togetherness' resulted in statements of belief which are 'only a game of multiple punning on key-words'.[60]

This last has not been an easy conclusion for me to reach given my own place, at one remove, in the processes of liturgical revision in the Church of England up to 1980. In many respects I am aware that it says nothing new.

In his last book, *The Development of the Anglican Liturgy, 1662–1980* (1989), my father acknowledged that, as long ago as 1958, the Church of England Liturgical Committee had referred in its report to Lambeth to the need for attention to be given to liturgical language 'to give expression to new knowledge and to be contemporary'.[61] In 1964, a small book by Basil Naylor entitled *Why Prayer Book Revision at All?* stressed the importance of engaging with philosophical discussions on the function of language, words and symbols. In 1978, the liturgical scholar Geoffrey Wainwright, in a paper entitled 'The Language of Worship',[62] begins by drawing attention to the widespread interest in language in the twentieth century, in philosophy in the work of Wittgenstein, the Anglo-Saxon study of linguistic analysis, Heidegger and Ricoeur; in anthropology in Malinowsky and Lévi-Strauss; and in the work of McLuhan as well as Saussure and Chomsky. Wainwright concludes with the somewhat bland, though nonetheless true, statement that 'liturgists may find insights from these secular disciplines which will help them to understand the functions of language in worship'.[63] Sadly, however, this seems rarely to have been the case. In practice the Anglican revision of liturgical language has suffered from a tendency to turn inwards, driven by the laudable intentions of ecumenism, the pursuit of the understandable, or the often less seemly processes and inevitable compromises of the synodical government of the Church. It is sometimes hard for theology and the Church, committed to its ancient traditions, to keep the correct balance, understood in Anglicanism in the balance between Scripture, tradition and reason.[64] It is true that the English language has become less attractive, narrower and more analytic in the last hundred years, while Western society has become increasingly post-literate and more secular in its habits. As Stella Brook in *The Language of the Book of Common Prayer* (1965) pointed out, and as we have seen in Walter Ong, the twentieth century saw an increasing division between spoken and written English, to the detriment of both. This has surely only increased in our digital age.[65] Such a division was certainly not the case in the age of Archbishop Cranmer, though the English of his *Prayer Book* was hardly the language of the common people of the time, yet still deeply rooted in its cadences and culture. Nevertheless Cranmer's prayers are founded upon an oral tradition that flourished in the drama of the Elizabethan and Jacobean theatre, and whose Anglo-Saxon roots are fed rather than diminished by the discipline of classical rhetoric such that, as C. S. Lewis put it, Latin was taught 'with a view to conversation as well as to reading, [and] ... many masters used it as a means of teaching "copiousness" and "eloquence" in English'.[66] It may be regretted that we no longer live in such an age, but that is no reason for abandoning the pursuit of a liturgical language and poetics for our own. This chapter has perhaps done little more than outline the difficulties in such a quest, and the shortcomings of those who have devoted themselves tirelessly to the practicalities of revising the liturgy of the Church of England up to the *ASB*. In the wider Church, perhaps, changing patterns of education and revised priorities have left Percy Dearmer's statement made in 1903 sadly all the more true. It will be left to the next chapter to follow the story in the Church of England up to the present time. Finally, a brief reflection on the eucharistic body will lead to a Conclusion that will seek to pursue the life of liturgical language and its poetics for the worshipping life of the Church in the years to come.

10

From 1980 to *Common Worship*

The change in the nature and tone in the discussion of liturgical language in the Church of England between the era of the *Alternative Service Book* of 1980 and the publication of *Common Worship* in 2000 was considerable and in some ways surprising. It indicated, to begin with, how quickly language and its priorities can change within a culture. In the years between the Second Vatican Council (1962–5) and 1980 the issue of gender-neutral and inclusive language was only beginning to be discussed seriously: a member of the 1976–81 Liturgical Commission and an ordained woman, Jean Mayland, recalls raising the issue for it was clear that the 'Commission had not responded to the new thinking in this area coming mainly from the United States and beginning to be an issue in England'.[1] The implication was that England and its liturgical practice in the established Church was beginning to be something of a cultural backwater in such matters.

Furthermore, the debates with traditionalists and defenders of the *Book of Common Prayer* at the time of the *ASB*, which we have discussed in previous chapters, reflect a concern for the lack of poetic quality in 'modern' language and, in retrospect, there was some truth in that, though the issues were oversimplified and lacked a proper sense of what is meant by 'poetics'. In the Liturgical Commission document of 1991 entitled *The Worship of the Church as It Approaches the Third Millennium* (GS Misc 374[2]), we read:

> We hope ... That some of the newer liturgical writing which is more pictorial and tangible, less abstract and conceptual, more evocative and rhythmical, less terse and tense than that of a generation ago, will help to bridge the gap between the Prayer Book and the twentieth-century liturgical tradition.[3]

Bringing the liturgy into modern English after the vernacularizing era of Vatican II did indeed highlight a shift towards the literal, regarded by many as a decline in the English language on the edge of the digital era of 'information' technology. The issue of the accessibility of language, as opposed to the language of mystery in which the matter of human understanding is not the real point inasmuch as the very words themselves are the carriers of the mystery, remains a matter of concern to be addressed more directly in this chapter. This matter will be discussed later particularly in the context of the 2015 *Additional Baptism Texts in Accessible Language*. Certainly the tenor of the discussion concerning language after 1980 shifted, although the increased, if often rather naive, acknowledgement of the place of the poetic and dramatic in the language of worship also brings its own questions. The following remarks in this chapter are largely in the form of a dialogue both with the liturgical texts and directives of *Common Worship*, with its emphasis on flexibility and at times encouragement of extempore prayer, and the essays in the two-volume *Companion to Common Worship* (2001/2006) edited by Paul Bradshaw, the co-editor with R. C. D. Jasper of the earlier *Companion to the Alternative Service Book* (1986).

What is becoming increasingly clear is that the contemporary debate about the nature of liturgical language has become considerably more complex and multilayered than the earlier often acrimonious arguments between supporters of the *Book of Common Prayer* and the liturgical revisions leading to the *ASB* seemed to suggest. And yet this debate still fails to grasp certain essential matters in the question of liturgical poetics that it has been the intention of this book to outline. Nevertheless two small collections of essays published in the early 1990s certainly indicated a change of atmosphere in the relationship between traditionalists adhering to the *Book of Common Prayer* and the liturgical 'reformers'. *Model and Inspiration: The Prayer Book Tradition Today* (1993), edited by Michael Perham, consisted largely of papers read at the PRAXIS consultation of November 1992. Prompted by the late Michael Vasey, PRAXIS came into being in 1990 under three sponsoring bodies, the Liturgical Commission itself, the more evangelical Group for the Renewal of Worship (GROW) and the more catholic Alcuin Club.[4] Seeking an 'Anglican ethos' in liturgical language, *Model and Inspiration* did not really carry the debate much further forward, having addressed the question, 'Can there not be a burying of hatchets and a healing of wounds?'[5] Colin James, the then Chairman of the Liturgical Commission, writes in his essay, not particularly helpfully or precisely, that 'in writing new liturgical texts we want them to be in a style that is rhythmical, evocative, memorable; pictorial and tangible'.[6] This does not take us very far.

The other collection of essays, also edited by Michael Perham, was entitled *The Renewal of Common Prayer: Unity and Diversity in Church of England Worship* (1993), was written entirely by members of the Liturgical Commission, and was rather more substantial in its discussion of the issue of language. In their essay 'Image, Memory and Text', Baroness Phyllis James,[7] Michael Perham and David Stancliffe admitted that 'our response to language is intensely subjective' yet nevertheless we should 'at least attempt to arrive at certain principles' governing the words used in worship.[8] Liturgical texts are never just texts pure and simple, and behind text lies texture or 'the pattern of experience' that shapes liturgy. This is not a bad start. In the liturgy are found words in action, both spoken and sung, texts with a particular texture that moves beyond words yet within which the beauty of language is intrinsic and not merely decorative. Nor are intelligibility and simplicity unquestionable virtues if the language is simply 'bland, pedestrian and unmemorable'.[9] Yet it is admitted that the language of 'common' prayer has largely ceased to be common to the great majority of people, even those nominally members of the Church of England. The resonances of prayer have simply faded from the common language of most people, as was certainly not the case in Elizabethan England. But then, it may be asked, how is the oddity and the traditional remoteness of liturgical language, as was discovered in the West when Greek continued to be preferred to the more common Latin,[10] to be preserved in a living tradition?

Still, the Anglican liturgy remains embedded in the theology and practice of two millennia of the Christian Church, of which the terms, rhythms and assumptions lie buried deep in its words and language. Even more, perhaps, it is embedded (though not fossilized) in five centuries of Anglican worship. Contemporary debates about such matters as gender-neutral and inclusive language have become far more complex than was imagined in the later twentieth century, and if we seek a language which is accessible to those people accustomed to neither theology nor literature, then the poetry sought by *Common Worship*, despite its pursuit of contemporary simplicity, in its employment of the writings of George Herbert and Bishop Lancelot Andrewes, not to speak of more ancient liturgical hymns and prayers or, more recently, the new prayers of Professor David Frost and others, must still seem remote, dense and often unintelligible. In its debate in 1994 that culminated in the publication of the Liturgical Commission Report entitled *Language and the Worship of the Church* (GS 1115), the General Synod of the Church of England acknowledged, in the words of Michael Perham,

> the need for a fresh approach to liturgical language, at the same time being more positive about historic texts and more creative and poetic in

> crafting new ones, while all the time having an eye to what was happening in the liturgical texts of other Churches and in ecumenical agreements ... the [Liturgical] Commission and the Synod were committed to a particular approach, not least to a policy of holding old and new together in one volume, and also to a presumption in favour of using the English Language Liturgical Consultation (ELLC) texts whenever possible.[11]

This, of course, was a very tall order, begging a number of questions, and not least, for our purposes, what precisely is meant by the term 'poetic'. Perham's words were clearly an attempt to hold together a large range of rather disparate elements. Whether all these together successfully constituted a 'fresh approach to liturgical language' is certainly questionable. Clearly the ethos of the years before the *ASB* had changed by 1994. Those years were characterized by a rather undefined concern for liturgy in 'contemporary language' and the perhaps naive hope that the Poet Laureate C. Day-Lewis could solve the problem of the Liturgical Commission's version of prayers, creeds and canticles entitled *Modern Liturgical Texts* (1967).[12] In fact *Language and the Worship of the Church* is a rather dull working paper, a characteristic product of committee thinking that is well intentioned but without much edge. A typical suggestion contained within it, freighted with background but without the necessary detail, is that 'a certain obliqueness in some central liturgical texts may help the church understand again the allusive character of religious language'.[13] It is not clear what this exactly means, though its implications are hardly comfortable in the context of a document which argues 'that language itself is neither logical nor controllable'.[14] *Language and the Worship of the Church* does, nevertheless, acknowledge the difficulty of providing a liturgy for a society that has almost entirely lost the resonances and habits of corporate worship that were still common in the earlier twentieth century and for which the traditionalist/modernist debates prior to the publication of the *ASB* are therefore virtually meaningless. Even, it has to be admitted, the 'familiar resonance' of the Lord's Prayer is quite unknown to many people who might still regard themselves as nominally Christian,[15] so that the rather alarming suggestion that 'nostalgia may be an important doorway to faith'[16] would seem at best unrealistic.

The issue of the *ASB*'s failure to address the matter of inclusive language resulted in the publication of a Liturgical Commission report entitled *Making Women Visible: The Use of Inclusive Language with the ASB* in 1988, which included a version of Anselm's 'Prayer to St Paul' that draws on 1 Thessalonians 2.7–8 in its lines, 'Among Christians you were like a nurse/ who not only cared for her sons.'[17] This Michael Vasey turns into a canticle, which may be sung responsorially, entitled 'A Song of St Anselm' that begins with the line, 'Jesus, as a mother you gather your people to you.'[18] It is undeniably a beautiful piece of writing, rooted in Scripture (the Gospel of Matthew, Isaiah, 1 Peter, the Gospel of John).

What strikes the current reader about this report, which does contain some excellent material on the nature of gendered language, is its parochialism and failure to engage with the serious feminist writing of the late 1980s by such major figures in feminist thought and philosophy as Julia Kristeva, Luce Irigaray and Michèle le Doeuff, or in the United States Elisabeth Schussler Fiorenza.[19] Instead, in its section on 'Women and Modern Society', it limits itself to looking back to the England of nineteenth-century women novelists and the late admission of women to Oxford degree courses in 1920.[20] Anglican liturgical revision and its language thus condemns itself to a narrow place in English culture and society that must beg many questions of the Church's wider theology and mission. In its concluding summary on the matter of inclusive language and those who felt excluded, by gender, from the language of the *ASB*, the Liturgical Commission made one highly debatable assertion as to the nature of liturgical language:

> The future *may* lie with those who feel excluded, but we believe liturgical language should reflect the mind of the Church, not be used as a tool to change basic attitudes. Those who consider attitudes wrong should seek to change them by other means; if they succeed, then liturgy should follow suit, reflecting the Church's new mind.[21]

There seems to be a logical impasse here. What exactly are these 'other means' by which attitudes may be changed and, if the liturgy reflects the mind of the Church, how is this mind to be changed outside the liturgy? Furthermore, though liturgy may indeed sustain the stability and continuity of the Church, why should it not also be an instrument of change and renewal, a continual address to society and culture? In this reference to 'those who feel excluded' one may begin to feel of the liturgy and its limited self-awareness regarding gendered language, up to the publication of *Common Worship*, rather like the Bible to the women in Margaret Atwood's dystopic *The Handmaid's Tale* (1985), published only three years before *Making Women Visible*. The narrator Offred, a 'handmaid', remarks:

> The Bible is kept locked up, the way people once kept tea locked up, so the servants wouldn't steal it. It is an incendiary device; who knows

> what we'd make of it, if we ever got our hands on it? We can be read to from it, by him, but we cannot read.[22]

Perhaps, at times, the liturgy too should reflect in its language a rage against injustice. But perhaps, too, liturgical scholars and reformers simply read too little fiction.

Nevertheless, these discussions about the issues of sensitivity to gender and the affirmation of the feminine in the liturgy were creative of certain new broader issues in liturgical language. Never simply a question of gender inclusiveness, such gender-aware language inevitably tends to become more metaphorically complex, demanding and 'poetic' even when found in *Patterns for Worship* (1989), with its emphasis on 'family services' and 'all age worship' and its passion for accessibility. Michael Perham goes so far as to describe *Patterns for Worship* as 'leaving the ASB mind-set behind, creating a new sort of poetic text' using 'poetry, memorability and resonance'.[23] To a certain degree this is the case. It certainly moves on from the already-dated language of the *ASB*.

Given this renewed sense of the poetic, albeit understood rather vaguely, it is therefore not altogether surprising to find, in Benjamin Gordon-Taylor's essay on the Calendar in the *Companion to Common Worship*,[24] that the liturgical seasons are described as views on God 'through a glass darkly', and Gordon-Taylor draws on the words of the American monk and writer Thomas Merton on liturgical time as 'humanly insecure, seeking its peace outside the structures of all that is established, visible and familiar, in the shape of a kingdom which is not seen'.[25] But one wonders how far such theological language and sense of liturgical time are accessible to modern minds which, as is often recognized in *Common Worship*, might come to church occasionally and with little sense of liturgy let alone theology. Should we, perhaps, be seeking new ways of articulating the strange and the elusive, the oblique and the allusive? In other words, should we be seeking a new form of ritual poetics for our culture and time? And as we move away from the belief that liturgical language should simply be clear and accessible to the understanding, are we not encountering a new, seemingly opposing, problem? For how, then, does such a fairly traditional (and rather Romantic) sense of the poetic in language that seeks to articulate and convey theological truths, as understood by Michael Perham and others, sit beside the other great influence behind *Patterns for Worship*, that is the report of the Commission of the Archbishop of Canterbury on Urban Priority Areas (UPAs) entitled *Faith in the City* (1985)? In this report we find these words:

> ... to give people a 1300 page *Alternative Service Book* is a symptom of the gulf between the Church and ordinary people in the UPAs. We have heard calls for short, functional service booklets or cards, prepared by people who will always ask 'if all the words are really necessary'.[26]

The plea in *Faith in the City* was for a liturgical language that was of the everyday, functional, 'more concrete and less philosophical, and also for a greater use of meaningful symbols'.[27] In such a functional context what exactly are these 'meaningful symbols'?

This demand does, of course, raise a number of radical questions for the nature and task of contemporary liturgical language. First of all *Faith in the City* clearly recognizes that we can no longer assume a society that is predominantly Christian or has any experience of the worship of the Church whatsoever. This is not only the case with regular weekly services but for the more occasional liturgy of baptism, marriage and so on. This, of course, was certainly not the case in the English Reformation. All clergy today are familiar with the discomfort felt by people who find themselves in church for an occasional service – a baptism or a funeral – in which the atmosphere is often emotionally highly charged but the words, embedded in an ancient tradition, are not only unfamiliar but effectively meaningless. Such words as 'sin' or 'salvation' cannot be assumed to be meaningful in liturgical contexts any longer. What, then, does the phrase in *Faith and the City*, 'if all the words are really necessary', precisely mean? Necessary for what, and for whom? Furthermore, from where do we now draw those 'meaningful symbols' referred to by Anne Dawtry and Carolyn Headley in their essay in the *Companion to Common Worship*? The Christian liturgy is freighted with symbolism that is sometimes thousands of years old, and its language, even in the *ASB*, is rarely less than concrete and even more rarely 'philosophical'. But if the symbols are now often simply inaccessible to those with little or no experience of liturgical worship, how easy is it for liturgical theology and practice to cast about for replacements that are more 'meaningful'? Finally, throughout *Common Worship* there is an acknowledgement of the linguistic riches available within the traditions of Anglican worship and the Christian Church. For the proposals for the celebration of the Day of Thanksgiving for the Institution of Holy Communion (*Corpus Christi*), Benjamin Gordon-Taylor simply notes, with satisfaction, 'the language is very rich'.[28] This, I fear, is not enough, not sufficiently precise. Indeed, it means nothing at all.

Such 'richness' we will return to in due course, but for now the question needs to be asked how this concept sits alongside the reductive principles that guide the 'commended' edition of *Patterns for Worship* (1995), an immensely popular volume that sold over ten thousand copies in less than two years after its publication. Its very appearance was a break with the past in liturgical publication, the cover being the reproduction of a red, white, blue and yellow Mondrian painting, its Sample Services all accompanied by Taffy cartoons which have dated very quickly. All this was a response to *Faith in the City*'s demand for liturgy to 'be more informal and flexible in its use of *urban language*'.[29] But it is not at all clear precisely what this term means, or even whether such 'urban language', whatever it is, is actually capable at any level of bearing the weight of demands upon the language of a formal Christian liturgy. We would need, I suppose, the genius of a William Tyndale and his capacity for everyday immediacy, the direct and simple, combined with poetic rhythm – and even this was to a large degree removed from daily life by the time of the broad sonorities of the still beloved King James Bible in the early seventeenth century.[30]

This, then, is the dilemma: that all such liturgical experiments tend to become exercises in reductionism. When *Patterns for Worship* was first published by the Liturgical Commission in November 1989, the *Daily Mail* flippantly commented:

> All those old dull Bible readings ... aren't you sick of them? Okay, swingers, let's put the snap, crackle and above all pop back into the gospelling. Little Jackanory-style stories from your cosy, cuddly vicar. Nothing too long. Nothing too solemn ...[31]

The heavy ironies, it seems to me, are clearly directed: these are prayers for an age that suffers from acute attention deficit, competing hopelessly with the superficial ethos of a 'pop' culture. When the Commended edition of *Patterns for Worship* was published in 1995 it suffered from the tension between the almost inevitable inward-looking and 'churchy' nature of common prayer with its concern for the 'form, dignity, and economy of words'[32] and the concern, emphasized by the radical cover design, to be evangelistic, trendy and outward looking. It clearly did meet a need (or was well marketed) for it sold out immediately on publication. However, its language still echoed the problems of the *ASB*, lacking a proper or consistent sense of the nature of liturgical poetics. For example, in the section for 'Thanksgivings' in Resource Sections, we find for 'Incarnation, Christmas, Annunciation, Mary':

> He is the Word of the Father, crying as a baby,
> Jesus is the Son of God:
> **We worship and adore you.**

He is robed in glory, wrapped in infant clothes;
Jesus is the Son of God:
We worship and adore you.

Lord of heaven and earth, laid in a manger;
Jesus is the Son of God:
We worship and adore you.

Strong in weakness,
Glorious in humility,
To him be all praise and glory.[33]

The difficulty with this is that it both modernizes with the rather awkward phrase 'crying as a baby', while at the same time it leaves untouched a traditional phrase such as 'laid in a manger' (how many unchurched 'swingers' know what a manger actually is?) as well as the theologically challenging oxymoron 'Glorious in humility'. The language is neither one thing nor the other. How far is liturgy here committed to the 'everyday language' described by Michael Perham,[34] and how far is that possible or desirable?

From the rather laboured and reductive world of *Patterns for Worship*, and its successor *New Patterns for Worship* (2002), it seems a long way to the poetic aspirations of *Common Worship* after the often deliberately dry and prosaic language of the *ASB* (although this criticism of the *ASB* was, to a degree, unjust). In her essay on 'Collects and Post Communion Prayers' in *Companion to Common Worship*, Vol. 1, Bridget Nichols, well known subsequently for her fine work on collects,[35] notes the conservative drift in *Common Worship*'s provision of modern collects following the revisions of the *ASB*:

> The compilers of CW have declared their intention of staying close to the BCP wherever possible. This has had noticeable effects. The relative clause, largely eliminated from the ASB, has returned. Sometimes an older phrase has been restored (for example at the end of the Ash Wednesday collect). There are some unfortunate instances where an archaic phrase has been retained in a way that puts strain on the collect as a whole. A full set of collects in traditional language has been compiled.[36]

The unease as regards the language and form of the *Common Worship* collects is clear and significant. Many of these collects deliberately return to the tradition of 1549 or 1662, using the medieval Sarum rite as Cranmer himself had done. Modern collects composed by David Frost, Michael Perham and others are written with self-conscious scriptural echoes and verbal ambiguities that, at their best, work well within a formal liturgy, but rarely move outside the great and self-conscious 'literary' poetic tradition of Lancelot Andrewes, George Herbert and the Metaphysical Poets. This is, of course, a largely Anglican tradition, but Bridget Nichols herself highlights the difficulty in her reference to the new collect composed for the commemoration of George Herbert, Priest, Poet (27 February).

> This new composition is an example of the best kind of evocative and imaginative collect-writing. It weaves allusions to those of Herbert's devotional poems which have become well-loved hymns ('King of glory, king of peace'; 'Teach me my God and King'; and 'Let all the world in every corner sing') into its texture. Finally, it reminds the worshipper both of the title of Herbert's collection of poems – *The Temple* – while also recalling his sense of the Temple or church building as an emblem for the framework of the spiritual life, dedicated in humility to the praise and worship of God.[37]

This comment illustrates precisely the dilemma for the 'poetics' of liturgical language. We are very far here from the issues of *Faith in the City* and *Patterns for Worship* – indeed, in a wholly different world. Those few who still regularly attend Anglican worship might well pick up the resonances of the hymns (probably without knowing that they were by George Herbert), but very few indeed of such worshippers would be 'reminded' of Herbert's *The Temple* or 'recall' his sense of the nature of the church building. We are here within a very donnish world, and the problem encountered by the earlier Liturgical Commission of the *ASB* in rather naively assuming that poets, simply because they are poets, would know how to write good liturgy remains.

An English poetic tradition is indeed embedded in Anglicanism, though it is largely pastoral rather than liturgical.[38] But how it is discovered under the highly dubious principle articulated by David Frost 'that worship of the Church should be in the language of the day'[39] is not by self-conscious donnishness or under the assumption that congregations in parishes will respond to echoes of an English poetic tradition. True poets begin at a different point – and that lesson was learnt by Tyndale, Cranmer and Andrewes – and recreate the tradition anew in their own way, and that is not liturgical. Two excellent modern examples would be the poems on the monastic daily offices by W. H. Auden (*Horae Canonicae*), and the more recent work of Hilary Davies (*Exile and the Kingdom*), both of which employ simple contemporary language in highly disciplined lyric poetic contexts to articulate the journey of the soul towards faith.[40] Neither of them would work for a moment within a liturgy, and it was never the intention of the poets that they should.

The problems with the collects in *Common Worship* quickly became apparent. The return to the forms of the *Book of Common Prayer* after twenty years of the *ASB* collects was not well received. Paul Roberts suggested:

> A literary miscalculation had been made. Rendering a sixteenth-century prayer into contemporary language must involve a shift of syntax, not merely of vocabulary, or the result risks sounding like the literary equivalent of mock Tudor architecture.[41]

Shifts in language are not only a question of vocabulary, but of syntax and even more subtle shifts – of how language is structured and *feels*. The 2003 report by the Liturgical Commission entitled *Common Worship: Additional Collects* (GS1493) is described by Paul Roberts as 'perhaps one of the most extensive exercises in original composition for the Liturgical Commission to embark upon in recent years'.[42] In its report, the Commission acknowledges the shortcomings of the *Common Worship* collects in significant, though somewhat contradictory, ways. Their syntax is too complicated and archaic; they are too long; their language is often 'inaccessible for certain contexts' (especially for children in a 'non-book' culture); and yet, at the same time they are too bland ('they end up saying very little, and take a long time to say it, in an unnecessarily complicated way').[43] These remarks are very much of their time and, especially in the final comment, are not altogether true. It is, perhaps, simply the fact that we are no longer an age that can digest a certain density and complexity in language – and much the same criticisms could be made of more or less the whole of the *Book of Common Prayer*, except that it was written in an age when literary digestions were more robust.

In response, the Commission suggests five criteria for the new Additional Collects; that they should be:

i. short
ii. simple in their syntax
iii. vivid and interesting in their themes and imagery
iv. accessible in the kind of language they use, and
v. to end up saying something which is clear and distinct.[44]

Finally, the initial relative clause in a collect, which has its origins in the Latin translations of the *Prayer Book* and was largely deleted in the *ASB* and reintroduced in *Common Worship*, was to be used but sparingly. The comment (14) on this matter in the report is indicative of the still unresolved dilemmas felt by the Commission.

> On the other hand, occasional use of a relative clause is probably still needed, as it forms part of the classic Anglican inheritance of collect-writing, where the petition is normally based on some prior spoken reflection on the nature and works of God. Sometimes a simple relative clause can achieve this, provided it is not at the expense of the flow of contemporary language. What is needed is a simple set of parameters governing the limits to complexity of the language which the collect uses to invoke the name of God.[45]

This, however, is an oversimplification of the situation. The relative clause (e.g. 'Blessed Lord, *who hast caused all holy scriptures to be written for our learning* ...' *BCP*, Advent II) is a Latinate construction that is taken into English. 'Contemporary English' is, on the whole, intolerant of Latin syntax, though the liturgical language of Anglicanism might still be thought of as sustaining such Latinisms as a characteristic of the 'odd' language of worship. We do not, as we have seen throughout this book, pray as we normally speak. Liturgy properly has its own particular poetics and, as we approach the mystery of God, language cannot be simply 'accessible', but must reflect also the inaccessibility of the divine who is yet near. Nor should we address God in the 'clear and distinct' manner in which we necessarily address the person selling us a railway ticket, where simplicity and precision are required and the purpose is to get to the right place at the right price.

Let us then compare two collects for the first Sunday in Advent – that from the *ASB* and the 2003 Additional Collect:

ASB: Almighty God,
give us grace to cast away the works of darkness
and to put on the armour of light,
now in the time of this mortal life,
in which your Son Jesus Christ
  came to us in great humility:
so that on the last day
when he shall come again in his glorious majesty
  to judge the living and the dead,

we may rise to the life immortal;
through him who is alive and reigns
with you and the Holy Spirit,
one God, now and for ever. Amen

Additional Collect:

Almighty God,
as your kingdom dawns,
turn us from the darkness of sin to the
light of holiness,
that we may be ready to meet you
in our Lord and Saviour, Jesus Christ.

The *ASB* prayer follows closely the 1549 collect that was composed by Cranmer using two ancient prayers from the Gregorian Sacramentary and the Gelasian Sacramentary.[46] There are certain modernizations of vocabulary (from 'quick' to 'living'), one or two terms that would need some explanation, perhaps in a sermon ('give us grace'), and the collect has a narrative complexity that requires some reflection, but which opens up theological matters that extend across the season of Advent: the two comings of Christ as the Christmas infant and as judge of all at the last, the distinction between humility and glory – and their implications for our participation in 'life'. The brevity and simplicity of the Additional Collect pares down the imagery so that it becomes less, not more, immediate, and certainly lacks the theology of Cranmer/*ASB*. The idea and image of the 'armour of light' gives an opening to reflection that 'light of holiness' does not. Furthermore, prayer does need time and should give space for reflection, so that the criterion of shortness can be a difficulty not a virtue.

The two collects might be said to say much the same thing in the end. But prayer must be a manner of saying, set in a larger dramatic context, and simplicity and accessibility may not necessarily allow us – any of us – to enter the mystery through the language. Time, as in the Holy Communion liturgy of 1559 which I discussed in Chapter 3,[47] in the *ASB* collect is complex and subtle – the 'now' of the fourth line linking us with the historical time of Christ, then opening to the eschatological time of the 'last day' when we will share in the life immortal. There is nothing of these dramatic shifts in the Additional Collect.

Yet the demand for accessibility in prayer seems insistent. On 1 September 2015 the *Additional Baptism Texts in Accessible Language* were authorized for use in the Church of England. *Common Worship* had shifted considerably from the initiation services of the *ASB*, while the theology of confirmation continued to be a vexed question.[48] But while theology remains unsettled, the desire for 'accessibility' remains undimmed. Liturgy must be accessible even if it does not really say anything. The Introduction to *Additional Baptism Texts* begins:

> The alternative Baptism Texts have been prepared and authorized in response to a motion by the Liverpool Diocesan Synod requesting texts in language that is more accessible to those who ask for baptism. It was recognized that the Decision and Prayer over the Water in the *Common Worship: Initiation Rites* were particularly difficult for many. The General Synod accepted this need, and these texts are the result of much careful work.[49]

The Introduction continues to articulate the problem that the 'language of faith' lies within a 'culture of understanding', yet this is not shared by many who continue to have a 'deep spiritual yearning and who ask for baptism because they want the very best for their children or for themselves'. But it is not at all clear what this means, and certainly it is not theologically clear at all. The result is that the language of these texts is reductive and wholly lacking in the mystery of what St John Chrysostom called 'the awesome mysteries about which it is forbidden to speak', 'this awesome rite of initiation' and 'the awesome and holy rites of initiation'.[50]

There are a number of difficulties within the project of looking for language that is 'accessible to those who are not used to being in church'. Such language tends to become somewhat legalistic in its terseness. It ought to presuppose that there has been some kind of instruction as to the nature of baptism and its theology, which otherwise becomes almost meaningless. Finally, the anxiety to be simple and clear fails to acknowledge clearly that behind any words used is a freight of tradition and theology within a community of which the mystery, if reduced to a plain literalism, actually begins to make less rather than more sense. Let us take the example of the first 'Prayer over the Water' (itself an odd phrase with reminiscences, to a Scotsman, of Bonnie Prince Charlie!)

> Loving Father,
> we thank you for your servant Moses,
> who led your people through the waters of the Red Sea
> to freedom in the Promised Land.
> We thank you for your Son Jesus,
> who has passed through the deep waters of death
> and opened for all the way of salvation.

Now send your Spirit,
that those who are washed in this water
may die with Christ and rise with him,
to find true freedom as your children,
alive in Christ for ever.[51]

The 'water' in this prayer is presented in three forms: the waters of the Red Sea, the 'waters of death' in Christ's Passion, and the actual water in the font to be used in baptism. There is a complex narrative here, realized on a number of different levels, which requires not simply clear understanding, but considerable imaginative agility. This can only be achieved by careful teaching and preparation and a response to the language that demands more life than is available in the reductive anxieties of this prayer. Baptism reflects more than a 'deep spiritual yearning'.

This chapter has been highly selective of the liturgical provisions offered in *Common Worship* and has been, perhaps, more critical than it might have been if my concerns had been wider than the forms of liturgical language used and the principles upon which they are based. The debate about language has moved on from the arguments between traditionalists and reformers prior to the publication of the *ASB* in 1980. Nevertheless they have left dilemmas that are far from resolved. We recognize that we are living at a time when there can be few assumptions about cultural familiarity with the tradition of 'common prayer' even within a shrinking church-going population. In an age when the Church of England, like many other churches, is conscious of its place as a missionary community, reaching out to the largely unchurched, then discussions about the nature of liturgical language will change, understanding it as a central element in evangelism speaking to those who share few if any assumptions about the biblical or theological mysteries that lie at the heart of liturgy. It is not clear that this is fully admitted in the processes of liturgical revision. If ritual poetics remain, at base, consistent from Hippolytus and Chrysostom to the present day, their context alters from the religiously saturated culture of the English Reformation to the largely secular society of the present time. In a popularly written book produced by the Group for the Renewal of Worship (GROW) entitled *Common Worship Today: An Illustrated Guide to Common Worship* (2001), we find the statement that 'the Church of England was formed with "common prayer" at its core, yet in more recent times it has been adapting to the new climate'.[52]

But this is not enough. Shakespeare, in whose age relatively few people were literate, could properly assume that every member of his audience was familiar with the Bible and the weekly liturgy of the English Reformation

Church. The contemporary Church of England, in a digital and 'IT' age when literacy is almost universal, can make no such assumption. It may be that 'liturgical language' itself is a thing of the past for the vast majority of the nominally Christian population. Suggestions as to its possible recovery will be given in the Conclusion. The anxiety to be accessible and simple is thus very largely missing the point. But when *Common Worship* tried to return to a more complex, 'traditional' and poetic language in its collects, it was criticized. Both projects are misguided. Rather, there is today a need to recover a genuine and authentic poetics of liturgy, in an age when neither poetry nor the Church are given much attention. As we have seen in this chapter, there is fine contemporary poetry being written, setting an excellent example but read, sadly, by few. In addition, within the Church of England, liturgical provisions for Holy Week, Easter, and the special seasons of the liturgical year were well provided for by the fine publications *Lent, Holy Week, Easter: Services and Prayers* (1984), and *The Promise of His Glory: Services and Prayers for the Season from All Saints to Candlemas* (1990), both closely linked to the *ASB* and in use before the publication of *Common Worship* in 2000. But these flourished rather narrowly *within* the worshipping Church community. As the Introduction to *Lent, Holy Week, Easter* states, in their task 'the [Liturgical] Commission began by attempting to analyse the needs of the Church'.[53] But when, in the next decade, the Church of England began stripping worship of its mystery in the interest of linguistic simplification and brevity, it was at the cost of the mystery that can only be carried by denser, less literal corporate language. The Liturgical Commission itself, after 1980, became less a bastion of liturgical scholarship, such that the nature of the study of liturgy itself became a vexed question. Where does it begin, and what can it presume?

Before turning to some very tentative answers to these questions in my Conclusion, I will offer a rather different chapter on the mystery of the eucharistic body as a theological meditation upon some of the issues raised within this book.

11

Reflections on the Eucharistic Body

This chapter began life in a book of which I was a co-editor, entitled *Embodiment: Phenomenological, Religious and Deconstructive Views on Living and Dying* (2014).

What is it doing here? *Embodiment* was a study in the philosophy of religion by British and continental philosophers and theologians exploring the relationship between human and divine existence as reflected in understandings of time, eternity and our experience of the body. Liturgical experience and its language lie at the very heart of such concerns. This historical discussion of the eucharistic body comes appropriately at the end of the present book which began with a relating of liturgical language with post-Petrarchan poetics and the vexed question of liturgy and performance in the early Church up to Amalarius of Metz, indicating that liturgical poetics are at the very centre of Western culture and self-understanding. Liturgy is indeed the deepest expression of the faith and beliefs of the Church, not an odd byway, its language expressive of the links between the human and the divine just as philosophy may consider the phenomenology of the incarnation or the concept of being. The Eucharist is indeed an utterance of the *plebs sancta Dei* – the holy common people of God – yet the common prayer of the Church, developed over two millennia, cannot be rested in principles of simplicity and immediacy of understanding, for its poetry is one of the finest instruments of human expression between time and eternity, participating in both the life of the everyday and the things of deepest mystery. In the eucharistic liturgy comes to life what the philosopher Jean-Luc Nancy calls the 'central proposition of Christianity: *verbum caro factum est* (in Greek in the text of St John's Gospel: λόγος σαρξ ἐγενετο)'.[1] For liturgical poetics are not propositional.

The earliest accounts that we have of the Eucharist strive to indicate the legitimate and proper character of Christian worship in the face of pagan suspicions. From the writing of St Paul and in the Gospels of Mark, Matthew and Luke we learn that, on the night of his betrayal, Jesus, in the context of a meal and in the presence of his disciples, took bread and wine and pronounced the mysterious words, 'this is my body' and 'this is my blood of the covenant'.[2] The biblical accounts differ slightly. In his *First Apology* (*c.* 150 CE), Justin Martyr, writing in Rome and within a well-established tradition of eucharistic practice, is clearly uncomfortably aware of the accusation that Christians drank human blood, and he makes it plain that the bread and wine over which thanks have been given are not 'common' but by 'a word of prayer' are the 'flesh and blood of [the] incarnate Jesus'. Liturgical language is not to be understood in a narrowly literal sense, but neither is it mere metaphor. For the Christian Eucharist is quite different, Justin insists, from the practices of the 'evil demons' of the mysteries of Mithras who 'commanded the same things to be done' but who engaged in false and lurid imitations of the words and actions of Jesus.[3] Some fifty years later in Carthage, in his *Apologeticum*, written in defence of Christian morality, Tertullian offers a satirical and grimly sarcastic account of the pagan reaction to the Eucharist:

> No doubt [the Christian] would say, 'You must get a child still very young, who does not know what it means to die, and can smile under your knife; and bread to collect the gushing blood ... Come, plunge your knife into the infant ... Or, if that is someone else's job, simply stand before a human being dying before it has really lived ... Take the fresh young blood, saturate your bread with it, and eat freely.[4]

Tertullian is using words and irony to attack gross pagan superstition, turning from the word made flesh to the flesh made word to write in defence of the Eucharist within which, as Justin Martyr expresses it, '[God] is well pleased with all the sacrifices in his name, which Jesus the Christ handed down to be done, namely in the Eucharist of the bread and the cup.'[5] Yet the enormity stubbornly remains that Christianity is a religion of the 'Word made flesh', insisting at the heart of its worship upon the language of the sacrifice of the real human flesh of the incarnate God.[6] Probably contemporary with Tertullian is the enormously influential work, discussed at length above in Chapter 5, the *Apostolic Tradition* of Hippolytus which claims to reflect in Rome 'the tradition which has remained until now' and which begins the anaphora with a statement asserting belief in the Word who 'was made flesh and demonstrated to be Thy Son', rehearsing again the scriptural words, 'Take, eat: this is my Body which is broken for you' and 'This is my Blood which is shed for you.'[7]

The key biblical verse regarding the incarnation of the Word is John 1.14, in the New Revised Standard Version, 'And the Word became flesh [o λόγος σαρξ ἐγενετο] and lived among us.' As the New Testament scholar C. K. Barrett has pointed out, the verb here cannot mean simply 'became' as the Word continues to be the subject of further statements, and he suggests that a closer rendering would be 'the Word came on the (human) scene – as flesh'.[8] The Word, or Logos (and by extension its presence in the words of the Eucharist), remains as the eternal Word in the mysterious paradox of the particularity of the incarnation. Thus our engagement with the eucharistic body in an act of consumption and what Charles Williams called 'co-inherence'[9] is a moment of eternity in time, at once the result of an event in history and yet always experienced in anticipation. We can see why time is such an important and delicate element within the liturgy. The eschatological dimension of the eucharistic meal is fundamental to our understanding of its fleshly nature. As Archbishop Rowan Williams has said of its 'shape', referring specifically to Gregory Dix's great work of liturgical imagination, *The Shape of the Liturgy*:

> Its central theme is the single movement of the Son to the Father, in eternity and in time: the outpouring of the Son to the Father in the Trinity ... with the great pivotal sign of the Lord's Supper summing up and holding the meaning of that journey and opening out on to the perspective of eternity again.[10]

Our words move between time and eternity, and it is this present and anticipatory nature of the eucharistic body, spoken in word and known, perhaps performed, only in the mystery of the sacrament, that enables the Fathers of the early Church to assert that we already live the life of the resurrection by virtue of baptism, in which we have already passed through the waters of death into new birth, and participation in the Lord's Supper.[11] St Maximus the Confessor (*c.* 580–662) gives more generous corporeal shape to the ancient Platonic sense of this life understood as a preparation for death and the next, more spiritual, manner of existence.[12] For, like St Paul, Ambrose, John Chrysostom and others before him, Maximus proclaims that by passing through the waters of baptism the Christian has already journeyed upon the path through death to the life beyond, emerging, like Christ at his Passion, with the resurrected body that is nothing short of the eucharistic body, consumed and being consumed in the Spirit. In short the Christian already lives the resurrection life which is yet to come, in both body and spirit, baptism made complete at the final resurrection when our mortal bodies will be raised from the dead.[13] The words that we utter in the Eucharist are both the language of our present life on earth and the language of heaven. They are thus the words of greatest truth. We live and speak thus on a dual level, corporeal and spiritual, in the present and in anticipation: and so, in the anaphora of Hippolytus, by utterance and by an act of remembrance [ἀναμνησις] we have become one with the body and blood of Christ, from which immediately follows the epiclesis in which we pray for the longed-for coming of the Holy Spirit whereby all the saints will be united finally with God.[14] There is a remarkable parallel to this shape of the early liturgy at the end of Jean-Luc Marion's philosophical (and deeply liturgical) reflection *The Erotic Phenomenon* (2003) when the experience of the flesh (the σαρξ of John 1.14) anticipates the child that is both witness and guarantee of the lovers' faithfulness – the seal of the Spirit that also stands in judgement. Thus, in the echoes of Trinitarian modes of thoughts that are to be found in Marion's narrative, paralleling those of the Eucharistic Prayer itself, the child as third party actually precedes us and guarantees, in spite of all fleshly weakness, the perfected end of the endless repetitions of love, pronouncing upon a last judgement.[15]

The congregation of the Eucharist participate in word and deed in the fleshly being of God incarnate, yet readily cross the boundaries of time and space. From the sixth century in the East and a little later in the West, the story of St Mary of Egypt circulated in monastic communities. Her life as told by St Sophronius (*c.* 560–638) is racy, multilayered and focused upon Mary as at once the eucharistic body and the body of flesh.[16] In the West, Mary became what Benedicta Ward has described as a 'liturgical icon of repentance', celebrated on the fifth Sunday of Lent, 'an icon in words of the theological truths about repentance'.[17]

At one level hers is a love story as the mysterious figure of Mary, the repentant prostitute and desert ascetic, entrances the priest Father Zossima in his search for true holiness. For him she is a dream woman, the very embodiment of the texts of Scripture (although she is illiterate), finally absorbed into the mystery of the sacrament as she eats but three grains of the lentils that he has brought for her sustenance as, for her, 'the grace of the Holy Spirit is sufficient to keep whole the substance of the soul'.[18] A delightful story both of divine miracles and human fascination, the narrative recounts the life of Mary from prostitute to saint living in the wilderness, feeding upon the psalms and words of Scripture and 'waiting for my God'.[19] As her story begins to draw to a close, she sends Father Zossima away for a year, bidding him meet her on the banks of the Jordan bringing with him the eucharistic elements. In their final meeting, Mary approaches the priest by crossing the Jordan in the manner of Jesus, walking on the water, begs his blessing and receives the sacrament, and disappears again as she came. A year later again, the priest comes once more only to find Mary lying dead with words written above her head giving instructions for her burial. Mary, it is written, died 'on the self-same night as the Passion of the Lord after making her communion of the Divine and Mysterious Supper'. In her the Word is made flesh as flesh becomes word. Zossima realizes also that the journey that had taken him twenty days, Mary had completed, after receiving the sacrament, in but one hour 'and then at once passed on to God'.[20] In the Eucharist time and eternity are met.

Mary's story, in many later tellings such as is to be found in Jacobus de Voragine's thirteenth-century *Golden Legend*, becomes overburdened with fantasy and miracle. But in Sophronius' narrative it is clearly a meditation on the nature of the liturgical word and the eucharistic body, the body of flesh and spirit that is capable of deep attractions yet which draws us into a sense of a present that is most profoundly characterized by divine anticipation. For her earthly 'lover', Father Zossima, there only remains the necessary word of proclamation to his brothers so that 'all marvelled to hear of God's wonders and kept the memory of the saint in fear and love'.[21] Sophronius is deeply aware that this celebration of Mary's life is suspended between the written text and the oral word. But its power lies essentially in the latter and its spokenness: 'But I have told in writing what I heard orally.'[22]

It has been said that 'reading the Lives of Harlots with unrepentant pleasure is risky business'.[23] Here words bite. The point is obvious, and not a new one. At the beginning of the third century Origen wrote a commentary on the Song of Songs which he read as a song 'recited in the character of a bride who was being married and burned with a heavenly love for her bridegroom, who is the Word of God',[24] and he was perfectly well aware of the risks involved in reading such spiritual texts to those still subject to 'the vexations of flesh and blood'. Yet, the risk that is inherent in the eucharistic body and its utterance in liturgical celebration is precisely the point, the paradox of the 'Word made flesh'. This is not language for the faint-hearted or those easily distracted. It is this power that drives also the erotic language of the *Canción de la subida del Monte Carmelo* of St John of the Cross, the dramatic and fleshly night visions of Dame Julian of Norwich, and the powerful sermons, in his turn, of St Bernard of Clairvaux on the Song of Songs.[25] The eucharistic body is, in John's words, '*con ansias en amores inflamada*' ('inflamed by love's desires'), the language drawn from the experience of erotic anticipation, yet in St John of the Cross's poem such desires are actually the entrance to the dark night of sensory purification in which 'the soul sings of the path she followed as she left behind attachment to herself and to created things'.[26]

Here indeed is poetry tipping into the dark power of a ritual poetics. In the writings of St John of the Cross, of Meister Eckhart, of Teresa of Avila and of all the late medieval Christian mystics we enter a profoundly Trinitarian world of which the energies are not motivated by the theological world of the creeds and councils of the Church, but are rather found in the form of a reverent, ultimately liturgical experiment, and a seeking to express and know the inner dynamism of the divine life with all its forces, its potential, its dangers, and its mystery.[27] The language used to express such Trinitarianism must of necessity be inconsistent, incomplete, and finally poetic.[28] But such mystical writing shares liturgical roots with the shape and even the language of the earliest eucharistic liturgies, a connection that has never been adequately recognized, and which finds its focus in the great moment at the heart of the Eucharistic Prayer when the congregation, together with angels and archangels and the whole company of heaven, in a moment of eternity lost in time, utter the Sanctus, the ancient great hymn of praise that has its origins in the vision of the Lord that is granted to Isaiah in the temple (Isaiah 6.1–3). The liturgical scholar E. C. Ratcliff argued that in Hippolytus' *Apostolic Tradition* the anaphora originally ended with the Sanctus. Few have accepted his insight, but it seems theologically to be profoundly correct as the Eucharist reaches its conclusion in the merging of the energies of the human, the spiritual and the divine in words that celebrate the final flooding of heaven and earth with the glory of God.[29]

It is this supreme moment of praise in the Eucharist that encapsulates in language the mystical tradition and its sense of the body. In a very real sense the Sanctus is nothing but pure 'language', making it nonsense to speak of the 'mystical experience'. There is no experience prior to language, nothing anterior that we strive to put into words. As Don Cupitt has expressed it:

> St John of the Cross did not first have a language-transcending experience and then subsequently try to put it into words. On the contrary, the very composition of the poem was *itself* the mystical experience. The happiness is *in the text*; it lies in the fact that John, in prison, has been able through the imagery of the poem to make religious happiness out of the various conflicting forces bearing upon him and the personal suffering he is undergoing. *Writing* is redemption ...[30]

Participating in the liturgy is taken even further as we move from text to orality. For the liturgy is an utterance of words, a *poiesis* or making, which is the realization not of the Word *made* flesh, for it is, in the Prologue of St John's Gospel, the Word who 'dwells among us' and whose glory 'we beheld' in, we might say, our very utterance: and it is the Word which comes to us as flesh in the incarnation and in the sacrament. Thus, in the twelfth century, Arnold of Bonneval (d. after 1156) is very precise in his description of the identification of the Eucharist and the Church (and without the Eucharist there is no Church), writing that:

> Christ calls this sacrament sometimes flesh and blood, sometimes bread, and sometimes his body ... By his body he meant to indicate both himself and his church, of which he is the head, and which he unites by the communion of flesh and blood.[31]

It is what Christ *says* and the power of his words that is important. But this does not imply that for the medieval Christian the Word is not also felt and known in the body. In the form of the bread and wine within the narrative of the eucharistic liturgy the Word 'becomes' (ἐγενετο) flesh in miracles of consecrated wafers dropping blood, actually and creepily, as Caroline Walker Bynum describes it:

> Miracles of bleeding hosts, which proliferate from the twelfth century on, sometimes have sinister overtones. The host becomes flesh to announce its violation; the bleeding is an accusation. When the nun Wilburgis (d. 1289) took the host to her enclosure to help her avoid sexual temptation, it revealed itself, in a quite common miracle, as a beautiful baby who spoke the words of the Song of Songs. But when another nun hid a host that she dared not swallow because she was in mortal sin it turned into flesh. The second miracle sounds a threatening note not present in the first.[32]

Certainly the increasingly graphic and bizarre forms of especially women's eucharistic piety in the twelfth and thirteenth centuries can and should be linked to various kinds of psychosomatic conditions yet, nevertheless, theologically they remain to a degree at least consistent with the doctrinal insistence on the reality of the incarnation and the paradox of the Word made flesh, the Word made real in human fleshly experience. Certainly many thirteenth-century theologians, such as James of Vitry and Thomas of Cantimpré, endorsed such graphic eucharistic piety as evidence of the falsity of the heretical claim that God was not present in the matter of human flesh.[33]

Nor is such extreme and complex eucharistic 'devotion' limited to the medieval period. A twentieth-century thinker as sophisticated as Simone

Weil, who very likely died as a result of anorexia nervosa, found it quite reasonable when she was told by her doctor of the nun who had nourished herself for an extended period on the holy Eucharist. One thinks again of the story of St Mary of Egypt. Weil's doctor is well aware of the dilemma, probably unwittingly using the ancient language of the (saving) wounds of Christ:

> I had the sensation that I was both giving her pleasure and doing her *harm*. This was how it was with this creature who was at war with her own life. If you did one side of her good, you wounded the other side.[34]

At her most extreme, Weil monstrously identifies wholly with the sacrificial flesh of the incarnate Lord, describing herself as a form of nourishment for soldiers dying at the front in the Second World War. She prays:

> That I may be unable to will any bodily movement, or even attempt at any movement, like a total paralytic. That I may be incapable of receiving any sensation, like someone who is completely blind, deaf, and deprived of all the senses. That I may be unable to make the slightest connection between two thoughts ... devoured by God, transformed into Christ's substance, and given for food to afflicted men whose body and soul lack every kind of nourishment. And let me be a paralytic – blind, deaf, witless, and utterly decrepit.[35]

Appalling though this may be Weil is, in fact, in a tradition of both men and women who identify utterly with the eucharistic body, a tradition that finds its origins in the Christ of the Passion and the Suffering Servant of the text of deutero-Isaiah.[36] It is also the terrifying extreme of liturgical language, of both pure language and where words are what they speak, a warning that when we stand on holy ground there is the fear of the Lord. It is not just nice or easy.

Weil's figure as the Suffering Servant is present everywhere in the literature of the lives of the early saints. In the fourth-century *Lausiac History* we find the story of the mad kitchen-maid who is the 'sponge of the monastery' upon whose (non)existence the community feeds and by which it is nourished. Providing food for others 'not one ever saw her chew anything during the years of her life ... without speaking little or much, though she was beaten with blows, insulted, laden with curses, and treated with disgust'.[37] And when it is finally revealed that upon her the well-being of all others depends, she disappears into the desert and is lost. She is the silence that is at the heart of all liturgical language.

Theologically and within the Church, it may be argued, this eucharistic tradition changed and very largely decayed after the Reformation and with the advent of modernity, to the extent that one notable Roman Catholic liturgical scholar, Louis Bouyer, in his influential book *Eucharist* (1966), entitles his penultimate chapter 'Modern Times: Decomposition and Reformation', writing of the 'un-eucharistic eucharist of the Reformers'.[38] Yet it was never entirely lost, and remained at the heart of Cranmer's liturgy as well as, in different ways, within even the secular traditions of art and literature in their recognition of the power of the image and the word. We have already seen how in the nineteenth century the recovery of the 'fiduciary' sense of language within Romanticism[39] prompted a spiritual renewal that learnt from a sense of the power of symbol as something close to sacrament and as that which partakes of the reality that it seeks to render intelligible and present. In the nineteenth century it is very evident how such a sense in Romanticism of the powerful capacity of language to realize, as Coleridge expressed it, 'in more than a metaphorical sense',[40] had a profound influence on the renovation of eucharistic devotion of the Oxford Movement, the liturgical recovery prompted by Dom Prosper Guéranger's refounding of the Benedictine Abbey of Solesmes in 1832 which formed the true beginning of the Liturgical Movement, and the theology of Cardinal John Henry Newman who was, in many ways, the guiding spirit behind the Second Vatican Council in the century after his death.

In drawing towards a conclusion, therefore, it is fitting to refer briefly to that Council, which took place in Rome between 1962 and 1965 and of which, significantly, the first published work was the Constitution on the Sacred Liturgy. What is emphasized in these documents is the corporate nature of the Eucharist, stressing like the medieval Church the elements of bread and wine, the body and blood of Christ, as symbols not only of humankind but of the whole mystical body which is the Church. Throughout there is the real presence of Christ. Christ is present in the 'sacrifice of Mass' in the person of the priest, in the 'Eucharistic species', in word and sacrament, Christ speaking when Holy Scripture is read in the church and, finally but not least, present in the speaking community of those gathered as the Church.[41] Furthermore, the importance of the eschatological dimension of the eucharistic body is clear, as in the ancient tradition inhabited by Maximus the Confessor and others, wherein the sense of anticipation sustains the life of the Eucharistic Prayer as the celebration of the narrative of the Last Supper, with its imagery of fleshly consumption, is followed by the invocation of the Holy Spirit in the epiclesis and the consummation of all things as we finally enter into our heritage in the company of the Virgin

Mary, all the saints and our brothers and sisters living and departed.[42] The 'Pastoral Constitution on the Church in the Modern World' from the documents of Vatican II states:

> The Lord left behind a pledge of this hope and strength for life's journey in that sacrament of faith where natural elements refined by man are changed into His glorified Body and Blood, providing a meal of brotherly solidarity and a foretaste of the heavenly banquet.[43]

And the language is all. Writing only one year after the conclusion of the Council, Louis Bouyer indicates in detail the continuity between the post-Vatican II eucharistic liturgies, both Catholic and Protestant, and the earliest texts which we have so often alluded to, Hippolytus' *Apostolic Tradition* in particular.[44] The anaphora, as the great act of thanksgiving for creation and redemption, contains the form found in Hippolytus with the mention of the body 'which will be given for you' as a deliberate anticipation of the Passion to come, an event which has now taken place in history involving the broken flesh of the incarnate Lord, and an anticipation of the banquet which is to come and guaranteed by the coming of the Holy Spirit. In words all time and space are embraced and inhabited.

The dependence of contemporary eucharistic formulations on the formulas of the early Church in the Roman rite and the Mozarabic and Gallican tradition sustains the early dynamic and necessary interplay between Word and flesh. As in the literature of the mystical tradition, the word is not dependent upon experience but the other way around. The Word (and therefore the words of the liturgy with their capacity for reference) are creative of the real presence of Christ in the eucharistic body in a paradox that sustains the miracle of the incarnation and is empowered by the dynamism of the inner life of the Trinity. In the words of the theologian Edward Schillebeeckx, like Bouyer writing immediately after the conclusion of Vatican II:

> The real presence of Christ in the Eucharist can therefore only be approached by *allowing* the form of bread and wine experienced phenomenally to *refer to* this presence (of Christ and of his Church) in a projective act of faith which is an *element of and in* faith in Christ's Eucharistic presence. The event in which Christ, really present in the Eucharist, appears, or rather, offers *himself* as food and in which the believer receives him as food therefore also includes a projective act of faith. This act does not bring about the real presence, but presupposes it as a metaphysical priority. Thus the 'sacramental form' is really the

> 'body of the Lord' proclaiming itself as food. Christ really gives himself as food for the believer. This 'sacramental form' only reaches its fulfilment in the meal in which we nourish ourselves on Christ to become a believing community.[45]

'Christ really gives himself as food for the believer.' The sentence captures well the paradox of the eucharistic body and the oddity of the language, known and acknowledged by Tertullian – a fleshly scandal entered into through the Word only by a willing suspension of disbelief.[46] It can be argued that as heirs of the Enlightenment and the primacy of instrumental reason, today we have inherited an attenuation of forms of embodiment and somatic experience to be found again only in engagement with ritual, its poetics, and liturgical sacramentality.[47] In secular forms of reflection from the Romantics to Zygmunt Bauman and Michel Foucault what can be broadly called 'modernity' has found its critics, a constant theme being that of disembodiment and with it the devaluation of ritual and liturgical utterance and participation. In such modernity we have lost the sense of a world that is created and given and replaced it with one that is without any doctrine of creation but perceived as commodity, to be used and perhaps rebuilt in a spiral of ecological decay. It reaches its apex, perhaps, in the nihilist social theory of the sociologist Jean Baudrillard on commodity consumption and the reduction of the body to an object of 'consumerist desire'.[48] We move from the dishonesty of *dissimulation*, which is the first step in sacramental decline, the point at which we can no longer believe what is still present, to 'feign not to have what one has',[49] to the deceit of *simulation*. If the first still perhaps implies a presence, the second admits merely to an absence. Simulation inevitably follows when the order of things in the world is no longer taken as 'given'. To simulate an illness is not simply to pretend, but actually to produce symptoms that were not previously present. Then, as Kafka once expressed it, lying turns into a universal principle,[50] and language is dead.

Herein lies the departure of the modern (and post-modern) world of simulacra and simulations from the creative reality of the eucharistic body. From the very beginning, in Christian witness, faith and participation in the breaking, the death – and resurrection – of the body of the Word made flesh, the scandal which was recognized by St Paul and after him Justin Martyr and Tertullian, the shocking mystery of the invitation to eat flesh and drink blood – symbolically? actually? – was the necessary heart of the matter of being human. The words spoken brought it into being and in human flesh the Word lives. We thus exist dynamically in the sensation of the present and the hope of the future. This mystery necessitates a language that is finally beyond our understanding, for what can these words possibly mean: 'Those who eat my flesh and drink my blood have eternal life, and I will raise them up on the last day; for my flesh is true food and my blood is true drink'?[51] Hardly surprisingly Jesus' disciples respond to them with incomprehension: 'This teaching is difficult; who can accept it?' Yet still we utter them in faith.

It is no accident that, in the stumbling beginnings of the modern science of anatomy, the cadavers used for dissection were those of criminals, often tortured to death before they became objects for examination on the dissecting table.[52] One of the great early examples of this in art is Rembrandt's painting *The Anatomy Lesson of Dr Nicholas Tulip* (1632), in which the enquiring Dr Tulip invades the side of the dead body on the table just as Thomas the doubter was invited to penetrate the wounded side of Jesus, now the Jesus of the resurrection body (John 20.24–25). Later the nightmare of *Frankenstein* (1818) sees the haunted and godless mind of science seeking to reanimate the dead criminal body, snatched from the grave, with ghastly consequences. But it is Christianity that supplies the perfect exemplar to science in the eucharistic body, the notion of the resurrection of the flesh in the word made flesh of liturgical poetics and celebration. It is thus that we move even beyond art and literature into a new poetics. Certainly modern science, caught in its own ambivalences, has perhaps missed the necessary paradox and true scandal of the sacrament. As David L. Martin has written:

> Marked within the very discursive structures of modern observational science seems to be an irresolvable ambivalence: on the one hand there is the desire to homogenize the difference of knowledge production through the one-to-one subject–object relationships of scientific classification; yet, on the other, there is the constant failure of these efforts to fully erase the heterogeneous from knowledge production.[53]

Such heterogeneity remains, insistently and in spite of all efforts to erase it or deconstruct it from within. It remains in the stubborn oddity of the language of worship and in the insistence of the Church from the very beginning to find human life and hope in the divine, kenotic movement of the Word found in the medium of the flesh, a journey which embraces the full humanity of the body and raises it so that it becomes what it is by virtue of what it shall be. The liturgical scholar Dom Gregory Dix was thus led to speak of us as *homo eucharisticus*, defined and ever renewed in and through the Eucharist.

Conclusion

Even by the standards of Henry VIII's turbulent reign, 30 July 1540 was a grim day. Robert Barnes, prior of the Augustinian friary in Cambridge, having sailed too close to the wind with regard to elements in Lutheran theology, was burnt at the stake for heresy. But to keep the theological balance right, the king executed three evangelicals and three papists at the same time. Two days earlier Thomas Cromwell, Henry's erstwhile all-powerful chief minister, had been beheaded for treason, professing at his death his adherence to 'the traditional faith'.[1] It was the eve of the great liturgical reforms of Thomas Cranmer and less than ten years to the appearance of the 1549 *Book of Common Prayer*, an event that provoked conservative riots in Devon, Hampshire, Oxfordshire, Buckinghamshire and Yorkshire by people demanding their Latin Mass back.

The Church of England in the twentieth century was, perhaps, a little more temperate in the manner of its religious and liturgical controversies, but still some comparisons may be made as the years of reform before and after the *Alternative Service Book* in 1980 experienced sometimes acrimonious and unkind debates. No one has actually been burnt at the stake or beheaded, and the response to the abolition of the Latin services on Whitsunday, 9 June 1549 might be but palely compared to the hurt and bereaved tone of Beryl Bainbridge's little essay in the *Daily Telegraph*, 16 November 1980, 'When Prayer goes Pop'.[2] Closer in spirit is an unkind letter written to my father which I discovered among his papers, that expressed the hope that he might 'rot in hell' as a result of his revisionary liturgical labours. Human nature, it seems, changes little when liturgy and its revision engages in the business of what Michael Foucault in his time explored as

> the question of power regarding discourse ... at a time when analyses in terms of the concept or object of the 'text', along with the accompanying methodology of semiology, structuralism, etc., were the prevailing fashion. Posing for discourse the question of power means basically to ask whom does discourse serve?[3]

That was certainly a life-and-death question in England in the sixteenth century. Whom does, indeed, the liturgy serve – God or the king, the Church or the people? Brian Cummings, in his book *The Literary Culture of the Reformation*, one of the most important and brilliant books on the relationship between literature and theology in recent years, roots the Reformation quarrel between theology and literature in the intertwined grammatical and theological debates between Erasmus and Luther after the publication of Erasmus' new Bible, the *Novum Instrumentum*, in 1516.[4] The secularization of language had begun in earnest although, even in the early fifteenth century, John Lydgate – court poet under Henry IV, Henry V and Henry VI, and monk – was, like Gerard Manley Hopkins centuries later, deeply aware of the conflict between his vocations as a poet and as a priest, as demonstrated in his five-part 'Testament of Dan John Lydgate'.[5]

The difficulties of translators of the Bible like William Tyndale were rooted in the fact that Latin was the established language of theology so that he was forced, effectively, to *invent* a theological language based on English, despite the fact that 'the terminology in which he learned English grammar was derived from Latin grammatical theory'.[6] Theological divisions were rooted in differences in grammar and signification between Hebrew, Greek, Latin and English. At the beginning of his book *The Obedience of a Christian Man* (1528), Tyndale makes the argument that just as 'God gave the children of Israel a law by the hand of Moses in their mother tongue',[7] so the Bible should be given to people in the same way – in short, in English. Indeed, he suggests (with questionable accuracy):

> For the Greek tongue agreeth more with the English than with the Latin. And the properties of the Hebrew tongue agreeth a thousand times more with the English than with the Latin.[8]

If Tyndale is here skating on rather thin ice, he was certainly perfectly well aware of the issues in syntax and grammar, and their dangerous relationship with theology, on the eve of the first fully vernacular liturgy in English. Words and grammar, when it came to the matter of grace and predestination, bit to the very marrow. Thus, on the other side of the fence, Thomas More, in his *Dialogue Concerning Heresies* (1530), goes back to Jerome's theory of translation,[9] as had the *Arundel Constitutions* of 1409, to warn against the translation of Scripture 'as in translacyon it is harde alwaye to kepe the same sentence hole'.[10]

It was against this volatile background that the 1549 *Book of Common Prayer* was promulgated, a central plank within the ideological issues of the day as England emerged from the turbulent reign of Henry VIII into the brief six years of Edward VI. Grammar and language, theology and politics could not be untangled. And, lest we become carried away with the glories of English and its literature as they were shortly to emerge in Elizabethan drama and poetry, we need to remember that no work on English grammar was published until William Bullokar's *Bref Grammar for English* (1586), the standard Latin grammar in schools, John Colet and William Lily's *Shorte Introduction of Grammar* and *Brevissima Institutio* (1548), remaining in place for many years to come. As Cummings has clearly demonstrated, Lily thought (grammatically) in Latin, trying to fit English into corresponding parts of Latin speech.[11] My point is not that there is not a flourishing vernacular literature, as we have seen in Chapter 6. It is rather that theology, and therefore liturgy, in the sixteenth century was a battleground within and between languages, with Latin grammar still pre-eminent, and enmeshed in volatile politics where sometimes what you did not say, or only said in a veiled manner, was as important as what you said. Luther himself was the master of paradox, and the later Anglican tradition in divines and poets like Lancelot Andrewes, George Herbert and John Donne, all deeply schooled in the English *Prayer Book*, produced poetry and prose that embody what Brian Cummings calls 'habits of syntax [that] form a complex theology but it is not one that is articulated directly'.[12] We might call it a language of deep poetic mystery – but, more pragmatically, it might also allow you to keep your head in an age when life was cheap. Reading a much-loved poem by George Herbert, 'Prayer (1)', which begins with the familiar line 'Prayer the Churches banquet, Angels age', Cummings sums it up with two negatives: 'It is a poem without proper syntax, and a poem which stops without ending. In that sense it is a trope for the gift of grace.'[13]

Let us explore what this suggests by two examples from literature (and in the second case also philosophy) – one Renaissance and one postmodern.[14] At the beginning of Christopher Marlowe's *Tragical History of Doctor Faustus* (1604)[15] we see Faustus in his study at first embracing and then dismissing 'Divinity', his musing set against the background of the grammatical logic of Peter Ramus (1515–72). He is reading Jerome's Bible and begins with two biblical quotations.

The reward of sin is death.

If we say that we have no sin
We deceive ourselves, and there is no truth in us.[16]

Reading them as a syllogism Faustus concludes that we must, inevitably, sin and therefore die. Thus he has had enough of Divinity.

> What doctrine call you this? *Che sera, sera.*
> 'What will be, shall be.' Divinity adieu![17]

Faustus' English subtly changes the Italian (*sera, sera*), moving from 'will' to 'shall'. The contingent 'will' becomes the necessary 'shall', changing the accepting shrug of the Italian phrase into the determinism of the English. Faustus (and Marlowe) know exactly what is going on – and in this tiny, almost unnoticed shift in language Faustus' fate is sealed.

My point here is to remind ourselves always that Cranmer and those responsible for the *Book of Common Prayer* were not simply in the business of producing fine, resonant poetry. In the (misguided) words of Ian Robinson they, like the translators of the King James Bible, were not simply trying to produce 'slow, measured rhythmic sentences, one for each step of creation, [that] convince one in a poetic way'.[18] Rather it was the tortuous, dangerous and hugely complex process of liturgical production and revision, carried out within the fraught mire of politics, that certainly made, as it happens, an enormous contribution to the development of English in a manner that was often, of necessity, as resistant to theology as it was expressive of it.

And so to the modern example. If Luther's reformation was, in some sense, all about grace, by which we are justified, the paradox of grace as a gift, freely given, has been revisited in our time by the philosopher Jacques Derrida. His 1992 book *Donner la mort* was translated into English as *The Gift of Death*, which plays upon the linguistic unease of the French – '*se donner le mort*' means to commit suicide, or in English we have the chilling phrase 'the kiss of death'. Derrida's point is that the gift is never 'free'. It always has its price. In Derrida's words:

> The truth of the gift (its being or its appearing such, its *as such* insofar as it guides the intentional signification or the meaning-to-say) suffices to annul the gift. The truth of the gift is equivalent to the non-gift or to the non-truth of the gift. This proposition obviously defies common sense. That is why it is caught in the impossible of a very singular double bind, the bond without bond of a bind and a non-bind. On the one hand, Mauss reminds us that there is no gift without bond, without bind, without obligation or ligature; but on the other hand, there is no gift that does not have to untie itself from obligation, from debt, contract, exchange, and thus from the bind.[19]

There is, we may say, nothing new under the sun. In a way Luther would have known exactly what Derrida is talking about. The gift is free, but never free. The word is recalcitrant. Grace that is not freely given is not grace, but yet there is always a price – the burden of choice or the freedom of determinism.

Are these tangles of grammar and theology at the root of the verdant blossoming of English in the *Book of Common Prayer* – and Shakespeare or Marlowe as well? And if so, what of today and the computerized language of our time? Susan Powell, in a fascinating essay entitled 'After Arundel: The First Half-Century of Print',[20] imagines what it would be like to stand in a fictional bookshop in England in 1526. The first *Prayer Book* is only just over twenty years away. This requires more than a little willing suspension of disbelief and patience with certain glaring anachronisms. Yet the exercise has its value. In the first place a small shop could then carry a more or less comprehensive list of books in print, as it is a mere fifty years since Caxton first printed a book. Most books are in English as Latin books (a small market anyway) are generally printed in Europe, and tend to be liturgical – missals, Books of Hours, and so on. Any Bibles in English are, at best, likely to be under the counter as the long shadow of the *Arundel Constitutions* has extended to more than one hundred years. Works by Wyclif and the Lollards are, of course, out. The vast majority of books, then, are devotional works printed by Caxton and Wynkyn de Worde, books such as the established favourite Walter Hilton's *Scale of Perfection*, written in English (and then translated into Latin) well over a hundred years before. Then there are sermons and saints' lives such as Caxton's translation of the thirteenth-century Jacobus de Voragine's *The Golden Legend*. Luther had been declared a heretic six years earlier, so his works were out, and nothing at all could be legally imported without the approval of the Lord Chancellor, Thomas Wolsey. More or less all of the books were deeply religious, and fairly conservative, and yet there were signs that things were on the move and the times were changing. Like lovers of the *Book of Common Prayer* after 1980, Thomas More in 1532, just six years after our visit to the bookshop in 1526, was lamenting the loss of the good old days before the appearance of the insidious biblical translations of Tyndale which proved as hard to suppress as garden weeds. Tyndale's New Testament was first printed in Worms in February 1526 with copies already appearing in England in March of the same year. They were likely to have been under the counter in our bookshop.[21] In his *Confutacyon of Tyndales Answere*, More wrote sadly of the good old days:

> For surely the very best waye were neyther to rede thys [the present book against Tyndale] nor theirs [the books of heretics], but rather the people vnlerned to occupye themselfe beside theyr other busynesse in prayour, good medytacyon, and redynge of suche Englysshe books as moste may norysshe and increase deuocyon. Of whyche kynde is Bonauenture of the *Lyfe of Cryste*, Gerson of the *Folowynge of Cryste*, and the deuoute contemplatyue booke of *Scala Perfeccionis* with such other lyke.[22]

In the same vein, if rather less elegantly, Beryl Bainbridge wrote after the publication of the *ASB*:

> I am not suggesting that the Church Commission [sic] should ape the Inquisition, but it might be better if it went backwards instead of forwards. If the Church would stop mucking about with the Prayer Book and cease worrying about popularity, its time might come again.[23]

Nostalgia is never far away in most discussions about liturgy.

But the differences between our bookshop visit in 1526 and again in 2017, as I write these words, would also be stark. Assuming that we are now in a large branch of one of the chain bookshops, the choice would be overwhelming though still controlled, if by different agencies. If we are looking for any kind of religious book we will have to search hard in a small corner on the top floor, and even then probably have to order the title we want. But popular fiction, travel books and computer manuals abound, apart from a predictable selection of literary 'classics'. The twentieth century has had its crisis of language, and we can read up in simplified textbooks on Saussure, Wittgenstein and perhaps J. L. Austin – though they are not prominent in the bibliographies of most liturgical books. If, as Anglicans, we have got over, to a certain extent, our nostalgia for the old days (mainly because not enough people actually attend church and remember them), we have made little progress in reflecting upon the nature of a liturgical language for the future. It is not the intention or purpose of this book to suggest one, but I hope that I have, at least, given some food for thought.

We certainly have to begin at a very different point from Cranmer. For us the enemy is not the interwoven vicissitudes of politics and theology within which a false step, a wrong tense or a verb out of place could cost you your life, but a deadening, dull indifference in a society and culture that is trained in measurable and economically viable outcomes for everything, including language. The language of worship cannot be simple or easily comprehensible, and where it is it will not last long as fashions change. Its problems open up into larger questions of art and theology in a society that is increasingly governed by emails, Twitter and the sound bite, none of which will readily adapt to use in church. I began this book by addressing the question of a poetics of liturgy, or a ritual poetics. The principles of that remain, and though they have been largely neglected in liturgical practice I do not think that they are impossible to recover, or perhaps rediscover. Liturgy at its best has always been bold, learning how to reveal the mystery even when hedging its bets and prepared to make compromises with the world outside the church walls. Liturgy in the Church is not an instrument of evangelism but, through its beauty, its intelligence, its paradoxes and evasive grammar suggesting mystery, it may still be arresting in an age of unbelief. A. D. Nuttall, no believer himself, wrote a chapter of his book *Overheard by God* as 'a plea to people to see what a knife-edge thing the Gospel of John is'.[24] I would like to see liturgy and its language in the same way – on a knife-edge with words that cut and ask, however they are spoken, to be overheard by God.

Appendix

Intercessory Prayer

Historical Outline

This brief essay has its origins in work that I carried out for the Doctrine Committee of the Scottish Episcopal Church in 2015 as part of a publication entitled *Prayer and Spirituality*[1] which was one of a series of booklets entitled Grosvenor Essays. These are intended for practical use in churches as well as to provide some theological and historical background for both clergy and laypeople in their Christian lives. I have included it at the end of this book to serve as a practical exercise in some of the issues on liturgical language that have been discussed in the preceding pages.

Intercessory prayer forms part of the earliest evidence we have for Christian liturgy, having its origins, most probably, in the Jewish *berakoth* or 'benedictions', expressions of praise or thanks to God that may be used either in the liturgy of the synagogue or in private prayer, including such domestic prayers as grace said before a meal. By the evidence of the earliest Christian reference, found in Justin Martyr's *First Apology* in the mid second century CE, intercession was part of the common prayers concluding the *synaxis*, that is the office of readings and prayers that precedes the celebration of the Eucharist. In his *Apology* Justin, with reference to 'prayers of the faithful' offered after baptism, speaks of offering up 'sincere prayers in common for ourselves, for the baptized person, and for all other persons wherever they may be' (1.65). St Ambrose (*c.* 339–97), refers to prayers of intercession as 'human utterance' to be said by the people in contrast to the rest of the Eucharist which is said by the priest.[2] With guidance from the medieval office of Prone[3] (employing intercessions for the people in the vernacular while the canon, in Latin, was recited silently), continental reformers like Calvin, Bucer and Hermann offered substantial prayers of intercession between the sermon and the Eucharistic Prayer – a pattern followed by Cranmer and thus the English *Prayer Book*. It is the pattern that is largely followed today in the worship of the Church of England and the wider Anglican Communion.

The inclusion of intercessions in the Eucharist appears to have been a slightly later development. Hippolytus' *Apostolic Tradition* has no intercessions in the Eucharistic Prayer, though other ancient liturgies do appear to include them within the Eucharist. It is most likely that they originate in the *diptychs*,[4] that is the practice going back to the reading by the deacon of the names of those who had brought an offering of bread for the Eucharist. Given that such offerings were vicarious, made on behalf of those who were dead, to the names of the living were added also the names of the departed beneficiaries of the offerings. From this grew the later custom of offerings for people still living (for example, godparents on behalf of their godchildren who were still catechumens). Later still the names of martyrs and saints for whom thanks should be given were also added.

So much for the history: but what of the theological rationale of the intercessory prayers in the anaphora? In the words of W. Jardine Grisbrooke,

> To remove all intercessory prayer from the memorial of Christ's one all-sufficient sacrifice cannot but obscure the fact that we can offer this like any other prayer, only as members of Christ, redeemed through that sacrifice, and in the power of that sacrifice.[5]

In other words such prayer assumes the co-inherence of all redeemed humanity in Christ, and this is a powerful argument for intercession within the Eucharist itself. Before participating in the Eucharist the prayer of intercession is a final and necessary act. For as Christ 'always lives to make intercession' (Hebrews 7.25), so we, as his Body, cannot help accepting his intercession as our own or participating in it. In the Eucharist, having laid aside all earthly care in the glory of the messianic banquet, at the same time we recover and attend to the world in its deepest reality, a truth constituted in intercession as a necessary preparation for communion.

What, then, of the language of our intercession? Here words are literally spoken between heaven and earth. As it is a gathering of all in God it must be rooted in doxology and offered as sacrifice. Through the words of intercession our daily lives and the life of the world are sanctified and made present in God, self-consciously a poetic – a making – within the act of communion.

The Greek word λιτη, from which is derived our term 'litany', usually found in Greek in the plural, means a 'prayer' or 'entreaty' and is commonly found in the language of Greek tragedy and drama from Aeschylus to Euripides. Although its origins are Homeric, it is clearly rooted in theatre and performance. The later word λιτανεια means something like an 'entreating'. As a prayer of petition and response it is not, thus, exclusively Christian but much older, its earliest known form in Christian liturgy, with the response *Kyrie eleison*, dating from the late fourth century in the *Apostolic Constitutions*. There is some evidence of its development in the West slightly earlier than this (as recorded in both Lactantius [*c.* 250–*c.* 325] and Eusebius [*c.* 260–*c.*340]), though it is sketchy and its form seems to have been remarkably similar to the pagan supplications of the Roman soldiers. Although there is evidence of a Western litany, the *Deprecatio Gelasii*, in the late fifth century, it was the Syrian Pope Sergius I (687–701) who much later imported from the East the Litany of the Saints, which supplanted all earlier forms and contained clear intercessory elements through invocations for mercy to the Trinity and pleas for intercession to the Virgin Mary, the prophets and the saints. It was this form of the Litany that migrated to the Irish *Stowe Missal* of the early eighth century, down to the Sarum Processional and through this route to Cranmer's Litany in 'our native English tongue', based on the Sarum Litany of the Saints. This Litany, which remains in the *Book of Common Prayer* today, was described by F. E. Brightman in *The English Rite* as 'one of the magnificencies of Christendom'.[6] Cranmer's Litany opens with a threefold supplication to the Trinity – God the Father of heaven, God the Son, redeemer of the world, and God, the Holy Ghost, proceeding from the Father and the Son – made by us 'miserable sinners'. From the lowest depths of sinful humanity, the words of prayer link heaven and earth.

Evidence for the use of intercession in the divine office dates from the end of the fourth century, and the practice of concluding each office with a series of suffrages or intercessory petitions can be dated as far back as the Rule of St Benedict (*c.* 526 CE).

Intercessions and Liturgical Revision

Liturgical revision of the Eucharist since Vatican II has generally shown a return to the intercession of the *synaxis* and a suppressing of intercession in the Eucharist itself. This was the case in the *Alternative Service Book* and its immediate predecessors. The practice is often for the laity to offer the intercessions – sometimes using the forms suggested (as, for example, in 1982 Liturgy of the Scottish Episcopal Church) but often with almost total freedom and with the apparent assumption that the intercessions can be offered by anyone without adequate training or instruction either theologically or linguistically. This is clearly not the case and I will conclude very briefly, therefore, with a few practical observations regarding the preparation of intercessions in either the Eucharist or the daily office, with particular regard to their language.

Some Practical Observations[7]

1 We should never forget the theological nature and purpose of intercessions in worship. In no sense are they a reminder to God of anything that might have been forgotten or an attempt to bully God into action. Their language is finally one of *offering* rather than *request*. We offer and bring before God ourselves, those for whom we care and the world. Lengthy words of introduction or explanation to the congregation are both unnecessary and distracting.
2 Careful attention should be given to the *structure* of intercessory prayers. Even when they are divided into categories their essentially *unified* nature should always be borne in mind. Prior to the *ASB* in the Church of England, the Series Two Holy Communion service (1967) offered a radical return to the principle of the old Roman *Orationes Solemnes*. Intercession is made for 'the whole Church of God in Christ Jesus, and for all men [*sic*] according to their needs',[8] divided into four sections: the Church, the nations of the world, the sick and afflicted, and the departed. Emphasis was made, however, on the prayers as a continuous whole, joined by a versicle and response which was, in fact, a restoration of the *Kyrie* to its use as a response to intercession.
3 Provision should be made for responses to be made, or perhaps petitions added and also, most importantly, periods of *silence*. Words in worship may often be silent and internal but still powerful. Silence also allows time for listening and attention. In biddings, silence and responses we are reminded that intercession is the prayer of the whole Church, not just of one person or voice, another aspect of its unified nature.
4 Intercession is never a condensed form of the week's news. As an intrinsic part of the flow of the liturgy, it is a gathering of all before God, a participation in human words in the intercessions of Christ himself, and a recognition that we truly see the world *sub specie aeternitate*.
5 Brevity is a virtue in intercessory prayer. The poetics of liturgy generally flourish best in conditions of verbal economy, as is the case in most poetics. Furthermore, as in all good writing and use of language, especially when it is corporate, care should be taken with composition – and it is always good to take some time before worship begins for quiet reflection and prayer before leading others in prayer.

These few brief reflections are not complicated and may seem, indeed, to a large extent self-evident. But taken together they suggest, very practically, the nature of a form of liturgical language or poetic that this book has sought to explore in the history and practice of the Church, with particular attention to the liturgy of the Church of England.

Bibliography

(GS – General Synod)

Walter M. Abbott, SJ, ed., *The Documents of Vatican II* (London: Geoffrey Chapman, 1972)

G. Abbott-Smith, *A Manual Greek Lexicon of the New Testament* (Edinburgh: T & T Clark, 1968)

Additional Baptism Texts in Accessible Language (London: Church House Publishing, online, 2015)

Michael Alexander, Ed. *The Earliest English Poems* (London: Penguin, 1966)

The Alternative Service Book (London: Clowes/SPCK/Cambridge University Press, 1980)

The Ancrene Riwle. Trans. M. B. Salu (London: Burns & Oates, 1955)

St Anselm, *The Prayers and Meditations of St. Anselm*. Trans. Benedicta Ward (Harmondsworth: Penguin, 1973)

Paul Arblaster, Gergely Juhász and Guido Latré, eds., *Tyndale's Testament* (Turnhout, Belgium: Brepols, 2002)

The Archbishop of Canterbury's Speech (London: Peter Cole, 1644)

Margaret Atwood, *The Handmaid's Tale* (London: Virago Press, 1987)

W. H. Auden, *Collected Shorter Poems, 1927–1957* (London: Faber & Faber, 1966)

J. L. Austin, *How to Do Things with Words*. Second revised edition (Oxford: Oxford University Press, 1975)

Kate Badie, 'The Prayer of Humble Access'. archive.churchsociety.org/Churchman/documents/Cman_120_2_Badie.

L. W. Barnard, *Justin Martyr: His Life and Thought* (Cambridge: Cambridge University Press, 1966)

C. K. Barrett, *The Gospel According to John: An Introduction* (London: SPCK, 1955)

Jean Baudrillard, *Selected Writings*. Ed. Mark Poster (Cambridge: Polity Press, 1988)

J. Beck, *La Musique des Troubadours* (Paris, 1910)

St Benedict, *The Rule of St Benedict*. Trans. Carolinne White (London: Penguin, 2008)

Dinah Birch, ed., *The Oxford Companion to English Literature*. Seventh edition (Oxford: Oxford University Press, 2009)

Harold Bloom, *The Anxiety of Influence: A Theory of Poetry* (New York: Oxford University Press, 1973)

Harold Bloom, *The American Religion* (New York: Touchstone Books, 1992)

Jacob Böhme, *The Key and Other Writings*. Trans. Peter Malekin, with the assistance of Lars Malmberg (Durham: The New Century Press, 1988)

John E. Booty, ed., *The Book of Common Prayer: 1559, The Elizabethan Prayer Book* (Charlottesville: University of Virginia Press, 2005)

Dom Bernard Botte, *From Silence to Participation* (Washington: Pastoral Press, 1973)

Louis Bouyer, *Eucharist: Theology and Spirituality of the Eucharistic Prayer*. Trans. Charles Underhill Quinn (Notre Dame: University of Notre Dame Press, 1968)

Paul F. Bradshaw, ed., *The New Westminster Dictionary of Liturgy and Worship* (Louisville: WJK Press, 2002)

Paul F. Bradshaw, ed., *Companion to Common Worship*. 2 vols (London: SPCK, 2001, 2006)

Paul F. Bradshaw, Maxwell E. Johnson and L. Edward Phillips, *The Apostolic Tradition: A Commentary* (Minneapolis: Fortress Press, 2002)

F. E. Brightman, *The English Rite*. 2 vols. (London: Rivingtons, 1915)

F. E. Brightman, ed., *The Preces Privatae of Lancelot Andrewes, Bishop of Winchester* (London: Methuen, 1903)

Stella Brook, *The Language of the Book of Common Prayer* (London: André Deutsch, 1965)

Colin Buchanan, *What Did Cranmer Think He Was Doing?* (Cambridge: Grove Books, 1976)

Colin Buchanan, Trevor Lloyd and Harold Miller, eds, *Anglican Worship Today: Collins Illustrated Guide to the Alternative Service Book* 1980 (London: Collins Liturgical Publications, 1980))

Virginia Burrus, *The Sex Lives of the Saints: An Erotics of Ancient Hagiography* (Philadelphia: University of Pennsylvania Press, 2004)

Charles C. Butterworth, *The English Primers (1529–1545)* (Philadelphia: University of Pennsylvania Press, 1953)

Caroline Walker Bynum, *Holy Feast and Holy Fast: The Religious Significance of Food to Medieval Women* (Berkeley: University of California Press, 1987)

Caroline Walker Bynum and Paul Freedman, eds, *Last Things: Death and the Apocalypse in the Middle Ages* (Philadephia: University of Pennsylvania Press, 2000)

Robert Carroll and Stephen Prickett, eds, *The King James Bible* (Oxford: Oxford University Press, 1997)

Stanley Cavell, *The Claim of Reason: Wittgenstein, Skepticism, Morality, and Tragedy*. New edition (Oxford: Oxford University Press, 1999)

Michel de Certeau, *The Mystic Fable. Volume 1. The Sixteenth and Seventeenth Centuries*. Trans. Michael B. Smith (Chicago: University of Chicago Press, 1992)

E. K. Chambers, *The Mediaeval Stage*. 2 vols (Oxford: Clarendon Press, 1903)

Church of England Liturgical Commission, *Modern Liturgical Texts* (London: SPCK, 1968)

Church of England Liturgical Commission, *The Alternative Service Book, 1980: A Commentary* (London: CIO Publishing, 1980)

Church of England Liturgical Commission, *Making Women Visible: The Use of Inclusive Language with the ASB* (GS 859. London: Church House Publishing, 1989)

Church of England Liturgical Commission, *The Worship of the Church as It Approaches the Third Millennium* (GS Misc 364, 1991)

Church of England Liturgical Commission, *Language and the Worship of the Church* (GS 1115, 1994)

Church of England Liturgical Commission, *Common Worship: Additional Collects* (GS 1493, 2003)

Church of England Liturgical Commission, *Alternative Baptism Texts* (2015)

S. T. Coleridge, *Collected Letters*. Vol. 1 (1785–1800). Ed. Earl Leslie Griggs (Oxford: Clarendon Press, 1966)

S. T. Coleridge, *Lay Sermons*. Ed. R. J. White. Collected Works, Vol. 6 (Princeton: Princeton University Press, 1972)

S. T. Coleridge, *Biographia Literaria* (1817). Ed. James Engell and W. Jackson Bate. Collected Works, Vol. 7 (Princeton: Princeton University Press, 1983)

Common Worship: Services and Prayers for the Church of England (London: Church House Publishing, 2000)

Adam G. Cooper, *The Body in St. Maximus the Confessor: Holy Flesh, Wholly Deified* (Oxford: Oxford University Press, 2005)

Rita Copeland, *Rhetoric, Hermeneutics and Translation in the Middle Ages* (Cambridge: Cambridge University Press, 1995)

John Coulson, *Newman and the Common Tradition: A Study in the Language of Church and Society* (Oxford: Clarendon Press, 1970)

Jeffrey N. Cox and Larry J. Reynolds, eds, *New Historical Literary Study: Essays on Reproducing Texts, Representing History* (Princeton: Princeton University Press, 1993)

John D. Cox, *Seeming Knowledge: Shakespeare and Skeptical Faith* (Waco: Baylor University Press, 2007)

John Edmund Cox, ed., *Miscellaneous Writings and Letters of Thomas Cranmer* (Cambridge: Cambridge University Press, 1846)

Thomas Cranmer, *The Two Books of Homilies Appointed to Be Read in Churches*. Ed. John Griffiths (Oxford: Oxford University Press, 1859)

Cranmer's Selected Writings. Ed. C. S. Meyer (London: SPCK, 1961)

J. A. Cruddon, *A Dictionary of Literary Terms* (London: Penguin, 1982)

David Crystal, *Linguistics, Language and Religion* (London: Burns & Oates, 1965)

David Crystal, *Begat: The King James Bible and the English Language* (Oxford: Oxford University Press, 2010)

Jonathan Culler, *Saussure* (London: Fontana, 1976)

Geoffrey J. Cuming, *A History of the Anglican Liturgy*. Second edition (London: Macmillan, 1982)

Geoffrey J. Cuming, *The Godly Order: Texts and Studies Relating to the Book of Common Prayer* (London: Alcuin Club/SPCK, 1983)

Geoffrey J. Cuming, ed., *Hippolytus: A Text for Students* (Bramcote: Grove Books, 1976)

Brian Cummings, *The Literary Culture of the Reformation: Grammar and Grace* (Oxford: Oxford University Press, 2002)

Brian Cummings, ed., *The Book of Common Prayer: The Texts of 1549, 1559, and 1662* (Oxford: Oxford University Press, 2011)

Don Cupitt, *Mysticism after Modernity* (Oxford: Blackwell, 1998)

David Daniell, *The Bible in English* (New Haven: Yale University Press, 2003)

Donald Davie, *A Gathered Church: The Literature of the English Dissenting Interest, 1700–1930* (London: Routledge & Kegan Paul, 1978)

Donald Davie, ed., *The Psalms in English* (Harmondsworth: Penguin, 1996)

Hilary Davies, *Exile and the Kingdom* (London: Enitharmon Press, 2016)

Horton Davies, *Worship and Theology in England: From Newman to Martineau, 1850–1900* (Princeton: Princeton University Press, 1962)

Horton Davies, *Worship and Theology in England: From Cranmer to Hooker, 1534–1603* (Princeton: Princeton University Press, 1970)

J. G. Davies, *The Secular Use of Church Buildings* (London: SCM Press, 1968)

J. G. Davies, ed., *A New Dictionary of Liturgy and Worship* (London: SCM Press, 1986)

R. T. Davies, ed., *Medieval English Lyrics: A Critical Anthology* (London: Faber & Faber, 1963)

Norman Davis, ed., *Paston Letters and Papers of the Fifteenth Century*. 3 vols. (Oxford: Oxford University Press, 1971–6)

Margaret Deanesly, *The Lollard Bible* (Cambridge: Cambridge University Press, 1920/1966)

Percy Dearmer, *The Parson's Handbook*. Fourth edition (London: Grant Richards, 1903)

Jacques Derrida, *Of Grammatology*. Trans. Gayatri Chakravorty-Spivak (Baltimore: Johns Hopkins University Press, 1976)

Jacques Derrida, *Given Time: 1. Counterfeit Money*. Trans. Peggy Kamuf (Chicago: University of Chicago Press, 1992)

Emily Dickinson, *The Complete Poems*. Ed. Thomas H. Johnson (London: Faber & Faber, 1970)

Dom Gregory Dix, *The Shape of the Liturgy* (Westminster: Dacre Press, 1945)

Dom Gregory Dix, ed., *The Treatise on The Apostolic Tradition of St. Hippolytus of Rome*. Revised Henry Chadwick (London: SPCK, 1968)

Dom Gregory Dix, *The Sacramental Life*. Ed. Simon Jones (Norwich: Canterbury Press, 2007)

The Doctrine Committee of the Scottish Episcopal Church, *Prayer and Spirituality*. Grosvenor Essay No. 12 (Edinburgh: Scottish Episcopal Church, 2016)

C. H. Dodd, 'Eucharistic Symbolism in the Fourth Gospel', *The Expositor*, 8th series, Vol. 2 (1911), 530–46

C. H. Dodd, *The Interpretation of the Fourth Gospel* (Cambridge: Cambridge University Press, 1970)

Eamon Duffy, *The Stripping of the Altars*. Second edition (New Haven: Yale University Press, 2005)

Eamon Duffy, *Marking the Hours: The English People and Their Prayers, 1240–1570* (New Haven: Yale University Press, 2006)

William Dunbar, *Poems*. Ed. James Kinsley (Oxford: Clarendon Press, 1958)

Early Christian Writings. Trans. Maxwell Staniforth (Harmondsworth: Penguin, 1968)

Mark Eary and Gilly Myers, eds, *Common Worship Today: An Illustrated Guide to Common Worship* (London: HarperCollins, 2001)

Burton Scott Easton, *The Apostolic Tradition of Hippolytus* (Cambridge: Cambridge University Press, 1934)

Mircea Eliade, *The Sacred and the Profane*. Trans. Willard R. Trask (New York: Harcourt Brace, 1959)

George Eliot, *Adam Bede* (1859) (London: Cassell and Company, 1907)

T. S. Eliot, *Selected Essays*. Third enlarged edition (London: Faber & Faber, 1951)

T. S. Eliot, *The Poems of T. S. Eliot: The Annotated Text.* Vol. 1. Ed. Christopher Ricks and Jim McCue (London: Faber & Faber, 2015)

Roger Ellis, ed., *The Medieval Translator* (Woodbridge: Boydell and Brewer, 1989)

English Language Liturgical Consultation, *Praying Together* (Norwich: Canterbury Press, 1988)

Vivienne Faull and Jane Sinclair, *Count Us In: Inclusive Language in Liturgy* (Bramcote: Grove Books, 1986)

Charles Feidelson, Jr, *Symbolism and American Literature* (Chicago: Chicago University Press, 1953)

Floyd V. Filson, *The Gospel According to St. Matthew.* Second edition (London: Adam & Charles Black, 1971)

Elisabeth Schüssler Fiorenza, *In Memory of Her: A Feminist Reconstruction of Christian Origins* (London: SCM Press, 1995)

Stanley Fish, *There's No Such Thing as Free Speech, and It's a Good Thing Too* (Oxford: Oxford University Press, 1994)

Ramona Fotiade, David Jasper and Olivier Salazar-Ferrer, eds, *Embodiment: Phenomenological, Religious and Deconstructive Views on Living and Dying* (Farnham: Ashgate, 2014)

Michel Foucault, *Power/Knowledge: Selected Interviews and Other Writings, 1972–1977* (New York: Pantheon Books, 1980)

Michel Foucault, *On the Government of the Living.* Trans. Graham Burchell (New York: Picador, 2012)

David L. Frost, *The Language of Series 3.* Grove Booklet No. 12 (Bramcote: Grove Books, 1973)

David L. Frost, *Making the Liturgical Psalter.* The Morpeth Lectures, 1980 (Bramcote: Grove Books, 1981)

Brother Gararde, *The Interpretation and Signification of the Mass* (1532)

Harold Charles Gardiner, *Mysteries' End: An Investigation of the Last Days of the Medieval Religious Stage* (New Haven: Yale University Press, 1946)

John Gassner, *Medieval and Tudor Drama* (New York: Bantam Books, 1968)

Anthony Gelston, 'A Note on the Text of the *Apostolic Tradition* of Hippolytus', *Journal of Theological Studies*, Vol. 39.1 (1988), 117.

Vincent Gillespie and Kantik Ghosh, eds, *After Arundel: Religious Writing in Fifteenth-Century England* (Turnhout, Belgium: Brepols, 2011)

Roger Grainger, *The Language of the Rite* (London: Darton, Longman & Todd, 1974)

Donald Gray, *Ronald Jasper: His Life, His Work and the ASB* (London: SPCK, 1997)

Douglas Gray, *Themes and Images in the Medieval English Religious Lyric* (London: Routledge, 1972)

Stephen Greenblatt, *Hamlet in Purgatory* (Princeton: Princeton University Press, 2001)

Arthur Greene, *Post-Petrarchism: Origins and Innovations of the Western Lyric Sequence* (Princeton: Princeton University Press, 1991)

W. Jardine Grisbrooke, 'Intercession at the Eucharist', *Studia Liturgica*, Vol. 4 (1965), 129–55; 5 (1966), 20–44, 87–103

O. B. Hardison, Jr, *Christian Rite and Christian Drama in the Middle Ages* (Baltimore: Johns Hopkins University Press, 1965)

Thomas Hardy, *The Collected Poems* (London: Macmillan, 1965)

Andrew W. Hass, David Jasper and Elisabeth Jay, eds, *The Oxford Handbook of English Literature and Theology* (Oxford: Oxford University Press, 2007)

Seamus Heaney, *New Selected Poems, 1966–1987* (London: Faber & Faber, 1990)

Thomas J. Heffernan and E. Ann Matter, eds, *The Liturgy of the Medieval Church* (Kalamazoo: TEAMS, 2001)

George Herbert, *The English Poems*. Ed. Helen Wilcox (Cambridge: Cambridge University Press, 2007)

Nathan Hitchcock, 'Saving Edward Taylor's Purse: Masculine Devotion in the *Preparatory Devotions*', *Literature and Theology*, Vol. 22.3 (September 2008), 339–53

Michael Hollis, *The Significance of South India* (London: Lutterworth Press, 1966)

Bruce Holsinger, 'Liturgy', in Paul Strohm, ed., *Middle English*. Oxford Twenty-First Century Approaches to Literature (Oxford: Oxford University Press, 2007), pp. 295–314

Richard Hooker, *The Works of Mr. Richard Hooker*. Arranged by John Keble. 3 vols (Oxford: Clarendon Press, 1865)

Gerard Manley Hopkins, *Poems*. Ed. Robert Bridges (London: Oxford University Press, 1931)

Gerard Manley Hopkins, *Poems and Prose*. Selected and ed. W. H. Gardner (Harmondsworth: Penguin, 1963)

J. Huizinga, *The Waning of the Middle Ages*. Trans. F. Hopman (London: Penguin, 1990)

International Consultation on English Texts, *Prayers We Have in Common*. Second revised edition (Philadelphia: Fortress Press, 1975)

Christopher Irvine, ed., *They Shaped Our Worship: Essays on Anglican Liturgists* (London: SPCK, 1998)

David Jasper, *Rhetoric, Power and Community: An Exercise in Reserve* (London: Macmillan, 1993)

David Jasper, *The Sacred Body: Asceticism in Religion, Literature, Art, and Culture* (Waco: Baylor University Press, 2009)

David Jasper, *The Sacred Community: Art, Sacrament and the People of God* (Waco: Baylor University Press, 2012)

David Jasper, *Literature and Theology as a Grammar of Assent* (Farnham: Ashgate, 2016)

David Jasper, ed., *Images of Belief in Literature* (London: Macmillan, 1984)

David Jasper and R. C. D. Jasper, eds, *Language and the Worship of the Church* (London: Macmillan, 1990)

R. C. D. Jasper, *Prayer Book Revision in England, 1800–1900* (London: SPCK, 1954)

R. C. D. Jasper, *The Development of the Anglican Liturgy, 1662–1980* (London: SPCK, 1989)

R. C. D. Jasper, ed., *The Renewal of Worship*. Joint Liturgical Group (London: Oxford University Press, 1965)

R. C. D. Jasper, ed., *The Eucharist Today: Studies on Series 3* (London: SPCK, 1974)

R. C. D. Jasper, ed., *Getting the Liturgy Right* (London: SPCK, 1982)

R. C. D. Jasper and Paul F. Bradshaw, eds, *A Companion to the Alternative Service Book* (London: SPCK, 1986)

R. C. D. Jasper and G. J. Cuming, *Prayers of the Eucharist: Early and Reformed*. Third edition (New York: Pueblo Publishing, 1987)

Hans Robert Jauss, '*La douceur du foyer*: The Lyric of the Year 1857 as a Pattern for the Communication of Social Norms', *Romantic Review*, Vol. 65 (1974), reprinted in Hans Robert Jauss, *Aesthetic Experience and Literary Hermeneutics*. Trans. Michael Shaw (Minneapolis: University of Minnesota Press, 1982), pp. 263–93.

St John of the Cross, *Dark Night of the Soul*. Trans. Mirabai Starr (London: Rider, 2002)

Lawrence J. Johnson, *Worship in the Early Church: An Anthology of Historical Sources*. Vol. 1 (Collegeville: Liturgical Press, 2009)

Cheslyn Jones, Geoffrey Wainwright and Edward Yarnold, SJ, *The Study of Liturgy* (London: SPCK, 1978)

Edmund D. Jones, ed., *English Critical Essays (Sixteenth, Seventeenth and Eighteenth Centuries)* (Oxford: Oxford University Press, 1965)

Joseph A. Jungmann, SJ, *The Mass of the Roman Rite: Its Origins and Development*. Trans. Francis A. Brunner. Revised Charles K. Riepe. Abridged edition (New York: Benziger Brothers Inc., 1959)

Joseph A. Jungmann, SJ, *The Early Liturgy to the Time of Gregory the Great*. Trans. Francis A. Brunner (London: Darton, Longman & Todd, 1959)

Franz Kafka, *The Trial*. Trans. Willa and Edwin Muir (Harmondsworth: Penguin, 1953)

Frederick R. Karl, *William Faulkner: American Writer* (New York: Weidenfeld & Nicholson, 1989)

Benjamin Hall Kennedy, *The Revised Latin Primer* (London: Longmans, Green, and Co., 1912)

Frank Kermode, *The Sense of an Ending: Studies in the Theory of Fiction* (New York: Oxford University Press, 1966)

Fergus Kerr, *Theology after Wittgenstein* (Oxford: Blackwell, 1986)

Theodor Klauser, *A Short History of the Western Liturgy*. Trans. John Halliburton. Second edition (Oxford: Oxford University Press, 1979)

Francesca Bugliani Knox and John Took, eds, *Poetry and Prayer*. The Power of the Word II (Farnham: Ashgate, 2015)

Jean-Yves Lacoste, *Experience and the Absolute: Disputed Questions on the Humanity of Man*. Trans. Mark Raftery-Skehan (New York: Fordham University Press, 2004)

William Langland, *Piers the Plowman*, B-Text. (Crowley) Early English Text Society. Ed. Walter W. Skeat (Oxford: Oxford University Press, 1869/1964)

William Langland, *Piers Plowman*, C-Text. Ed. Derek Pearsall (Berkeley: University of California Press, 1978)

Language and Liturgy in the Church (Edinburgh: Scottish Episcopal Church, 1998)

Philip Larkin, *The Less Deceived* (Hull: The Marvell Press, 1966)

D. H. Lawrence, *Selected Literary Criticism*. Ed. Anthony Beal (London: Heinemann, 1967)

Jean Leclerq, 'Les Méditations eucharistiques d'Arnauld de Bonneval', *Recherches de théologie ancienne et médiévale*, Vol. 13 (1946)

Jean Leclerq, *The Love of Learning and the Desire for God: A Study in Monastic Culture*. Trans. Catharine Misrahi (New York: Fordham University Press, 1982)

Lent, Holy Week, Easter: Services and Prayers (London: Church House Publishing, 1984)

C. S. Lewis, *The Allegory of Love* (Oxford: Oxford University Press, 1936. Reprinted, 1968)

C. S. Lewis, *Poetry and Prose in the Sixteenth Century*. The Oxford History of English Literature, Vol. IV (Oxford: Clarendon Press, 1954/1990)

Liber Eliensis. Ed. D. J. Stewart (London, 1848)

H. G. Liddell and Robert Scott, *A Greek–English Lexicon*. Fifth edition (Oxford: Clarendon Press, 1864)

Henry Littlehales, ed., *The Prymer, or, Prayer-Book of the Lay People in the Middle Ages*. 2 vols (London: Longmans, Green & Co., 1891, 1892)

Charles Lloyd, ed., *Formularies of Faith Put Forth by Authority During the Reign of Henry VIII* (Oxford: Clarendon Press, 1825)

Henri Cardinal de Lubac, *Corpus Mysticum: The Eucharist and the Church in the Middle Ages*. Trans. Gemma Simmonds CJ, with Richard Price and Christopher Stephens (London: SCM Press, 2006)

Diarmaid MacCulloch, *Thomas Cranmer: A Life* (New Haven: Yale University Press, 1996)

Diarmaid MacCulloch, *Silence: A Christian History* (London: Allen Lane, 2013)

Sara Maitland, *A Book of Silence* (London: Granta, 2008)

Peter Malekin, 'Wordsworth and the Mind of Man', in J. R. Watson, ed., *An Infinite Complexity: Essays in Romanticism* (Edinburgh: Edinburgh University Press, 1983), pp. 1–25

Peter Malekin and Ralph Yarrow, *Consciousness, Literature and Theatre: Theory and Beyond* (London: Macmillan, 1997)

Judith Maltby, *Prayer Book and People in Elizabethan and Early Stuart England* (Cambridge: Cambridge University Press, 2000)

Jean-Luc Marion, *Prolegomena to Charity*. Trans. Stephen E. Lewis (New York: Fordham University Press, 2002)

Jean-Luc Marion, *The Erotic Phenomenon*. Trans. Stephen E. Lewis (Chicago: University of Chicago Press, 2007)

Jean-Luc Marion, *The Essential Writings*. Ed. Kevin Hart (New York: Fordham University Press, 2013)

Christopher Marlowe, *The Complete Plays*. Ed. J. B. Steane (Harmondsworth: Penguin, 1969)

William Marshall, *Scripture, Tradition and Reason: A Selective View of Anglican Theology Through the Centuries* (Dublin: The Columba Press, 2010)

David Martin and Peter Mullen, eds, *No Alternative: The Prayer Book Controversy* (Oxford: Basil Blackwell, 1981)

David L. Martin, *Curious Visions of Modernity: Enchantment, Magic and the Sacred* (Cambridge, MA: The MIT Press, 2011)

F. O. Matthiessen, ed., *The Oxford Book of American Verse* (New York: Oxford University Press, 1968)

Ernest W. McDonnell, *The Beguines and Beghards in Medieval Culture, with Special Emphasis on the Belgian Scene* (New Brunswick, NJ: Rutgers University Press, 1954)

Sallie McFague, *Speaking in Parables: A Study in Metaphor and Theology* (Philadelphia: Fortress Press, 1975)

Bernard McGinn, *The Mystical Thought of Meister Eckhart* (New York: Crossroad Publishing, 2001)

Andrew B. McGowan, *Ancient Christian Worship: Early Church Practices in Social, Historical, and Theological Perspective* (Grand Rapids: Baker Acdemic, 2014)

James C. McKusick, *Coleridge's Philosophy of Language* (New Haven: Yale University Press, 1986)

Marshall McLuhan, *The Gutenberg Galaxy: The Making of Typographic Man* (Toronto: University of Toronto Press, 1962)

Thomas Merton, *The Wisdom of the Desert* (London: Sheldon Press, 1974)

Thomas Merton, *Meditations on Liturgy* (London: Mowbray, 1976)

John Milbank, *The Word Made Strange: Theology, Language and Culture* (Oxford: Blackwell, 1997)

Margaret R. Miles, *The Word Made Flesh: A History of Christian Thought* (Oxford: Blackwell, 2005)

J. Hillis Miller, *The Form of Victorian Fiction* (Notre Dame: Notre Dame University Press, 1968)

Anthony Milton, *Catholic and Reformed: The Roman and Protestant Churches in English Protestant Thought, 1600–1640* (Cambridge: Cambridge University Press, 1995)

Stephen D. Moore, *Poststructuralism and the New Testament: Derrida and Foucault at the Foot of the Cross* (Minneapolis: Fortress Press, 1994)

Brian Morris, ed., *Ritual Murder* (Manchester: Carcanet Press, 1980)

James Mozley, 'Bishop Andrewes' Sermons', *The British Critic*, Vol. 31 (January 1842), 169–205

Walter Nash, *Rhetoric: The Wit of Persuasion* (Oxford: Basil Blackwell, 1989)

J. H. Newman, *An Essay in Aid of a Grammar of Assent* (1870). Ed. I. T. Ker (Oxford: Clarendon Press, 1985)

Bridget Nichols, *Liturgical Hermeneutics: Interpreting Liturgical Rites in Performance* (Frankfurt: Peter Lang, 1996)

Bridget Nichols, ed., *The Collect in the Churches of the Reformation* (London: SCM Press, 2010)

Richmond Noble, *Shakespeare's Biblical Knowledge and Use of the Book of Common Prayer* (New York: Octagon Books, 1970)

Christopher Norris, *Deconstruction: Theory and Practice* (London: Methuen, 1982)

A. D. Nuttall, *Overheard by God: Fiction and Prayer in Herbert, Milton, Dante and St. John* (London: Methuen, 1980)

Walter J. Ong, SJ, *Orality and Literacy* (London: Routledge, 1982)

Origen, *Selected Works*. Trans. Rowan A. Greer (Mahwah, NJ: Paulist Press, 1979)

Robert Ornstein, *The Moral Vision of Jacobean Tragedy* (Madison: University of Wisconsin Press, 1965)

George Orwell, *Nineteen Eighty-Four* (London: Penguin, 1954)

G. R. Owst, *Literature and Pulpit in Medieval England* (Oxford: Basil Blackwell, 1966)

Elaine Pagels, *Beyond Belief: The Secret Gospel of Thomas* (London: Macmillan, 2003)

Patterns for Worship (London: Church House Publishing, 1995)

Bernard C. Pawley, ed., *The Second Vatican Council: Studies by Eight Anglican Observers* (London: Oxford University Press, 1967)

Michael Perham, ed., *Towards Liturgy 2000* (London: SPCK, 1989)

Michael Perham, ed., *Model and Inspiration: The Prayer Book Tradition Today* (London: SPCK, 1993)

Michael Perham, ed., *The Renewal of Common Prayer: Unity and Diversity in Church of England Worship* (London: SPCK, 1993)

Petrarch (Francesco Petrarca), *Selections from the* Canzoniere *and Other Works*. Trans. Mark Musa (Oxford: Oxford University Press, 1985)

S. Pétrement, *Simone Weil: A Life*. Trans. E. Crauford (London: Mowbray, 1977)

Philip H. Pfatteicher, *The School of the Church: Worship and Christian Formation* (Valley Forge, PA: Trinity Press International, 1995)

Philip H. Pfatteicher, *Liturgical Spirituality* (Valley Forge, PA: Trinity Press International, 1997)

Catherine Pickstock, *After Writing: On the Liturgical Consummation of Philosophy* (Oxford: Blackwell, 1998)

Alejandro Planchart, ed., *The Repertory of Tropes at Winchester*. 2 vols (Princeton: Princeton University Press, 1977)

Plato, *Phaedrus*. Trans. Walter Hamilton (London: Penguin, 1973)

H. F. M. Prescott, *Jerusalem Journey: Pilgrimage to the Holy Land in the Fifteenth Century* (London: Eyre & Spottiswoode, 1954)

Francis Procter and Walter Howard Frere, *A New History of the Book of Common Prayer* (London: Macmillan, 1949)

The Psalms: A New Translation for Worship (London: Church Information Office/Collins, 1977)

F. J. E. Raby, *The Poetry of the Eucharist* (London: Mowbray, 1957)

Karl Rahner, *Theological Investigations*, Vol. 4. Trans. Kevin Smith (London: Darton, Longman & Todd, 1974)

Ian Ramsey, *Religious Language*. Third impression (London: SCM Press, 1973)

Gail Ramshaw, *Liturgical Language: Keeping it Metaphoric, Making it Inclusive* (Collegeville: Liturgical Press, 1996)

E. C. Ratcliff, 'The Sanctus and the Pattern of the Early Anaphora', *Journal of Ecclesiastical History*, Vol. 1.1 (April 1950), 29–36, Vol. 1.2 (October 1950), 125–34

E. C. Ratcliff, *Liturgical Studies*. Ed. A. H. Couratin and D. H. Tripp (London: SPCK, 1976)

Paul Ricoeur, *The Symbolism of Evil*. Trans. Emerson Buchanan (Boston, MA: Beacon Press, 1967)

Paul Ricoeur, *The Rule of Metaphor*. Trans. Robert Czerny (Toronto: University of Toronto Press, 1977)

Edward Robinson, *The Language of Mystery* (London: SCM Press, 1987)

Ian Robinson, *The Survival of English: Essays in Criticism of Language* (Cambridge: Cambridge University Press, 1973)

David Rosenberg, ed., *Congregation: Contemporary Writers Read the Jewish Bible* (New York: Harcourt Brace Jovanovich, 1987)

Timothy Rosendale, *Liturgy and Literature in the Making of Protestant England* (Cambridge: Cambridge University Press, 2007)

Geoffrey Rowell, *The Liturgy of Christian Burial*. Alcuin Club Collections, No. 59 (London: SPCK, 1977)

Nicholas Sagovsky, 'The Language of Worship', in Colin Buchanan, Trevor Lloyd and Harold Miller, eds, *Anglican Worship Today* (London: Collins, 1980), pp. 44–6.

Robert P. Scharlemann, *Inscriptions and Reflections: Essays in Philosophical Theology* (Charlottesville: University of Virginia Press, 1989)

E. Schillebeeckx, OP, *The Eucharist*. Trans. N. D. Smith (London: Sheed & Ward, 1968)

Christine Catharina Schnusenberg, *The Relationship between the Church and the Theatre, Exemplified by Selected Writings of the Church Fathers and by Liturgical Texts until Amalarius of Metz – 775–852 AD* (New York: University Press of America, 1988)

David Scott, *A Quiet Gathering* (Newcastle upon Tyne: Bloodaxe Books, 1986)

Deborah K. Shuger, *Sacred Rhetoric: The Grand Christian Style in the English Renaissance* (Princeton: Princeton University Press, 1988)

Thomas Frederick Simmons, ed., *The Lay Folks Mass Book* (London: Early English Text Society/N. Trübner & Co., 1879)

Ulrich Simon, *Sitting in Judgement, 1913–1963* (London: SPCK, 1978)

A. D. Snyder, *Coleridge on Logic and Learning* (New Haven: Yale University Press, 1929)

B. D. Spinks, 'The Consecratory Epiclesis in the Anaphora of St. James', *Studia Liturgica*, Vol. 11.3/4 (1976), 19–32.

Barry Spurr, *The Word in the Desert* (Cambridge, Lutterworth, 1995)

George Steiner, *After Babel: Aspects of Language and Translation* (Oxford: Oxford University Press, 1975)

Kenneth Stephenson, *Jerusalem Revisited: The Liturgical Meaning of Holy Week* (Washington DC: Pastoral Press, 1988)

Daniel B. Stevick, *Language in Worship: Reflections on a Crisis* (New York: The Seabury Press, 1970)

Annie Sutherland, *English Psalms in the Middle Ages, 1300–1450* (Oxford: Oxford University Press, 2015)

Daniel S. Swift, *Shakespeare's Common Prayers: The Book of Common Prayer and the Elizabethan Age* (Oxford: Oxford University Press, 2013)

Ramie Targoff, *Common Prayer: The Language of Public Devotion in Early Modern England* (Chicago: University of Chicago Press, 2001)

Anthony C. Thiselton, *New Horizons in Hermeneutics* (London: HarperCollins, 1992)

R. S. Thomas, 'A Frame for Poetry', *Times Literary Supplement*, 3 March 1966, p. 169.

R. S. Thomas, *Laboratories of the Spirit* (London: Macmillan, 1975)

John Tinsley, 'Tell It Slant', *Theology*, Vol. 83 (1983), 163–70

David Torevell, *Losing the Sacred: Ritual, Modernity and Liturgical Reform* (London: T & T Clark, 2000)

Robert M. Torrance, *The Spiritual Quest: Transcendence in Myth, Religion, and Science* (Berkeley: University of California Press, 1994)

Cyril Tourneur, *The Revenger's Tragedy* (1607). Ed. Brian Gibbons (London: Ernest Benn, 1967)

R. C. Trench, *On the Study of Words* and *English Past and Present* (London: J. M. Dent, 1927)

Denys Turner, *The Darkness of God: Negativity in Christian Mysticism* (Cambridge: Cambridge University Press, 1995)

William Tyndale, *The Obedience of a Christian Man* (1528). Ed. David Daniell (Harmondsworth: Penguin, 2000)

William Tyndale, *Tyndale's New Testament* (1534). Ed. David Daniell (New Haven: Yale University Press, 1995)

Brian Vickers, *In Defence of Rhetoric* (Oxford: Clarendon Press, 1988)

Geoffrey Wainwright, 'The Language of Worship', in Cheslyn Jones, Geoffrey Wainwright and Edward Yarnold, SJ, eds, *The Study of Liturgy* (London: SPCK, 1978), pp. 465–72.

Heather Walton, ed., *Literature and Theology: New Interdisciplinary Spaces* (Farnham: Ashgate, 2011)

Benedicta Ward, SLG, *Harlots of the Desert: A Study of Repentance in Early Monastic Sources* (Kalamazoo: Cistercian Publications, 1987)

Frederick E. Warren, trans., *The Sarum Missal in English*. 2 vols (London: Alcuin Club Collections/A. R. Mowbray & Co., 1913)

J. R. Watson, *The Victorian Hymn* (Durham: University of Durham Press, 1981)

J. R. Watson, *Awake My Soul: Reflections on Thirty Hymns* (London: SPCK, 2005)

Paul A. Welsby, *Lancelot Andrewes, 1555–1626* (London: SPCK, 1958)

James Boyd White, *When Words Lose Their Meaning: Constitutions and Reconstitutions of Language, Character, and Community* (Chicago: Chicago University Press, 1984)

John Wilkinson, *Egeria's Travels* (London: SPCK, 1971)

Charles Williams, *The Descent of the Dove: A Short History of the Holy Spirit in the Church* (London: Longmans, Green & Co., 1939)

Rowan Williams, *Being Disciples: Essentials of the Christian Life* (London: SPCK, 2016)

Edith Wyschogrod, *Saints and Postmodernism* (Chicago: University of Chicago Press, 1990)

Edward Yarnold, SJ, *The Awe-Inspiring Rites of Initiation: Baptismal Homilies of the Fourth Century* (Slough: St Paul Publications, 1971)

Karl Young, *The Drama of the Medieval Church*. 2 vols. (Oxford: The Clarendon Press, 1933)

Katherine Zieman, *Singing the New Song: Literacy and Liturgy in Late Medieval England* (Philadelphia: University of Pennsylvania Press, 2008)

Ariel Zinder, 'Hebrew Liturgical Poetry – Beyond the Borders of Decorum'. Unpublished paper given at the meeting of the International Society for Religion, Literature and Culture, University of Glasgow, September, 2016.

Previously Published Chapters

An earlier version of Chapter 1 was published as 'Heaven in Ordinary, Man Well Dressed' in the online periodical *Ignaziana*, edited by the Ignatian Spirituality Center of the Institute of Spirituality at the Pontifical Gregorian University in Rome, 2017.

A different form of Chapter 5 is to be included in a Festschrift volume for Peter Malekin, published by Brill.

Chapter 8 has its origins in an essay entitled 'Liturgy and Language', published in Catherine A. Runcie, ed., *The Free Mind: Essays and Poems in Honour of Barry Spurr* (Sydney: Edwin Lowe Publishing, 2016), pp. 212–20.

Chapter 11 is a revised form of an essay contributed to Ramona Fotiade, David Jasper and Olivier Salazar-Ferrer, eds, *Embodiment: Phenomenological, Religious and Deconstructive Views on Living and Dying* (Farnham: Ashgate, 2014), pp. 131–42.

Notes

Introduction

1 G. J. Cuming, *A History of Anglican Liturgy*. Second edition (London: Macmillan, 1982), p. 10.

2 Brother Gararde, *The Interpretation and Signification of the Mass* (1532), quoted in Cuming, *ibid.*, pp. 4–5.

3 Katherine Zieman, *Singing the New Song: Literacy and Liturgy in Late Medieval England* (Philadelphia: University of Pennsylvania Press, 2008): Annie Sutherland, *English Psalms in the Middle Ages: 1300–1450* (Oxford: Oxford University Press, 2015).

4 Timothy Rosendale, *Liturgy and Literature in the Making of Protestant England* (Cambridge: Cambridge University Press, 2007): Ramie Targoff, *Common Prayer: The Language of Public Devotion in Early Modern England* (Chicago: University of Chicago Press, 2001): Daniel Swift, *Shakespeare's Common Prayers: The Book of Common Prayer and the Elizabethan Age* (Oxford: Oxford University Press, 2013).

Poetry and the Language of Prayer and Worship

1 An earlier version of this chapter was given as a lecture in Heythrop College, London, November 2016, as part of the series of conferences entitled Power of the Word.

2 George Sampson, Introduction to R. C. Trench, *On the Study of Words*, and *English Past and Present* (London: J. M. Dent, 1927).

3 See James C. McKusick, *Coleridge's Philosophy of Language* (New Haven: Yale University Press, 1986), pp. 33–41.

4 See Catherine Pickstock, *After Writing: On the Liturgical Consummation of Philosophy* (Oxford: Blackwell, 1998). See also John Milbank, *The Word Made Strange: Theology, Language and Culture* (Oxford: Blackwell, 1997), Ch. 4, 'The Linguistic Turn as a Theological Turn', pp. 84–120.

5 S. T. Coleridge, *Collected Letters*, Vol. 1 (1785–1800). Ed. Earl Leslie Griggs (Oxford: Clarendon Press, 1966), pp. 351–2.

6 See John Coulson, *Newman and the Common Tradition* (Oxford: Clarendon Press, 1970), pp. 14–37; David Jasper, *Literature and Theology as a Grammar of Assent* (Farnham: Ashgate, 2016), pp. 15, 32.

7 See A. D. Snyder, *Coleridge on Logic and Learning* (New Haven: Yale University Press, 1929), p. 138.

8 Michael Perham, ed., *Towards Liturgy 2000* (London: SPCK, 1989), p. 67.

9 Preface, *The Alternative Service Book* (London: Clowes/SPCK/Cambridge University Press, 1980), p. 11.

10 S. T. Coleridge, *The Statesman's Manual* (1816), in *Lay Sermons*. Ed. R. J. White. Collected Works, Vol. 6 (Princeton: Princeton University Press, 1972), p. 29. Ezekiel 1.15–21.

11 See, Philip H. Pfatteicher, *The School of the Church: Worship and Christian Formation* (Valley Forge, PA: Trinity Press International, 1995), p. 29; *The Poems of T. S. Eliot: The Annotated Text*, Vol. 1 (London: Faber & Faber, 2015), p. 31.

12 Pickstock, *After Writing*, p. xii.

13 Pfatteicher, *School of the Church*, p. viii.

14 *Ibid.*, p. 68.

15 See Jean-Yves Lacoste, *Experience and the Absolute: Disputed Questions on the Humanity of Man*. Trans. Mark Raftery-Skehan (New York: Fordham University Press, 2004).

16 Gail Ramshaw, *Liturgical Language: Keeping It Metaphoric, Making It Inclusive* (Collegeville: Liturgical Press, 1996), p. 10.

17 John E. Booty, ed., *The Book of Common Prayer: 1559, The Elizabethan Prayer Book* (Charlottesville: University of Virginia Press, 2005), p. 332.

18 George Herbert, *The English Poems*. Ed. Helen Wilcox (Cambridge: Cambridge University Press, 2007), pp. 371–2.

19 *Ibid.* p. 371.

20 'Make not an ell, by trifling in thy wo.' *Ibid.*, p. 62. Shakespeare uses it in *Romeo and Juliet* (1597), 'O, here's a wit of cheveril, that stretches from an inch narrow to an ell broad.' Act 2, Sc. 4, line 88.

21 *Constitution on the Sacred Liturgy*, 34, in Walter M. Abbott, SJ, ed., *The Documents of Vatican II* (London: Geoffrey Chapman, 1972), p. 149. See also David Crystal, *Linguistics, Language and Religion* (London: Burns & Oates, 1965), pp. 152–3.

22 *Common Worship: Services and Prayers for the Church of England* (London: Church House Publishing, 2000), p. 181.

23 David L. Frost, *The Language of Series 3*. Grove Booklet No. 12 (Bramcote: Grove Books, 1973), p. 10.

24 *Ibid.*

25 See also R. C. D. Jasper and Paul F. Bradshaw, eds, *A Companion to the Alternative Service Book* (London: SPCK, 1986), pp. 203–4.

26 Frost, *Language of Series 3*, p. 10.

27 Paul Ricoeur, *The Rule of Metaphor*. Trans. Robert Czerny (Toronto: University of Toronto Press, 1977), p. 6.

28 *Ibid.*, p. 7.

29 Origen, *Selected Works*. Trans. Rowan A. Greer (Mahwah NJ: Paulist Press, 1979), p. 217.

30 *Ibid.*, p. 218; Hebrews 5.14.

31 Coleridge, *Statesman's Manual*, p. 30.

32 Socrates tells Phaedrus that 'Lysias or any other writer, past or future, who claims that clear and permanently valid truth is to be found in a written speech, lays himself open to reproach, whether that reproach is actually levelled at him or not.' Plato, *Phaedrus*. Trans. Walter Hamilton (London: Penguin, 1973), p. 100.

33 Louis Bouyer, *Eucharist*. Trans. Charles Underhill Quinn (Notre Dame: University of Notre Dame Press, 1968), p. 380 (emphases added). See also Joseph A. Jungmann, *The Mass of the Roman Rite: Its Origins and Development*. Trans. Francis A. Brunner. Revised Charles K. Riepe. Abridged edition. (New York: Benziger Brothers Inc, 1959), pp. 37–45.

34 Pickstock, *After Writing*, p. 173.

35 On 'stretched' language, see also Sallie McFague, *Speaking in Parables: A Study in Metaphor and Theology* (Philadelphia: Fortress Press, 1975), p. 13.

36 See J. A. Cruddon, *A Dictionary of Literary Terms* (London: Penguin, 1982), pp. 60–1.

37 *Ibid*., pp. 40–1.

38 *Ibid*., pp. 471–2.

39 *Poems of Gerard Manley Hopkins*. Ed. Robert Bridges (London: Oxford University Press, 1931), p. 19.

40 For further study of rhetoric and English poetry see Deborah K. Shuger, *Sacred Rhetoric: The Christian Grand Style in the English Renaissance* (Princeton: Princeton University Press, 1988); Brian Vickers, *In Defence of Rhetoric* (Oxford: Clarendon Press, 1988); Walter Nash, *Rhetoric: The Wit of Persuasion* (Oxford: Basil Blackwell, 1989); David Jasper, *Rhetoric, Power and Community: An Exercise in Reserve* (London: Macmillan, 1993). Chapter 5 of my book deals particularly with the language of the 1549 *Book of Common Prayer*.

41 Cuddon, *Dictionary*, pp. 598–603.

42 See Pickstock, *After Writing*, pp. 213–14.

43 See Jasper and Bradshaw, *Companion to the Alternative Service Book*, p. 243.

44 Quoted in Stella Brook, *The Language of the Book of Common Prayer* (London: Andre Deutsch, 1965), pp. 19–20.

45 George Orwell, *Nineteen Eighty-Four* (London: Penguin, 1954), p. 241 (emphasis added).

46 *Cranmer's Selected Writings*. Ed. C. S. Meyer (London: SPCK, 1961), p. 2.

47 See Donald Davie, *A Gathered Church: The Literature of the English Dissenting Interest, 1700–1930* (London: Routledge & Kegan Paul, 1978), p. 24.

48 See, Crystal, *Linguistics, Language and Religion*, Ch. XII, 'Language and Logical Positivism', pp. 157–89.

The Poetics of Liturgy

1 Karl Rahner, 'Poetry and the Christian', *Theological Investigations*, Vol. 4. Trans. Kevin Smyth (London: Darton, Longman & Todd, 1974), pp. 357–67, at p. 365.

2 The volumes, now three in number, derive from a series of conferences inaugurated by Heythrop College, University of London, in 2011 and are published by Ashgate/Routledge.

3 David Lonsdale, 'Poetry and Prayer: A Survey of Some Twentieth-Century Studies', in Francesca Bugliani Knox and John Took, eds, *Poetry and Prayer*. The Power of the Word II (Farnham: Ashgate, 2015), p. 33.

4 Francesca Bugliani Knox, Introduction to *Poetry and Prayer*, p. 3. Underhill, of course, is best known for such books as *Mysticism* (1911) and *Worship* (1936), though she was also an underrated novelist.

5 Rahner, 'Poetry and the Christian', p. 358 (first emphasis added).

6 T. S. Eliot, *Selected Essays*. Third enlarged edition (London: Faber & Faber, 1951), p. 389.

7 S. T. Coleridge, *Biographia Literaria* (1817). Ed. James Engell and W. Jackson Bate. Collected Works, Vol. 7 (Princeton: Princeton University Press, 1983), Vol. 1, p. 304. This is, of course, specifically what Coleridge terms the 'primary imagination'.

8 R. S. Thomas, *Laboratories of the Spirit* (London: Macmillan, 1975), p. 10.

9 The image of the flowering cross is ancient, such as on the designs of the Ruthwell Cross in Scotland, probably dating from the eighth century, and containing verses from 'The Dream of the Rood', an Anglo-Saxon poem saturated in the liturgy of Passiontide. See Michael Alexander, ed., *The Earliest English Poems* (Harmondsworth: Penguin, 1966), p. 105.

10 *King James Bible*, 'The Translators to the Reader'. Ed. Robert Carroll and Stephen Prickett (Oxford: Oxford University Press, 1997), p. lvi.

11 See further Richard McLauchlan, 'Saturday Prayers: R. S. Thomas and the Search for a Silent God', in Knox and Took, *Poetry and Prayer*, pp. 182–4.

12 Jay Parini, 'Poetry as Immanence: How Language Informs Reality', in *ibid.*, p. 72.

13 Seamus Heaney, *New Selected Poems, 1966–1987* (London: Faber & Faber, 1990), p. 90.

14 Quoted in Michael Perham, 'Liturgical Revision 1981–2000', in Paul F. Bradshaw, ed., *Companion to Common Worship*, Vol. 1 (London: SPCK, 2001), p. 29.

15 Introduction to *Alternative Baptism Texts* (Church of England Liturgical Commission, 2015), p. 1.

16 David Scott, *A Quiet Gathering* (Newcastle upon Tyne: Bloodaxe Books, 1986), p. 36.

17 Philip Larkin, *The Less Deceived* (Hull: The Marvell Press, 1966), p. 29.

18 Rahner, 'Poetry and the Christian', p. 365.

19 Lonsdale, 'Poetry and Prayer', p. 32.

20 Eliot, *Selected Essays*, p. 391. (I have changed Eliot's odd spelling 'Corneile'.)

21 William Shakespeare, *Hamlet*, Act 3, Sc. 3, line 38. I am drawing here upon the fine essay by Małgorzata Gregorzewska, 'Prayer, Poetry and Silence: A Musical Correspondence', in Knox and Took, *Poetry and Prayer*, pp. 134–6.

22 The New Revised Standard Version renders this, 'standing by himself was praying.' In this case it seems that the KJV is closer to the Greek original.

23 See Jean-Luc Marion, *Prolegomena to Charity*. Trans. Stephen E. Lewis (New York: Fordham University Press, 2002), p. 26. 'Satan, or the perfect idiot: ἴδιος, the one who assumes his particularity as a proper good, who appropriates his own identity to such a point that he first does not want and then is not able to "leave himself," that is to say, to inhabit distance.'

24 *Hamlet*, Act 3, Sc. 3, lines 97–8.

25 George Eliot, *Adam Bede* (1859) (London: Cassell and Company, 1907), pp. 7–8.

26 Jean Leclerq, *The Love of Learning and the Desire for God: A Study in Monastic Culture*. Trans. Catharine Misrahi (New York: Fordham University Press, 1982), pp. 236–54. Quoted in Mark S. Burrows, '"Prayer is the Little Implement": Poetic

Speech and the Gestures of Prayer in Christian Traditions', in Knox and Took, *Poetry and Prayer*, p. 48.

27 Published first as *The Psalms: A New Translation for Worship* (London: Church Information Office/Collins, 1977).

28 David L. Frost, *Making the Liturgical Psalter*. The Morpeth Lectures, 1980 (Bramcote: Grove Booklets, 1981), p. 37.

29 *Ibid.*, p. 35.

30 *The Rule of St. Benedict*. Trans. Carolinne White (Harmondsworth: Penguin, 2008), 9, p. 28.

31 *Iron in the Soul* was used for the English title of the third part of Jean-Paul Sartre's trilogy *Les Chemins de la liberté* (1945–9). The French title is *La Mort dans l'âme*.

32 See John Hollander, 'Psalms', in David Rosenberg, ed., *Congregation: Contemporary Writers Read the Jewish Bible* (New York: Harcourt Brace Jovanovich, 1987), pp. 294–5.

33 *Ibid.*, p. 294.

34 See Paul Ricoeur, *The Symbolism of Evil*. Trans. Emerson Buchanan (Boston, MA: Beacon Press, 1967), pp. 353–7.

35 *Patterns for Worship* (London: Church House Publishing, 1995), p. 12.

36 D. H. Lawrence, *Selected Literary Criticism*. Ed. Anthony Beal (London: Heinemann, 1967), pp. 6–7.

37 Thomas Hardy, *The Collected Poems* (London: Macmillan, 1965), p. 403. See J. R. Watson, *The Victorian Hymn* (Durham: University of Durham Press, 1981), p. 6.

38 Watson, *Victorian Hymn*, p. 9.

39 Isaac Watts, quoted in Donald Davie, *A Gathered Church: The Literature of the English Dissenting Interest, 1700–1930* (London: Routledge & Kegan Paul, 1978), p. 24.

40 J. R. Watson, *Awake My Soul: Reflections on Thirty Hymns* (London: SPCK, 2005), pp. 92–3.

41 Hardy, *Collected Poems*, p. 439.

42 In October 1878, Hopkins wrote to R. W. Dixon: 'What I had written I burnt before I became a Jesuit and resolved to write no more, as not belonging to my profession, unless it were by the wish of my superiors; so for seven years I wrote nothing …' *Gerard Manley Hopkins: Poems and Prose*. Selected and ed. W. H. Gardner (Harmondsworth: Penguin, 1963), p. 187.

43 Thomas Merton, 'Poetry and Contemplation: A Reappraisal' (1958), quoted in Sarah Law, 'Thomas Merton's Poetry and Prayer', in Knox and Took, *Poetry and Prayer*, p. 190.

44 Originally published under the title *Seasons of Celebration*.

45 A. D. Nuttall, *Overheard by God: Fiction and Prayer in Herbert, Milton, Dante and St. John* (London: Methuen, 1980), p. 142.

46 *Ibid.*

47 *Ibid.*, p. 143.

A Ritual Poetics and the Demands of Liturgical Language

1 David Cockerell, 'Why Language Matters', in David Martin and Peter Mullen, eds, *No Alternative: The Prayer Book Controversy* (Oxford: Basil Blackwell, 1981), pp. 96–113.

2 See below, especially Chs 8 and 9.

3 In a letter of 21 December 2016.

4 Arthur Greene, *Post-Petrarchism: Origins and Innovations of the Western Lyric Sequence* (Princeton: Princeton University Press, 1991), p. 109.

5 *Ibid.*, p. 17.

6 See Donald Davie, ed., *The Psalms in English* (Harmondsworth: Penguin, 1996).

7 Frank Kermode, *The Sense of an Ending: Studies in the Theory of Fiction* (New York: Oxford University Press, 1966), p. 39.

8 See, most famously, the 'Mutabilitie Cantos' of the fragmentary Book VII of Spenser's *Faerie Queen* (1609).

9 Petrarch (Francesco Petrarca), *Selections from the* Canzoniere *and Other Works*. Trans. Mark Musa (Oxford: Oxford University Press, 1985), p. 21.

10 Archibald MacLeish famously suggested that a poem should not mean, but be. See Hans Robert Jauss, '*La douceur du foyer*: The Lyric of the Year 1857 as a Pattern for the Communication of Social Norms', *Romantic Review*, Vol. 65 (1974), 201.

11 Greene, *Post-Petrarchism*, p. 11.

12 Mircea Eliade, *The Sacred and the Profane*. Trans. Willard R. Trask (New York: Harcourt, Brace, 1959), pp. 68–70.

13 Greene, *Post-Petrarchism*, p. 195.

14 See further J. Hillis Miller, *The Form of Victorian Fiction* (Notre Dame: Notre Dame University Press, 1968).

15 *The Poems of T. S. Eliot: The Annotated Text*, Vol. 1. Ed. Christopher Ricks and Jim McCue (London: Faber & Faber, 2015), pp. 5, 179.

16 Personal letter, see above, note 2.

17 Charles Feidelson, Jr, *Symbolism and American Literature* (Chicago: University of Chicago Press, 1953), pp. 18–19.

18 In F. O. Matthiessen, ed., *The Oxford Book of American Verse* (New York: Oxford University Press, 1968), p. 381.

19 Greene, *Post-Petrarchism*, p. 27.

20 Petrarch, *Selections from the* Canzoniere, Sonnet 122, p. 40.

21 Although it is true that the best modern critical edition of the *Book of Common Prayer* (1549, 1559, 1662) is by a professor of English Literature, Brian Cummings, rather than a liturgist (Oxford: Oxford University Press, 2011).

22 See also Nathan Hitchcock, 'Saving Edward Taylor's Purse: Masculine Devotion in the *Preparatory Devotions*', *Literature and Theology*, Vol. 22.3 (September 2008), 339–53.

23 Greene, *Post-Petrarchism*, p. 109.

24 Judith Maltby, Foreword to *The Book of Common Prayer: 1559, The Elizabethan Prayer Book*. Ed. John E. Booty (Charlottesville: University of Virginia Press, 2005), pp. x–xi.

25 Brian Cummings, ed., *The Book of Common Prayer: The Texts of 1549, 1559, and 1662* (Oxford: Oxford University Press, 2011), pp. 136–7.

26 *Ibid.*, p. 137.

27 One is reminded of the great purple passage at the end of Dom Gregory Dix's *The Shape of the Liturgy* (Westminster: Dacre Press, 1945), p. 744. 'Was ever another command so obeyed? ... from the pinnacles of earthly greatness to the refuge of fugitives in the caves and dens of the earth. Men have found no better things than this to do ...'

28 Cummings, *Book of Common Prayer*, p. 137.

29 F. E. Brightman, *The English Rite* (London: Rivingtons, 1915), Vol. II, p. 692. See also R. C. D. Jasper and G. J. Cuming, *Prayers of the Eucharis: Early and Reformed*. Third edition (New York: Pueblo Publishing, 1987), pp. 88–92.

30 Louis Bouyer, *Eucharist: Theology and Spirituality of the Eucharistic Prayer*. Trans. Charles Underhill Quinn (Notre Dame: University of Notre Dame Press, 1968), p. 268.

31 B. D. Spinks, 'The Consecratory Epiclesis in the Anaphora of St. James', *Studia Liturgica*, Vol. 11.3/4 (1976), 19–32.

32 Quoted in C. S. Lewis, *Poetry and Prose in the Sixteenth Century* (Oxford: Clarendon Press, 1954), p. 217.

33 *Ibid.*

34 See, G. J. Cuming, *A History of Anglican Liturgy*. Second edition (London: Macmillan, 1982), pp. 15–29.

35 See below, Chapter 6, 'Liturgical Language and the Vernacular in Late Medieval England', pp. 75–89.

36 See, for example, Dominic Baker-Smith, 'Exegesis: Literary and Divine', in David Jasper, ed., *Images of Belief in Literature* (London: Macmillan, 1984), pp. 172–4.

37 Lewis, *Poetry and Prose in the Sixteenth Century*, pp. 60–1.

38 Baker-Smith, 'Exegesis', p. 172.

39 *Ibid.*, p. 173.

40 Sir Philip Sidney, *Apology for Poetry* (1595), in Edmund D. Jones, ed., *English Critical Essays (Sixteenth, Seventeenth and Eighteenth Centuries)* (Oxford: Oxford University Press, 1965), pp. 1–54. See also, Baker-Smith 'Exegesis', p. 176.

41 *The Archbishop of Canterbury's Speech* (London: Peter Cole, 1644), p. 7; Baker-Smith, 'Exegesis', p. 175.

42 Article 22 of the Thirty Nine Articles. See Stephen Greenblatt, *Hamlet in Purgatory* (Princeton: Princeton University Press, 2001). See further on *Hamlet* and Purgatory, Chapter 7, 'Literature and the Prayer Books of the English Reformation', below, pp. 97–100.

43 John Keats in a letter to Richard Woodhouse, 27 October 1818.

44 Greene, *Post-Petrarchism*, p. 139.

45 Samuel Taylor Coleridge, *Lay Sermons*. Ed. R. J. White. Collected Works, Vol. 6 (Princeton: Princeton University Press, 1972), p. 30.

Liturgy and Performance

1 Floyd V. Filson, *The Gospel According to St. Matthew*. Second edition (London: Adam & Charles Black, 1971), p. 95.

2 Rowan Williams, *Being Disciples: Essentials of the Christian Life* (London: SPCK, 2016), p. 37.

3 Joseph A. Jungmann, SJ, *The Early Liturgy to the Time of Gregory the Great*. Trans. Francis A. Brunner (London: Darton, Longman & Todd, 1959), p. 11.

4 Andrew B. McGowan, *Ancient Christian Worship: Early Church Practices in Social, Historical, and Theological Perspective* (Grand Rapids: Baker Academic, 2014), pp. 65–110.

5 *Ibid.*, p. 65.

6 Ariel Zinder, 'Hebrew Liturgical Poetry – Beyond the Borders of Decorum.' Unpublished paper given at the meeting of the International Society for Religion, Literature and Culture, University of Glasgow, September 2016, pp. 1–2.

7 *Ibid.*, p. 2.

8 See Jacques Derrida, *Of Grammatology*. Trans. Gayatri Chakravorty-Spivak (Baltimore: Johns Hopkins University Press, 1976), pp. 195–200.

9 Zinder, 'Hebrew Liturgical Poetry', pp. 11–12.

10 R. C. D. Jasper and G. J. Cuming, *Prayers of the Eucharist: Early and Reformed*. Third edition (New York: Pueblo Publishing, 1987), p. 7. On *berakah*, see further below, p. 53.

11 *Ibid.*, p. 8.

12 This early dating is admittedly highly contentious, and it has been placed as late as the third century, though this seems unlikely. The first codex, dating from 1067, was discovered in Constantinople in 1873.

13 *The Didache*, in *Early Christian Writings*. Trans. Maxwell Staniforth (Harmondsworth: Penguin, 1968), p. 234.

14 *Ibid.*, p. 231.

15 C. H. Dodd, 'Eucharistic Symbolism in the Fourth Gospel', *The Expositor*, 8th series, Vol. 2 (1911), 530–46, and *The Interpretation of the Fourth Gospel* (Cambridge: Cambridge University Press, 1970), pp. 138–9.

16 *The Didache*, p. 232. More recently Lawrence J. Johnson suggests, 'Allow the prophets to give thanks as they wish.' *Worship in the Early Church: An Anthology of Historical Sources*. Vol. 1 (Collegeville: Liturgical Press, 2009), p. 38.

17 Jasper and Cuming, *Prayers of the Eucharist*, p. 75.

18 Theodor Klauser, *A Short History of the Western Liturgy*. Trans. John Halliburton. Second edition (Oxford: Oxford University Press, 1979), p. 21.

19 *Ibid.*, p. 22 (emphasis added).

20 See Dom Gregory Dix, *The Shape of the Liturgy* (Westminster: Dacre Press, 1945), p. 744.

21 See Paul F. Bradshaw, Maxwell E. Johnson and L. Edward Phillips, *The Apostolic Tradition: A Commentary* (Minneapolis: Fortress Press, 2002), p. 6.

22 Geoffrey J. Cuming, ed., *Hippolytus: A Text for Students* (Bramcote: Grove Books, 1976), p. 8.

23 See Klaus, *Western Liturgy*, pp. 37–8.

24 Bradshaw, Johnson and Phillips, *Apostolic Tradition*, p. 7.

25 Dom Gregory Dix, ed., *The Treatise on The Apostolic Tradition of St. Hippolytus of Rome*. Revised Henry Chadwick (London: SPCK, 1968), p. 19.

26 See, Henry Chadwick, Preface to the Second edition of Dix, *Apostolic Tradition*, p. i.

27 *Ibid.*

28 Tertullian, *Apologeticum* 1: xxxix, in Johnson, *Worship in the Early Church*, Vol. 1, p. 117.

29 See George Guiver, 'Intercession', in Paul Bradshaw, ed., *The New Westminster Dictionary of Liturgy and Worship* (Louisville: WJK Press, 2002), p. 255; W. Jardine Grisbrooke, 'Intercession', in J. G. Davies, ed., *A New Dictionary of Liturgy and Worship* (London: SCM Press, 1986), pp. 281–2.

30 See above, p. 49.

31 Jasper and Cuming, *Prayers of the Eucharist*, p. 53.

32 *Ibid.*, pp. 60–1.

33 *Ibid.* Jasper and Cuming point out that this is from the final thirteenth-century form of the liturgy of Alexandria, preserved in five medieval manuscripts, though they argue for its construction from the early form of the *Liturgy of St. Mark* (p. 57).

34 See F. E. Brightman, *The English Rite*. Vol. 1 (London: Rivingtons, 1915), pp. 190–9, suggesting their origins in 1604.

35 Cyprian *On the Lord's Prayer* (*c.* 251/2 CE), in Johnson, *Worship in the Early Church*, p. 152.

36 H. G. Liddell and Robert Scott, *A Greek–English Lexicon*. Fifth edition (Oxford: Clarendon Press, 1864), p. 1503; G. Abbott-Smith, *A Manual Greek Lexicon of the New Testament* (Edinburgh: T & T Clark, 1968), p. 455.

37 See also Geoffrey Wainwright, 'The Periods of Liturgical History', in Cheslyn Jones, Geoffrey Wainwright and Edward Yarnold, SJ, eds, *The Study of Liturgy* (London: SPCK, 1978), p. 35.

38 Klauser, *Western Liturgy*, pp. 82–3.

39 See St Basil the Great, *On the Holy Spirit*, 73, in Lawrence J. Johnson, *Worship in the Early Church*, p. 222.

40 Mary Berry, 'Hymns', in Davies, *A New Dictionary of Liturgy and Worship*, p. 262.

41 Sergius baptized Caedwalla, King of the West Saxons, in 689, and ordered St Wilfrid to be restored to his see (*c.* 700).

42 Klauser, *Western Liturgy*, p. 84.

43 Florus, *Adversus Amalarium*, quoted in Henri Cardinal de Lubac, *Corpus Mysticum: The Eucharist and the Church in the Middle Ages*. Trans. Gemma Simmonds, CJ, with Richard Price and Christopher Stephens (London: SCM Press, 2006), p. 265.

44 O. B. Hardison, Jr, *Christian Rite and Christian Drama in the Middle Ages*. (Baltimore: Johns Hopkins University Press, 1965), p. 45.

45 See John Wilkinson, *Egeria's Travels* (London: SPCK, 1971). Such devotions in Jerusalem continued into the pilgrimage culture of the later Middle Ages, a tradition beautifully caught in H. F. M. Prescott's recovery of the pilgrim journeys of Friar Felix Fabri in her book *Jerusalem Journey: Pilgrimage to the Holy Land in the Fifteenth Century* (London: Eyre & Spottiswoode, 1954). See also David Jasper, *The Sacred Community: Art, Sacrament and the People of God* (Waco: Baylor University

Press, 2012), Ch. 4, 'The Community in Pilgrimage: Egeria and Her Fellow Travellers', pp. 45–64.

46 Kenneth Stevenson, *Jerusalem Revisited: The Liturgical Meaning of Holy Week* (Washington DC, Pastoral Press, 1988).

47 Douglas Jones, Introduction to *Lent, Holy Week, Easter: Services and Prayers* (London: Church House Publishing, 1984), p. 3. These services were never formally authorized by the Church of England, though widely used. They were 'commended by the House of Bishops'.

48 Amalarius, quoted in Hardison, *Christian Rite and Christian Drama*, pp. 47–8.

49 See above, Geoffrey Wainwright, p. 132.

50 See Christine Catharina Schnusenberg, *The Relationship between the Church and the Theatre, Exemplified by Selected Writings of the Church Fathers and by Liturgical texts until Amalarius of Metz – 775–852 AD* (New York: University Press of America, 1988), p. 210.

51 See Hardison, *Christian Rite and Christian Drama*, p. 43. 'Amalarius and his followers were not theologians in the sense in which the word is applied to the Scholastics of the high Middle Ages. In modern terms, their work is closer to literary criticism than to theology.'

52 Amalarius, quoted in Schnusenberg, *The Relationship between the Church and the Theatre*, pp. 224–5. The translation is my own with the help of Professor George Newlands.

53 See *ibid.*, p. 210.

54 Aelred of Rievaulx, quoted in Hardison, *Christian Rite and Christian Drama*, pp. 78–9. See also E. K. Chambers, *The Mediaeval Stage* (Oxford: Oxford University Press, 1903), Vol. 1, p. 81.

55 Joseph A. Jungmann, SJ, *The Mass of the Roman Rite: Its Origins and Development*. Trans. Francis A. Brunner. Revised Charles K. Riepe. Abridged edition. (New York: Benziger Brothers Inc., 1959), p. 69.

56 See further, with an example of an Easter resurrection play from the *Regularis Concordia*, John Gassner, *Medieval and Tudor Drama* (New York: Bantam Books, 1968), pp. 37–8.

57 Jungmann, *Mass of the Roman Rite*, p. 70.

58 Louis Bouyer, *Eucharist: Theology and Spirituality of the Eucharistic Prayer.* Trans. Charles Underhill Quinn (Notre Dame: University of Notre Dame Press, 1968), p. 443.

59 See above, pp. 5, 11.

60 See above, note 28.

Hippolytus and The Apostolic Tradition

1 It was, in fact, a volume in a series called Studies in Literature and Religion published by Macmillan of which I was then the General Editor. Peter Malekin, I should say, was a close colleague and friend of mine for many years.

2 T. S. Eliot, 'Burnt Norton II', in *The Poems of T. S. Eliot: The Annotated Text*. Ed. Christopher Ricks and Jim McCue (London: Faber & Faber, 2015), Vol. 1, p. 181.

3 See above, pp. 50–3.

4 See Lawrence J. Johnson, *Worship in the Early Church: An Anthology of Historical Sources*. Vol. 1 (Collegeville: Liturgical Press, 2009), p. 194; Dom Gregory Dix, ed., *The Treatise on The Apostolic Tradition of St. Hippolytus of Rome*. Revised Henry Chadwick (London: SPCK, 1968), p. xi.

5 Burton Scott Easton, Introduction to *The Apostolic Tradition of Hippolytus* (Cambridge: Cambridge University Press, 1934), p. 1.

6 Dix, *Apostolic Tradition*, pp. 40–1.

7 See the translation of R. C. D. Jasper and G. J. Cuming, *Prayers of the Eucharist: Early and Reformed*. Third edition (New York: Pueblo Publishing, 1987), p. 37.

8 John Wilkinson, *Egeria's Travels* (London: SPCK, 1971), pp. 136–8.

9 O. B. Hardison, Jr, *Christian Rite and Christian Drama in the Middle Ages* (Baltimore: Johns Hopkins University Press, 1965), p. 78.

10 See Malekin and Yarrow, *Consciousness, Literature and Theatre*, pp. 130–1, 176.

11 Peter Malekin, 'Wordsworth and the Mind of Man', in J. R. Watson, ed., *An Infinite Complexity: Essays in Romanticism* (Edinburgh: Edinburgh University Press, 1983), pp. 12–13.

12 Dix, *Apostolic Tradition*, p. xv. As a formidably learned liturgist Dix's scholarly reputation has not been enhanced in the field of liturgical studies by his capacity to shift into a poetic register in his writing, at which point more empirically minded and historically trained scholars become nervous. A classic instance of this is the celebrated passage at the end of *The Shape of the Liturgy* (1945) which describes the manifold ways in which the Eucharist has been 'performed' 'just to *make* the *plebs sancta Dei* – the holy common people of God'. To celebrate is truly to create. *The Shape of the Liturgy* (Westminster: Dacre Press, 1945), p. 744.

13 Dix, *Apostolic Tradition*, p. 2.

14 J. G. Davies, *The Secular Use of Church Buildings* (London: SCM Press, 1968), pp. 8–9.

15 *Ibid.*, p. 9.

16 Malekin and Yarrow, *Consciousness, Literature and Theatre*, p. 126.

17 *Ibid.*, pp. 128–9.

18 Comparison may be made here with the critical reading of the 1559 Holy Communion liturgy in Chapter 3, see above, pp. 39–44.

19 Jasper and Cuming note that the Latin here has no verb.

20 Malekin and Yarrow, *Consciousness, Literature and Theatre*, pp. 129–33.

21 'O, for a Muse of fire, that would ascend
The brightest heaven of invention;
A kingdom for a stage, princes to act
And monarchs to behold the swelling scene!'
Henry V, Act 1, Prologue, lines 1–4.

22 Franc Chamberlain, 'Embodying Spirit: Nihilism and Spiritual Renovation in the European Theatre, 1890–1990', PhD Diss., University of East Anglia, 1992, quoted in Malekin and Yarrow, *Consciousness, Literature and Theatre*, p. 131. The comment relates specifically to the theatre of the Spanish playwright Ramón María del Valle-Inclán y de la Peña.

23 Jasper and Cuming, *Prayers of the Eucharist*, p. 35.

24 Malekin, 'Wordsworth', p. 13.

25 See Jasper and Cuming, *Prayers of the Eucharist*, p. 33.

26 *Didache*, in *Early Christian Writings*. Trans. Maxwell Staniforth (Harmondsworth: Penguin, 1968), p. 231.

27 This detachment seems close to what Thomas Merton in his study of the spirituality of the Desert Fathers describes as 'purity of heart', known as 'an intuitive grasp of one's own inner reality' and resulting in *quies* or 'rest'. *The Wisdom of the Desert* (London: Sheldon Press, 1974), p. 8. Such 'detachment' is central also in the spiritual teachings of the *Philokalia*.

28 Malekin and Yarrow, *Consciousness, Literature and Theatre*, p. 133.

29 *Ibid.*, p. 135. Jerzy Grotowski was an innovative Polish theatre director and theorist.

30 I recall how a former Bishop of Ely, Peter Walker, seemed to become almost invisible and inaudible as he spoke the words of the Eucharist. The poet W. H. Auden, a man who 'did not parade his devotion', in his last years in Christ Church, Oxford, appreciated such spirit in performance. See Peter Walker, '*Horae Canonicae*: Auden's Vision of a Rood – a Study in Coherence', in David Jasper, ed., *Images of Belief in Literature* (London: Macmillan, 1984), p. 59.

31 W. B. Yeats, 'Among School Children'.

32 Dare one say it, the same might be said, dramatically, of Jesus Christ in the resurrection?

33 Malekin and Yarrow, *Consciousness, Literature and Theatre*, p. 138.

34 See, Dom Bernard Botte, *From Silence to Participation* (Washington: Pastoral Press, 1973); Ronald Jasper, 'Silence in Worship', in R. C. D. Jasper, ed., *Getting the Liturgy Right* (London: SPCK, 1982), pp. 51–6. A more recent general interest in silence is reflected in such works as Diarmaid MacCulloch, *Silence: A Christian History* (London: Allen Lane, 2013); Sara Maitland, *A Book of Silence* (London: Granta, 2008)

35 Malekin and Yarrow, *Consciousness, Literature and Theatre*, p. 142.

36 Matthew 26.26–28; Mark 14.22–24; Luke 22.17–20; 1 Corinthians 11.24–25.

37 Dix, *Apostolic Tradition*, p. 8.

38 Easton, *Apostolic Tradition*, p. 36.

39 This is the translation suggested by Jasper and Cuming, *Prayers of the Eucharist*, p. 35.

40 Malekin and Yarrow, *Consciousness, Literature and Theatre*, p. 149.

41 See David Jasper, *The Sacred Community: Art, Sacrament and the People of God* (Waco: Baylor University Press, 2012), pp. 4–8.

42 E. C. Ratcliff, 'The Sanctus and the Pattern of the Early Anaphora', *Journal of Ecclesiastical History*, Vol. 1.1 (April 1950), 29–36, Vol. 1.2 (October 1950), 125–34. Reprinted in E. C. Ratcliff, *Liturgical Studies*, ed. A. H. Couratin and D. H. Tripp (London: SPCK, 1976), pp. 18–40.

43 Malekin and Yarrow, *Consciousness, Literature and Theatre*, p. 148.

44 Robert M. Torrance, *The Spiritual Quest: Transcendence in Myth, Religion, and Science* (Berkeley: University of California Press, 1994), p. 54. See also Malekin and Yarrow, *Consciousness, Literature and Theatre*, p. 151.

45 Jacob Böhme, *The Key and Other Writings*. Trans. Peter Malekin, with the assistance of Lars Malmberg (Durham: The New Century Press, 1988).

46 Malekin, Introduction, *The Key and Other Writings*, p. 12.

47 *Ibid.*, p. 3.

48 Malekin and Yarrow, *Consciousness, Literature and Theatre*, p. 133.

49 Geoffrey J. Cuming, ed., *Hippolytus: A Text for Students* (Bramcote: Grove Books, 1976), p. 10.

50 G. Abbott-Smith, *A Manual Greek Lexicon of the New Testament*. Third edition (Edinburgh: T & T Clark, 1937), p. 369. 'τουτο ποιειτε, ὁσακις ἐαν πινητε, ἐις την ἐμην ἀναμνησιν.' 1 Corinthians 11.25.

51 Cuming, *Hippolytus*, p. 5.

52 Anthony Gelston, 'A Note on the Text of the *Apostolic Tradition* of Hippolytus', *Journal of Theological Studies*, Vol. 39.1 (1988), 117.

Liturgical Language and the Vernacular in Late Medieval England

1 See G. J. Cuming, *A History of Anglican Liturgy*. Second edition (London: Macmillan, 1982), p. 14.

2 Preface to the 1549 *Book of Common Prayer*. Ed. Brian Cummings (Oxford: Oxford University Press, 2011), p. 4.

3 John E. Booty, ed., *The Book of Common Prayer: 1559, The Elizabethan Prayer Book* (Charlottesville: University of Virginia Press, 2005), p. 8. See further Daniel S. Swift, *Shakespeare's Common Prayers: The Book of Common Prayer and the Elizabethan Age* (Oxford: Oxford University Press, 2013).

4 Bruce Holsinger, 'Liturgy', in Paul Strohm, ed., *Middle English*. Oxford Twenty-First Century Approaches to Literature ((Oxford: Oxford University Press, 2007), pp. 295–314, at p. 312.

5 Eamon Duffy, *The Stripping of the Altars*. Second edition (New Haven: Yale University Press, 2005), p. 11.

6 Holsinger, 'Liturgy', p. 296.

7 See above, p. 9; David L. Frost, *The Language of Series* 3. Grove Booklet No. 12 (Bramcote: Grove Books, 1973), p. 10. See further James Boyd White, *When Words Lose Their Meaning: Constitutions and Reconsitutions of Language, Character, and Community* (Chicago: Chicago University Press, 1984).

8 Andrew Hass, 'Discipline Beyond Disciplines', in Heather Walton, ed., *Literature and Theology: New Interdisciplinary Spaces* (Farnham: Ashgate, 2011), pp. 19–36, at p. 23.

9 Trans. H. M. Hubbell (Loeb Classical Library), quoted in Rita Copeland, 'The Fortunes of "Non Verbum Pro Verbo": Or, Why Jerome Is Not a Ciceronian', in Roger Ellis, ed., *The Medieval Translator* (Woodbridge: Boydell and Brewer, 1989), pp. 15–36, at p. 18.

10 *Ibid.*, p. 29.

11 Annie Sutherland, *English Psalms in the Middle Ages, 1300–1450* (Oxford: Oxford University Press, 2015), p. 160.

12 *Ibid.*, p. 28.

13 *Cranmer's Selected Writings*. Ed. C. S. Meyer (London: SPCK, 1961), p. 2.

14 See Margaret Deanesly, *The Lollard Bible* (Cambridge: Cambridge University Press, 1920. Reprinted 1966), Chapter XIII, 'Bible reading by the orthodox, 1408–1526', pp. 319–50.

15 John Edmund Cox, ed., *Miscellaneous Writings and Letters of Thomas Cranmer* (Cambridge: Cambridge University Press, 1846), pp. 169–70. See also Ramie

Targoff, *Common Prayer: The Language of Public Devotion in Early Modern England* (Chicago: University of Chicago Press, 2001), pp. 26–7.

16 The MS. Cotton Cleopatra C. 6, British Museum, is dated *c.* 1240.

17 *The Ancrene Riwle*. Trans. M. B. Salu (London: Burns & Oates, 1955), p. 7.

18 Roger Wieck, 'The Book of Hours', in Thomas J. Heffernan and E. Ann Matter, eds, *The Liturgy of the Medieval Church* (Kalamazoo: TEAMS, 2001), pp. 475–6. See also, Holsinger, 'Liturgy', pp. 302–3.

19 Geoffrey J. Cuming, *The Godly Order: Texts and Studies Relating to the Book of Common Prayer* (London: Alcuin Club/SPCK, 1983), p. 26. See also Charles C. Butterworth, *The English Primers (1529–1545)* (Philadelphia: University of Pennsylvania Press, 1953).

20 Quoted in Butterworth, *English Primers*, p. 257.

21 Henry Littlehales, *The Prymer, or, Prayer-Book of the Lay People in the Middle Ages*. 2 vols (London: Longmans, Green & Co., 1891, 1892).

22 *Ibid.*, Vol. II, p. vii.

23 Cuming, *Godly Order*, p. 26.

24 Littlehales, *Prymer*, Vol. II, p. xii.

25 Norman Davis, ed., *Paston Letters and Papers of the Fifteenth Century.* 3 vols. (Oxford: Oxford University Press, 1971–6), Vol. I, p. 39.

26 See Eamon Duffy, *Marking the Hours: English People and Their Prayers, 1240–1570* (New Haven: Yale University Press, 2006), pp. 107–18.

27 Quoted in Littlehales, *Prymer*, Vol. II, p. vii.

28 Butterworth, *English Primers*, p. 3.

29 Thomas Frederick Simmons, ed., *The Lay Folks Mass Book* (London: Early English Text Society/N. Trübner & Co., 1879), p. xvii.

30 *Ibid.*, p. xx.

31 Deanesley, *Lollard Bible*, pp. 212–13.

32 Simmons, *Lay Folks Mass Book*, p. 46; British Museum, Royal MS. 17 B xvii, lines 487–91. Spelling slightly modernized.

33 *Ibid.*, p. 16, lines 167–8.

34 *Ibid.*, pp. 149–50.

35 Dinah Birch, ed., *The Oxford Companion to English Literature*. Seventh edition (Oxford: Oxford University Press, 2009), p. 613.

36 C. S. Lewis writes of Lydgate: 'As a poet of courtly love Lydgate bears a double character. In his style, and in the construction of his poems, he is the pupil of Chaucer. His conception of poetical language, and sometimes his achievement, are based on [Chaucer's] way of writing ... In this respect Lydgate claims a place in the high central tradition of our poetry and at times ... He makes good the claim.' *The Allegory of Love* (Oxford: Oxford University Press, 1936, reprinted 1968), p. 239.

37 J. Huizinga, *The Waning of the Middle Ages*. Trans. F. Hopman (London: Penguin, 1990. First published 1924), p. 263.

38 Holsinger, 'Liturgy', p. 310.

39 This is one of the homilies that can with some confidence be ascribed to Cranmer himself. *The Two Books of Homilies Appointed to Be Read in Churches*. Ed. John Griffiths (Oxford: Oxford University Press, 1859), pp. 48–65.

40 See, R. T. Davies, Introduction to *Medieval English Lyrics: A Critical Anthology* (London: Faber & Faber, 1963), pp. 24, 31.

41 *Ibid.*, p. 51.

42 *Liber Eliensis*. Ed. D. J. Stewart (London, 1848), p. 202.

43 Davies, *Medieval English Lyrics*, p. 53.

44 Douglas Gray, *Themes and Images in the Medieval English Religious Lyric* (London: Routledge, 1972), p. 12. See also Holsinger, 'Liturgy', p. 303.

45 See, G. R. Owst, *Literature and Pulpit in Medieval England* (Oxford: Basil Blackwell, 1966), especially Ch. IX, 'A Literary Echo of the Social Gospel', pp. 548–93.

46 Herebert died in 1333 and 17 of his English paraphrases of Latin hymns survive. There are 136 pieces attributed to Ryman (late fifteenth century). See Davies, *Medieval English Lyrics*, p. 23.

47 *Ibid.*, pp. 94–5; *The Sarum Missal in English*. Trans. Frederick E. Warren. 2 vols (London: Alcuin Club Collections/A. R. Mowbray & Co., 1913), Part I, p. 234.

48 William Dunbar, *Poems*. Ed. James Kinsley (Oxford: Clarendon Press, 1958), pp. 7–8.

49 Owst, *Literature and Pulpit*, p. 532.

50 *Ibid.*, p. 575.

51 Simmons, *Lay Folks Mass Book*, p. lxx.

52 William Langland, *Piers Plowman*, C-text, v., lines 45–7. Ed. Derek Pearsall (Berkeley: University of California Press, 1978), p. 99.

53 *Piers Plowman*. B-text. (Crowley) Early English Text Society. Ed. Walter W. Skeat (Oxford: Oxford University Press, 1869/1964), p. 79, lines 401–4 (spelling slightly modernized). See also the comment in Targoff, *Common Prayer*, p. 64.

54 David Daniell, *The Bible in English* (New Haven: Yale University Press, 2003), pp. 100–1.

55 Holsinger, 'Liturgy', p. 312.

56 In this regard the works of E. K. Chambers (*The Medieval Stage*. 2 vols [1903]) and Karl Young (*The Drama of the Medieval Church*. 2 vols [1933]) remain foundational studies, if now dated.

57 See Harold Charles Gardiner, *Mysteries' End: An Investigation of the Last Days of the Medieval Religious Stage* (New Haven: Yale University Press, 1946), and O. B. Hardison, Jr, *Christian Rite and Christian Drama in the Middle Ages* (Baltimore: Johns Hopkins University Press, 1965), p. 290.

58 Hardison, *Christian Rite and Christian Drama*, pp. 290–2, at p. 290.

59 Stephen Greenblatt, *Hamlet in Purgatory* (Princeton: Princeton University Press, 2001); Swift, *Shakespeare's Common Prayers*.

60 Hardison, *Christian Rite and Christian Drama*, p. 292.

61 E. K. Chambers, *The Medieval Stage* (Oxford: Clarendon Press, 1903), Vol. 2, pp. 179–80.

62 *Ibid.*, Vol. 2, p. 147.

63 See above, pp. 55–9.

64 See Joseph A. Jungmann, SJ, *The Mass of the Roman Rite: Its Origins and Development*. Trans. Francis A. Brunner. Revised Charles K. Riepe. Abridged edition (New York: Benziger Brothers, Inc., 1959), pp. 67–70; Hardison, *Christian Rite and Christian Drama*, pp. 37–79.

65 Quoted in Jungmann, *Mass of the Roman Rite*, p. 68.

66 Hardison, *Christian Rite and Christian Drama*, p. 43.

67 See Karl Young, *The Drama of the Medieval Church* (Oxford: Clarendon

Press, 1933), Vol. 1, p. 119; also the example of St Ethelwold's *Regularis Concordia*, see above, pp. 58–9.

68 See further Hardison, *Christian Rite and Christian Drama*, pp. 178–219.

69 Young, *Drama of the Medieval Church*, Vol. 1, pp. 179–97, at p. 179.

70 See Alejandro Planchart, ed., *The Repertory of Tropes at Winchester*. 2 Vols (Princeton: Princeton University Press, 1977), Vol. 2, pp. 301–2.

71 See John Gassner, *Medieval and Tudor Drama* (New York: Bantam Books, 1968), p. 35, which draws upon a tenth-century manuscript from the monastery of St Gall.

72 Young, *Drama of the Medieval Church*, Vol. 1, p. 195. See also J. Beck, *La Musique des Troubadours* (Paris, 1910), pp. 23–4.

73 R. C. D. Jasper and Paul F. Bradshaw, eds, *A Companion to the Alternative Service Book* (London: SPCK, 1986), p. 266.

74 Bridget Nichols, 'The Collect in English: Vernacular Beginnings', in Bridget Nichols, ed., *The Collect in the Churches of the Reformation* (London: SCM Press, 2010), p. 17.

75 Cuming, *Godly Order*, p. 49.

76 See, Nichols, 'The Collect in English', p. 13.

77 See Butterworth, *English Primers*.

78 C. S. Lewis, *Poetry and Prose in the Sixteenth Century*. The Oxford History of English Literature, Vol. IV (Oxford: Clarendon Press, 1954/1990), pp. 217–20. See also D. L. Frost, 'Liturgical Language: Cranmer to Series 3', in R. C. D. Jasper, ed., *The Eucharist Today: Studies on Series 3* (London: SPCK, 1974), pp. 151–6.

79 Cox, *Miscellaneous Writings and Letters of Thomas Cranmer*, p. 494.

80 Diarmaid MacCulloch, *Thomas Cranmer: A Life* (New Haven: Yale University Press, 1996), p. 328.

81 F. E. Brightman, *The English Rite*. 2 vols (London: Rivingtons, 1915), Vol. 1, p. lxvii.

82 Cox, *Miscellaneous Writings and Letters of Thomas Cranmer*, p. 412.

83 Geoffrey Cuming, 'Thomas Cranmer, Translator and Creative Writer', in David Jasper and R. C. D. Jasper, eds, *Language and the Worship of the Church* (London: Macmillan, 1990), pp. 110–19, at p. 112.

84 Cuming, *Godly Order*, p. 60.

85 Brightman, *English Rite*, Vol. 1, p. 202.

86 William Tyndale, *New Testament of 1534*. Ed. David Daniell (New Haven: Yale University Press, 1995), pp. 238–9.

87 Brightman, *English Rite*, Vol. 1, pp. 201–2.

88 Charles Lloyd, ed., *Formularies of Faith Put Forth by Authority During the Reign of Henry VIII* (Oxford: Clarendon Press, 1825), p. 238.

89 Cuming, *Godly Order*, p. 60.

90 Cox, *Miscellaneous Writings and Letters of Thomas Cranmer*, p. 180.

91 Judith Maltby, *Prayer Book and People in Elizabethan and Early Stuart England* (Cambridge: Cambridge University Press, 2000), p. 28.

92 Duffy, *Stripping of the Altars*, p. 11.

Literature and the Prayer Books of the English Reformation

1 See above, page 23, for the poem in full.

2 Liturgical change has never of course, been entirely absent in the Church of England. I have not given attention, for example, since this does not really contribute to my argument, to the *Proposed Prayer Book* of 1927–8, let alone the liturgical revisions of the previous centuries. See R. C. D. Jasper, *The Development of the Anglican Liturgy, 1662–1980* (London: SPCK, 1989); G. J. Cuming, *A History of the Anglican Liturgy*. Second edition (London: Macmillan, 1982).

3 For example: Richmond Noble, *Shakespeare's Biblical Knowledge and Use of the Book of Common Prayer* (New York: Octagon Books, 1970); Ramie Targoff, *Common Prayer: The Language of Public Devotion in Early Modern England* (Chicago: University of Chicago Press, 2001); Brian Cummings, ed., *The Book of Common Prayer: The Texts of 1549, 1559, and 1662* (Oxford: Oxford University Press, 2011); Daniel S. Swift, *Shakespeare's Common Prayers: The Book of Common Prayer and the Elizabethan Age* (Oxford: Oxford University Press, 2013).

4 Brian Cummings, Introduction to *The Book of Common Prayer*, p. xxxiv.

5 See above, p. 9.

6 *The Alternative Service Book* (London: Clowes/SPCK/Cambridge University Press, 1980), p. 128. In Rite B in the *ASB*, the words remain, though only in brackets.

7 See above, Chapter 1, p. 10.

8 See further J. Gunstone, 'The Act of Penitence', in R. C. D. Jasper, ed., *The Eucharist Today: Studies on Series 3* (London: SPCK, 1974), p. 79.

9 James Boyd White, *When Words Lose Their Meaning: Constitutions and Reconstitutions of Language, Character, and Community* (Chicago: University of Chicago Press, 1984), p. 11.

10 *The Book of Common Prayer: 1559*. Ed. John E. Booty (Charlottesville: University of Virginia Press, 2005), p. 262.

11 Katie Badie, 'The Prayer of Humble Access', p. 103. archive.churchsociety.org/Churchman/documents/Cman_120_2_Badie.

12 *Ibid.*, p. 350.

13 For something of a modern parallel in the post-communion prayer in the *Alternative Service Book*, 'Father of all, we give you thanks and praise ...', see above, Chapter 1, pp. 14–15.

14 Colin Buchanan argues that it was Cranmer's attempt to lay emphasis on the people's *reception* of the elements rather than their *consecration. What Did Cranmer Think He Was Doing?* (Cambridge: Grove Books, 1976), pp. 23–5.

15 See Badie, 'Prayer of Humble Access', p. 106.

16 Cuming, *History of the Anglican Liturgy*, p. 43.

17 Dom Gregory Dix, *The Shape of the Liturgy* (Westminster: Dacre Press, 1945), p. 656. For a more recent assessment of Cranmer's eucharistic theology in the 1552 (and subsequently 1559) *Prayer Books*, see Diarmaid MacCulloch, *Thomas Cranmer: A Life* (New Haven: Yale University Press, 1996), pp. 504–12 (and the significance of Bucer and Peter Martyr) and 620–1.

18 '*ut peccata que ex carne et sanguine contraximus, caro mundet, sanguis lauet domini nostri ihesu Christi.*' F. E. Brightman, *The English Rite*. 2 vols (London: Rivingtons, 1915), Vol. 1, p. lxxv.

19 Badie, 'Prayer of Humble Access', p. 110. There are probable echoes also of Leviticus 17.11.

20 William Shakespeare, *Macbeth*, Act 5, Sc. 1.

21 See Swift, *Shakespeare's Common Prayers*, pp. 3–5.

22 Christopher Marlowe, *The Tragical History of Doctor Faustus*, Act 5, Sc. 2, lines 156–8, 176–8. *The Complete Plays*. Ed. J. B. Steane (Harmondsworth: Penguin, 1969), pp. 336–7.

23 Quoted in MacCulloch, *Thomas Cranmer*, p. 153.

24 *Doctor Faustus*, Act 5, Sc. 2, line 181.

25 Booty, *Book of Common Prayer*, pp. 9–10.

26 Judith Maltby, *Prayer Book and People in Elizabethan and Early Stuart England* (Cambridge: Cambridge University Press, 1998), pp. 36–8.

27 Booty, *Book of Common Prayer*, p. 68.

28 See Francis Procter and Walter Howard Frere, *A New History of the Book of Common Prayer* (London: Macmillan, 1949), p. 424.

29 See MacCulloch, *Thomas Cranmer*, p. 328.

30 Booty, *Book of Common Prayer*, pp. 68–9.

31 William Shakespeare, *King Lear*. Act 1, Sc. 2, lines 140–5.

32 John D. Cox, *Seeming Knowledge: Shakespeare and Skeptical Faith* (Waco: Baylor University Press, 2007), p. 38.

33 Geoffrey Cuming, 'Thomas Cranmer, Translator and Creative Writer', in David Jasper and R. C. D. Jasper, eds, *Language and the Worship of the Church* (London: Macmillan, 1990), p. 111.

34 Stella Brook, *The Language of the Book of Common Prayer* (London: André Deutsch, 1965), p. 38.

35 See further below, pp. 100–3.

36 T. S. Eliot, 'Lancelot Andrewes' (1926), reprinted in *Selected Essays*. Third enlarged edition (London: Faber & Faber, 1951), pp. 341–53.

37 See above, p. 87.

38 C. S. Lewis, *Poetry and Prose in the Sixteenth Century*. The Oxford History of English Literature, Vol. IV (Oxford: Clarendon Press, 1954/1990), pp. 218–19.

39 *Ibid.*, p. 219.

40 Stephen Greenblatt, *Hamlet in Purgatory* (Princeton: Princeton University Press, 2001). For Greenblatt's contribution to Shakespeare and the Eucharist, see, 'Shakespeare Bewitched', in Jeffrey N. Cox and Larry J. Reynolds, eds, *New Historical Literary Study: Essays on Reproducing Texts, Representing History* (Princeton: Princeton University Press, 1993), pp. 108–35.

41 William Shakespeare, *Hamlet*, Act 1, Sc. 5, line 91.

42 See Swift, *Shakespeare's Common Prayers*, p. 159.

43 *Hamlet*, Act 5, Sc. 2.

44 Swift, *Shakespeare's Common Prayers*, pp. 141–2.

45 *Hamlet*, Act 5, Sc. 1.

46 See Swift, *Shakespeare's Common Prayers*, p. 155.

47 *Hamlet*, Act 5, Sc. 1, lines 178–89.

48 See, for example, the painting of the *Repentant Magdalene* (*c.* 1640) gazing upon a skull, by Georges du Mesnil de la Tour (1593–1652), discussed in David Jasper, *The Sacred Body: Ascetism in Religion, Literature, Art, and Culture* (Waco: Baylor University Press, 2009), pp. 91–2.

49 Eamon Duffy, *The Stripping of the Altars*. Second edition (New Haven: Yale University Press, 2005), p. 474.

50 Booty, *Book of Common Prayer*, p. 310.

51 Cyril Tourneur, *The Revenger's Tragedy*, Act 3, Sc. 5, lines 83–5.

52 *Hamlet*, Act 5, Sc. 1.

53 Duffy, *Stripping of the Altars*, p. 475.

54 See Geoffrey Rowell, *The Liturgy of Christian Burial*. Alcuin Club Collections, No. 59 (London: SPCK, 1977), pp. 84–93.

55 Robert Ornstein, *The Moral Vision of Jacobean Tragedy* (Madison: University of Wisconsin Press, 1965), p. 223.

56 Richard Drake, quoted in Paul A. Welsby, *Lancelot Andrewes, 1555–1626* (London: SPCK, 1958), pp. 264–5.

57 R. W. Church, quoted in *ibid*. p. 267.

58 James Mozley, 'Bishop Andrewes' Sermons', *The British Critic*, Vol. 31 (January 1842), p. 189.

59 T. S. Eliot, 'Lancelot Andrewes', pp. 347–8.

60 See above note 7, on James Boyd White, *When Words Lose Their Meaning*.

61 It might be noted in passing that this prayer is very similar in its function to the Jewish Piyyut, see above Chapter 4, p. 48.

62 *The Preces Privatae of Lancelot Andrewes, Bishop of Winchester*. Ed. F. E. Brightman (London: Methuen, 1903), p. 23.

63 The 'Prayer of Chrysostom', dating from the ninth century, which is appended to the Litany in the 1559 *Prayer Book* (as it was by its translator Cranmer to his 1544 Litany), ends with, '… granting us in this world knowledge of thy truth, and in the world to come life everlasting.' Booty, *Book of Common Prayer*, p. 74.

64 Brightman, Introduction to the *Preces Privatae*, p. l.

65 Bishop Lancelot Andrewes, quoted in Eliot, 'Lancelot Andrewes', p. 350.

66 T. S. Eliot, 'Journey of the Magi', in *The Poems of T. S. Eliot: The Annotated Text*. Vol. 1. Ed. Christopher Ricks and Jim McCue (London: Faber & Faber, 2015), p. 101.

67 *The Works of Mr. Richard Hooker*. Arranged by John Keble. 3 vols (Oxford: Clarendon Press, 1865), Vol. II, p. 117.

68 *Ibid*., p. 120.

69 David Scott, 'The Book of Common Prayer 1549'.

Language and Liturgical Revision in the Church of England

1 Henceforth, *ASB*.

2 Barry Spurr, 'An Australian Prayer Book', in David Martin and Peter Mullen, eds, *No Alternative: The Prayer Book Controversy* (Oxford: Basil Blackwood, 1981), pp. 162–74.

3 *Ibid*., pp. 163, 164.

4 The phrase is taken from the cover notes of another collection of essays on liturgical reform, edited by Brian Morris, *Ritual Murder* (Manchester: Carcanet Press, 1980).

5 David Martin, 'Identity and a Changed Church', in *No Alternative*, p. 17.

6 See David L. Frost, *The Language of Series 3*. Grove Booklet No. 12 (Bramcote: Grove Books, 1973), p. 5.

7 C. S. Meyer, ed., *Cranmer's Selected Writings* (London: SPCK, 1961), p. 91.

8 Quoted in George Steiner, *After Babel: Aspects of Language and Translation* (Oxford: Oxford University Press, 1975), p. 245.

9 See above, pp. 12–13.

10 David Daniell, Introduction to *Tyndale's New Testament* (New Haven: Yale University Press, 1995), p. xxi.

11 Meyer, *Cranmer's Selected Writings*, p. 2.

12 See, James Boyd White, *When Words Lose Their Meaning: Constitutions and Reconstitutions of Language, Character, and Community* (Chicago: Chicago University Press, 1984), Chapter 1, 'A Way of Reading', pp. 1–23.

13 See Horton Davies, *Worship and Theology in England: From Newman to Martineau, 1850–1900* (Princeton: Princeton University Press, 1962); R. C. D. Jasper, *Prayer Book Revision in England, 1800–1900* (London: SPCK, 1954).

14 For a brief and excellent review of this crisis in language and theology, see Stephen D. Moore, *Poststructuralism and the New Testament: Derrida and Foucault at the Foot of the Cross* (Minneapolis: Fortress Press, 1994), pp. 13–41. More will be said of this in the next chapter.

15 Stephen Neill, 'Liturgical Continuity and Change in the Anglican Churches', in Martin and Mullen, *No Alternative*, p. 5. Of the great Cambridge liturgist E. C. Ratcliff, Neill observes that although he was learned 'he was never much in love with the Anglican tradition'.

16 Brian Cummings, ed., *The Book of Common Prayer: The Texts of 1549, 1559, and 1662* (Oxford: Oxford University Press, 2011), p. xxv.

17 Neill, 'Liturgical Continuity and Change', p. 7.

18 Stanley Fish, *There's No Such Thing as Free Speech, and It's a Good Thing Too* (Oxford: Oxford University Press, 1994), p. 242.

19 See Kevin Hart, Introduction to Jean-Luc Marion, *The Essential Writings* (New York: Fordham University Press, 2013), p. 21.

20 Bridget Nichols, *Liturgical Hermeneutics: Interpreting Liturgical Rites in Performance* (Frankfurt: Peter Lang, 1996), p. 258.

21 See J. L. Austin, *How to Do Things with Words*. Second revised edition (Oxford: Oxford University Press, 1975). Performative utterances for Austin are neither true nor false. The same cannot be said for liturgical language.

22 Nichols, *Liturgical Hermeneutics*, p. 259. (Emphasis added.)

23 *Ibid*., pp. 261–2.

24 Martin Warner, 'Philosophy, Implicature and Liturgy', in David Jasper and R. C. D. Jasper, eds, *Language and the Worship of the Church* (London: Macmillan, 1990), p. 150.

25 D. Z. Phillips, 'Mystery and Meditation: Reflections on Flannery O'Connor and Joan Didion', in David Jasper, ed., *Images of Belief in Literature* (London: Macmillan, 1984), p. 25.

26 John Coulson, *Newman and the Common Tradition: A Study in the Language of Church and Society* (Oxford: Clarendon Press, 1970), p. 4.

27 See above, pp. 4, 11.

28 '... that willing suspension of disbelief for the moment, which constitutes poetic faith'. S. T. Coleridge, *Biographia Literaria* (1817), Vol. 7. Ed. James Engell

and W. Jackson Bate. Collected Works, Vol. 7 (Princeton: Princeton University Press, 1983), Vol. 2, p. 6.

29 Coulson, *Newman and the Common Tradition*, p. 4.

30 *Ibid.*, p. 20.

31 J. H. Newman, *An Essay in Aid of a Grammar of Assent* (1870). Ed. I. T. Ker (Oxford: Clarendon Press, 1985), p. 223.

32 See further, Philip H. Pfatteicher, *The School of the Church: Worship and Christian Formation* (Valley Forge, PA: Trinity Press International, 1995), p. 115.

33 Emily Dickinson, *The Complete Poems*. Ed. Thomas H. Johnson (London: Faber & Faber, 1970), pp. 506–7. See also the article by John Tinsley, 'Tell It Slant', *Theology*,Vol. 83 (1983), 163–70.

34 See Jean-Luc Marion, *Prolegomena to Charity*. Trans. Stephen E. Lewis (New York: Fordham University Press, 2002).

35 Jean-Yves Lacoste, *Experience and the Absolute: Disputed Questions on the Humanity of Man*. Trans. Mark Raftery-Skehan (New York: Fordham University Press, 2004), p. 194.

36 See further David Jasper, *The Sacred Community: Art, Sacrament, and the People of God* (Waco: Baylor University Press, 2012).

37 R. S. Thomas, 'A Frame for Poetry', *Times Literary Supplement*, 3 March 1966, p. 169.

The Background to The Alternative Service Book

1 Percy Dearmer, *The Parson's Handbook*. Fourth edition (London: Grant Richards, 1903), p. 1.

2 J. L. Houlden, 'Liturgy and Her Companions: A Theological Appraisal', in R. C. D. Jasper, ed., *The Eucharist Today: Studies on Series 3* (London: SPCK, 1974), p. 170.

3 *Ibid.*, p. 174.

4 *Language and Liturgy in the Church* (Scottish Episcopal Church, 1998), p. 13. See also James Boyd White, *When Words Lose Their Meaning: Constitutions and Reconstitutions of Language, Character, and Community* (Chicago: University of Chicago Press, 1984).

5 Jonathan Culler, *Saussure* (London: Fontana, 1976), p. 39.

6 See, for example, *Begat: The King James Bible and the English Language* (Oxford: Oxford University Press, 2010); *Linguistics, Language and Religion* (London: Burns & Oates, 1965); 'Linguistics and Liturgy', *Church Quarterly*, Vol. 2 (1969), 23–30; 'Language in the Church', *The Tablet*, 16 June 1984, 570–2.

7 David Crystal, 'Liturgical Language in a Sociolinguistic Perspective,' in David Jasper and R. C. D. Jasper, eds, *Language and the Worship of the Church* (London: Macmillan, 1990), pp. 121–2.

8 See above, pp. 112–13.

9 Martin Warner, 'Philosophy, Implicature and Liturgy', in Jasper and Jasper, *Language and the Worship of the Church*, p. 150.

10 Ian Ramsey, *Religious Language*. Third Impression (London: SCM Press, 1973), p. 109.

11 *Ibid.*, p. 180.

12 Fergus Kerr, *Theology after Wittgenstein* (Oxford: Basil Blackwell, 1986), p. 3.

13 *Ibid.*, p. 10.

14 *Ibid.*, p. 141.

15 *Ibid.*, p. 140. The seemingly ineradicable presence of Gnosticism in the Western Christian tradition is another story. See, for example, Harold Bloom, *The American Religion* (New York: Touchstone Books, 1992).

16 Stanley Cavell, *The Claim of Reason: Wittgenstein, Skepticism, Morality, and Tragedy*. New edition (New York: Oxford University Press, 1999), pp. xvi–xvii. Emphasis added.

17 Christopher Norris, *Deconstruction: Theory and Practice* (London: Methuen, 1982), p. 23.

18 Dom Gregory Dix, ed., *The Treatise on The Apostolic Tradition of St. Hippolytus of Rome*. Ed. Henry Chadwick (London: SPCK, 1968), p. 10.

19 Walter J. Ong, SJ, *Orality and Literacy* (London: Routledge, 1982), p. 26. Also, Marshall McLuhan notes in *The Gutenberg Galaxy: The Making of Typographic Man* (Toronto: University of Toronto Press, 1962), p. 164, that 'print, as it were, translated the dialogue of shared discourse into packaged information, a portable commodity'. Prayer Books in the sixteenth and seventeenth centuries were certainly portable commodities, yet liturgy is not 'packaged information' but the living word expressed in community. The English liturgy was enlivened by its place on the cusp of the medieval written manuscript and the printed book.

20 Gail Ramshaw, *Liturgical Language: Keeping It Metaphoric, Making It Inclusive* (Collegeville: Liturgical Press, 1996), p. 9.

21 Anthony C. Thiselton, *New Horizons in Hermeneutics* (London: HarperCollins, 1992), p. 598.

22 See Michael Hollis, *The Significance of South India* (London: Lutterworth Press, 1966), Ch. VI, 'The Worship of the Church', pp. 44–9; Stephen Neill, 'Liturgical Change and Continuity', in David Martin and Peter Mullen, eds, *No Alternative: The Prayer Book Controversy* (Oxford: Basil Blackwell, 1981), p. 6.

23 Not of least significance was the establishment of the still-extant Joint Liturgical Group which produced its first publication in 1965, *The Renewal of Worship*, with contributions from the Church of England, the Presbyterian Church of England, the Church of Scotland, the Baptist Union of Great Britain and Ireland, the Congregational Union of England and Wales, and the Scottish Episcopal Church.

24 Ulrich Simon, *Sitting in Judgement, 1913–1963* (London: SPCK, 1978), p. 118.

25 Daniel B. Stevick, *Language in Worship: Reflections on a Crisis* (New York: The Seabury Press, 1970), p. 160.

26 *Ibid.*, p. 161.

27 *Ibid.*, p. 160

28 Ong, *Orality and Literacy*, pp. 38–9.

29 Benjamin Hall Kennedy, *The Revised Latin Primer* (London: Longmans, Green, and Co., 1912), pp. iii–iv.

30 Ong, *Orality and Literacy*, p. 40.

31 Ian Robinson, *The Survival of English: Essays in Criticism of Language* (Cambridge: Cambridge University Press, 1973), pp. 22–65.

32 Ong, *Orality and Literacy*, p. 97.

33 See Ong, *ibid.*, pp. 64–5.

34 Roger Grainger, *The Language of the Rite* (London: Darton, Longman & Todd, 1974), p. 10.

35 *Ibid.*, p. 11. A literary reader might hear faint echoes, or rather anticipations, of Derridean *différance* here.

36 *Ibid.*, p. 78.

37 *Ibid.*, p. 136.

38 R. C. D. Jasper and Paul F. Bradshaw, eds, *A Companion to the Alternative Service Book* (London: SPCK, 1986), p. 82.

39 Robinson, *Survival of English*, p. 15.

40 T. S. Eliot, 'Tradition and the Individual Talent' (1919), in *Selected Essays*. Third enlarged edition (London: Faber & Faber, 1951), pp. 13–22; Harold Bloom, *The Anxiety of Influence: A Theory of Poetry* (New York: Oxford University Press, 1973).

41 Edward Robinson, *The Language of Mystery* (London: SCM Press, 1987), p. 31.

42 See above, pp. 14–15.

43 Michael Perham, 'The Language of Worship', in Michael Perham, ed., *Towards Liturgy 2000* (London: SPCK, 1989), p. 67.

44 See above, p. 9. David L. Frost, *The Language of Series 3*. Grove Booklet No. 12 (Bramcote: Grove Books, 1973), p. 10.

45 Preface to the *Alternative Service Book* (London: Clowes/SPCK/Cambridge University Press, 1980), p. 11.

46 See above, p. 4. S. T. Coleridge, *The Statesman's Manual* (1816) in *Lay Sermons*. Ed. R. J. White. Collected Works, Vol. 6 (Princeton: Princeton University Press, 1972), p. 29.

47 Ramshaw, *Liturgical Language*, p. 7.

48 *Ibid.*, p. 8.

49 Quoted in Frederick R. Karl, *William Faulkner: American Writer* (New York: Weidenfeld & Nicolson, 1989), p. 118. The remark has taken on darker implications in the post-truth politics of our own times.

50 Ramshaw, *Liturgical Language*, p. 10.

51 *Ibid.*, p. 20.

52 See above, pp. 112–13.

53 Ramshaw, *Liturgical Language*, p. 18.

54 *Ibid.*, p. 28.

55 See Robert P. Scharlemann, *Inscriptions and Reflections: Essays in Philosophical Theology* (Charlottesville: University of Virginia Press, 1989), pp. 30–53.

56 Ramshaw, *Liturgical Language*, p. 38.

57 See Massey H. Shepherd, 'The Liturgy', in Bernard C. Pawley, ed., *The Second Vatican Council: Studies by Eight Anglican Observers* (London: Oxford University Press, 1967), pp. 149–74; Donald Gray, *Ronald Jasper: His Life, His Work and the ASB* (London: SPCK, 1997), Ch. 6, 'Ecumenical Liturgical Work', pp. 74–91.

58 Quoted in the Introduction to R. C. D. Jasper, ed., *The Renewal of Worship*. Joint Liturgical Group (London: Oxford University Press, 1965), p. 1.

59 See, *Prayers We Have in Common*. Second revised edition (Philadelphia: Fortress Press, 1975).

60 Quoted in Barry Spurr, *The Word in the Desert* (Cambridge: Lutterworth, 1995), p. 36.

61 R. C. D. Jasper, *The Development of the Anglican Liturgy, 1662–1980* (London: SPCK, 1989), p. 286.

62 In Cheslyn Jones, Geoffrey Wainwright and Edward Yarnold, SJ, eds, *The Study of Liturgy* (London: SPCK, 1978), pp. 465–72.

63 *Ibid.*, p. 465.

64 See the excellent book by William Marshall, *Scripture, Tradition and Reason: A Selective View of Anglican Theology Through the Centuries* (Dublin: The Columba Press, 2010).

65 Stella Brook, *The Language of the Book of Common Prayer* (London: André Deutsch, 1965), pp. 218–19.

66 C. S. Lewis, *Poetry and Prose in the Sixteenth Century. The Oxford History of English Literature*, Vol. IV (Oxford: Clarendon Press, 1954/1990), p. 60.

From 1980 to Common Worship

1 Michael Perham, 'Liturgical Revision 1981–2000', in Paul F. Bradshaw, ed., *Companion to Common Worship*, Vol. 1 (London: SPCK, 2001), p. 26.

2 General Synod, Miscellaneous Papers.

3 Church of England Liturgical Commission Report, *The Worship of the Church as It Approaches the Third Millennium* (GS Misc 364, 1991), p. 5.

4 Perham, 'Liturgical Revision', p. 32. The Alcuin Club was founded in 1897 and its liturgical publications remain important today. It was significant in its involvement in the proposed revisions of the *Prayer Book* in the early twentieth century.

5 Michael Perham, ed., *Model and Inspiration: The Prayer Book Tradition Today* (London: SPCK, 1993), p. 13.

6 Colin James, in *ibid.*, p. 36.

7 The writer P. D. James. A member of the Liturgical Commission, she was also Vice-President of the Prayer Book Society.

8 Michael Perham, ed., *The Renewal of Common Prayer: Unity and Diversity in Church of England Worship* (London: SPCK, 1993), p. 27.

9 *Ibid.*, p. 34.

10 See above, p. 50.

11 Perham, 'Liturgical Revision', p. 35. The English Language Liturgical Consultation (ELLC) was established in 1985 as a group of national associations of ecumenical liturgists in the English-speaking world. Its predecessor was the International Consultation on English Texts (ICET), established in 1969.

12 Paul Bradshaw, 'Services and Service Books', in *Companion to Common Worship*, Vol. 1, p. 18.

13 Church of England Liturgical Commission, *Language and the Worship of the Church* (GS 1115, 1994), p. 30.

14 *Ibid.*, p. 33.

15 Clergy conducting weddings in church or officiating at funerals, usually in crematoria, quickly discover this.

16 *Ibid.*, p. 38.

17 *The Prayers and Meditations of St. Anselm*. Trans. Benedicta Ward (Harmondsworth: Penguin, 1973), p. 141.

18 Church of England Liturgical Commission, *Making Women Visible: The Use*

of Inclusive Language with the ASB (GS 859). (London: Church House Publishing, 1989), p. 59.

19 Particularly important is Schüssler Fiorenza's slightly later, seminal work *In Memory of Her: A Feminist Reconstruction of Christian Origins* (London: SCM Press, 1995).

20 *Making Women Visible*, pp. 6–7.

21 *Ibid.*, p. 65.

22 Margaret Atwood, *The Handmaid's Tale* (London: Virago Press, 1987), p. 98.

23 Michael Perham, 'Liturgical Revision', pp. 31, 30.

24 Bradshaw, *Companion to Common Worship*, Vol. 1, pp. 38–51, 47–8.

25 Thomas Merton, *Meditations on Liturgy* (London: Mowbray, 1976), p. 40.

26 Quoted in Perham, 'Liturgical Revision', p. 29.

27 Anne Dawtry and Carolyn Headley, 'A Service of the Word', in Bradshaw, *Companion to Common Worship*, Vol. 1, p. 60.

28 Benjamin Gordon-Taylor, 'Times and Seasons', in *ibid.*, Vol. 2, p. 103.

29 Quoted in Trevor Lloyd, 'New Patterns for Worship', in *ibid.*, Vol. 2, p. 109 (emphasis added).

30 See David Daniell, Introduction to *Tyndale's New Testament* (New Haven: Yale University Press, 1995).

31 Quoted in Lloyd, 'New Patterns for Worship', p. 111.

32 Introduction to *Patterns for Worship* (London: Church House Publishing, 1995), p. 5.

33 *Patterns for Worship*, p. 133.

34 See above, p. 127.

35 Bridget Nichols, ed., *The Collect in the Churches of the Reformation* (London: SCM Press, 2010).

36 Bridget Nichols, 'Collects and Post Communion Prayers', in Bradshaw, *Companion to Common Worship*, Vol. 1, p. 182.

37 *Ibid.*, p. 199

38 See David Scott, 'Pastoral Tradition in Religious Poetry', in Andrew W. Hass, David Jasper and Elisabeth Jay, eds, *The Oxford Handbook of English Literature and Theology* (Oxford: Oxford University Press, 2007), pp. 726–41.

39 Quoted in *Making Women Visible*, p. 13.

40 W. H. Auden, *Horae Canonicae*, in *Collected Shorter Poems, 1927–1957* (London: Faber & Faber, 1966), pp. 323–37; Hilary Davies, *Exile and the Kingdom* (London: Enitharmon Press, 2016), pp. 95–108.

41 Paul Roberts, 'The Additional Collects', in Bradshaw, *Companion to Common Worship*, Vol. 2, p. 122.

42 *Ibid.*, p. 127.

43 Church of England Liturgical Commission, *Common Worship: Additional Collects* (GS 1493, 2003), p. 3.

44 *Ibid.*

45 *Ibid.*, p. 5.

46 See R. C. D. Jasper and Paul F. Bradshaw, eds, *A Companion to the Alternative Service Book* (London: SPCK, 1986), p. 269; F. E. Brightman, *The English Rite*. 2 vols (London: Rivingtons, 1915), Vol. 1, p. 200.

47 See above, pp. 39–40.

48 See Simon Jones and Phillip Tovey, 'Initiation Services', in Bradshaw, *Com-*

panion to Common Worship, Vol. 1, p. 178. 'Behind all this lies a lack of clear theology of the place of confirmation. The Church of England seems to hold on to it as a necessity, but with little theological justification. One hundred and fifty years of debate have still not led to a conclusion, and the debate looks set to continue.' In the twentieth century the debate on confirmation was focused in the arguments between Dom Gregory Dix and Geoffrey Lampe.

49 *Additional Baptism Texts in Accessible Language* (London: Church House Publishing, online 2015), p. 1.

50 St John Chrysostom, quoted in Edward Yarnold, SJ, *The Awe-Inspiring Rites of Initiation: Baptismal Homilies of the Fourth Century* (Slough: St Paul Publications, 1971), p. 55.

51 *Additional Baptism Texts*, p. 37.

52 Mark Eary and Gilly Myers, eds, *Common Worship Today: An Illustrated Guide to Common Worship* (London, HarperCollins, 2001), p. 78.

53 Douglas Jones, Introduction, *Lent, Holy Week, Easter: Services and Prayers* (London: Church House Publishing, 1984), p. 1.

Reflections on the Eucharistic Body

1 Jean-Luc Nancy, '*Verbum Caro Factum*', in Ramona Fotiade, David Jasper and Olivier Salazar-Ferrer, eds, *Embodiment: Phenomenological, Religious and Deconstructive Views on Living and Dying* (Farnham: Ashgate, 2014), p. 157.

2 Mark 14.22–24; Matthew 26.26–29; Luke 22.7–13; 1 Corinthians 11.23–25.

3 See R. C. D. Jasper and G. J. Cuming, *Prayers of the Eucharist: Early and Reformed*. Third edition (New York: Pueblo Publishing Company, 1987), pp. 25–30; Elaine Pagels, *Beyond Belief: The Secret Gospel of Thomas* (London: Macmillan, 2003), pp. 19–20; L. W. Barnard, *Justin Martyr: His Life and Thought* (Cambridge: Cambridge University Press, 1966), pp. 147–8.

4 Tertullian, *Apologeticum* 7, quoted in Pagels, *Beyond Belief*, p. 18.

5 Justin Martyr, *Dialogue with Trypho* 117.1, quoted in Jasper and Cuming, *Prayers of the Eucharist*, p. 28.

6 See, Margaret R. Miles, *The Word Made Flesh: A History of Christian Thought* (Oxford: Blackwell, 2005).

7 Dom Gregory Dix, ed., *The Treatise on The Apostolic Tradition of St. Hippolytus of Rome*. Revised Henry Chadwick (London: SPCK, 1968), pp. 7–8. Dix agrees with the earlier edition in English, edited by Burton Scott Easton, in translating the first statement as a present tense: 'My Body which is broken for you.' (See *The Apostolic Tradition of Hippolytus*. Trans. Burton Scott Easton. [Cambridge: Cambridge University Press, 1934], p. 36.) More recent English editions read this as a future tense. See Jasper and Cuming, *Prayers of the Eucharist*, p. 35, which has, 'which shall be broken for you'. This question of tense – present or future – as we shall see, is of some importance.

8 C. K. Barrett, *The Gospel According to John: An Introduction*. (London: SPCK, 1955), p. 138.

9 See Charles Williams, *The Descent of the Dove: A Short History of the Holy Spirit in the Church* (London: Longmans, Green & Co., 1939), p. 1. 'The visible

beginning of the Church is at Pentecost, but that is only a result of its actual beginning – and ending – in heaven.'

10 Rowan Williams, Foreword to Dom Gregory Dix, *The Sacramental Life*. Ed. Simon Jones (Norwich: Canterbury Press, 2007), p. ix.

11 See also, as part of his discussion of 'regimes of truth', Michel Foucault, *On the Government of the Living*. Trans. Graham Burchell (New York: Picador, 2012), Lecture 7, on Tertullian and baptism, pp. 142–66.

12 See Adam G. Cooper, *The Body in St. Maximus the Confessor: Holy Flesh, Wholly Deified* (Oxford: Oxford University Press, 2005), Ch. 5, 'Corporeality and the Christian', pp. 206–50. Also, Edward Yarnold, SJ, *The Awe-Inspiring Rites of Initiation: Baptismal Homilies of the Fourth Century* (Slough: St Paul Publications, 1971).

13 This anticipatory image is graphically discovered in St Bernard of Clairvaux's sermons for the Feast of All Saints, and his description of the saints who wait on their beds of rest, their souls longing for the glorified body which will join them at the great final day when their bliss will be glorified and they will take their places at the great messianic feast. See Anna Harrison, 'Community Among the Dead: Bernard of Claivaux's *Sermons for the Feast of All Saints*', in Caroline Walker Bynum and Paul Freedman, eds, *Last Things: Death and the Apocalypse in the Middle Ages* (Philadelphia: University of Pennsylvania Press, 2000), pp. 192–4.

14 Dix, *The Apostolic Tradition*, p. 9.

15 See Jean-Luc Marion, *The Erotic Phenomenon*. Trans. Stephen E. Lewis (Chicago: University of Chicago Press, 2007), p. 198; David Jasper, *The Sacred Body: Asceticism in Religion, Literature, Art, and Culture* (Waco: Baylor University Press, 2009), pp. 179–84.

16 *The Life of St. Mary of Egypt* is reprinted in English in Benedicta Ward, SLG, *Harlots of the Desert: A Study of Repentance in Early Monastic Sources* (Kalamazoo: Cistercian Publications, 1987), pp. 35–56. See also Virginia Burrus, *The Sex Lives of the Saints: An Erotics of Ancient Hagiography* (Philadelphia: University of Pennsylvania Press, 2004), pp. 147–54; Jasper, *Sacred Body*, pp. 69–80.

17 Ward, *Harlots of the Desert*, p. 26.

18 *Ibid.*, p. 54.

19 Compare Psalm 55.6–8. 'Truly, I would flee far away; I would lodge in the wilderness.'

20 Ward, *Harlots of the Desert*, p. 55.

21 *Ibid.*, p. 56.

22 *Ibid.*

23 Burrus, *Sex Lives of Saints*, p. 155.

24 Origen, *The Prologue to the Commentary on the Song of Songs*, in *Selected Works*. Trans. Rowan A. Greer (Mahwah, NJ: Paulist Press, 1979), p. 217.

25 For a modern instance of this 'paradox' of spirituality and the eucharistic body see the novel by Ron Hansen, *Mariette in Ecstasy* (1991).

26 St John of the Cross, *Song of the Ascent of Mount Carmel*, reprinted in Don Cupitt, *Mysticism after Modernity* (Oxford: Blackwell, 1998), pp. 72–3; *Dark Night of the Soul*. Trans. Mirabai Starr (London: Rider, 2002), p. 33.

27 See Bernard McGinn, *The Mystical Thought of Meister Eckhart*. (New York: Crossroad Publishing, 2001), p. 90.

28 When Jesus utters the words to his disciples, 'Do this in remembrance of me' (1 Corinthians 11.24), the verb that he uses is 'ποιειτε'.

29 E. C. Ratcliff, 'The Sanctus and the Pattern of the Early Anaphora', in *Liturgical Studies*, Ed. A. H. Couratin and D. H. Tripp (London: SPCK, 1976), pp. 18–40.

30 Cupitt, *Mysticism after Modernity*, p. 74. Denys Turner in *The Darkness of God: Negativity in Christian Mysticism* (Cambridge: Cambridge University Press, 1995) goes even further and denies that there is any such thing as mystical 'experience'. Rather, through language there is only realized a silence or negativity which is the darkness of God.

31 Jean Leclercq, 'Les Méditations eucharistiques d'Arnauld de Bonneval', *Recherches de théologie ancienne et médiévale*, Vol. 13 (1946), 53. See also Caroline Walker Bynum, *Holy Feast and Holy Fast: The Religious Significance of Food to Medieval Women* (Berkeley: University of California Press, 1987), pp. 62–4.

32 Bynum, *Holy Feast and Holy Fast*, p. 63.

33 For more arguments for the 'fleshly' and miraculous experience of the Eucharist as a guard against heresy, see Ernest W. McDonnell, *The Beguines and Beghards in Medieval Culture, with Special Emphasis on the Belgian Scene* (New Brunswick, NJ: Rutgers University Press, 1954), pp. 310, 315, 330, 415.

34 S. Pétrement, *Simone Weil: A Life*. Trans. E. Crauford (London: Mowbray, 1977), p. 178.

35 Quoted in Ann Loades, 'Simone Weil – Sacrifice: A Problem for Theology', in David Jasper, ed., *Images of Belief in Literature* (London: Macmillan, 1984), p. 126.

36 Isaiah 53.1–12. 'Surely he has borne our infirmities and carried our diseases; yet we accounted him stricken, struck down by God, and afflicted' (v. 4).

37 Text reproduced in Michel de Certeau, *The Mystic Fable. Volume I. The Sixteenth and Seventeenth Centuries*. Trans. Michael B. Smith (Chicago: University of Chicago Press, 1992), pp. 32–3. See also Edith Wyschogrod, *Saints and Postmodernism* (Chicago: University of Chicago Press, 1990), Ch. 1, 'Why Saints?', pp. 1–30.

38 Louis Bouyer, *Eucharist: Theology and Spirituality of the Eucharistic Prayer*. Trans. Charles Underhill Quinn (Notre Dame: University of Notre Dame Press, 1968), pp. 380–442.

39 See above, on S. T. Coleridge, pp. 4, 11.

40 S. T. Coleridge, *The Statesman's Manual* (1815), in ed. R. J. White, *Lay Sermons*. Collected Works, Vol. 6. (Princeton: Princeton University Press, 1972), p. 29.

41 *The Documents of Vatican II*. Ed. Walter M. Abbott, SJ (London: Geoffrey Chapman, 1972), pp. 140–1.

42 I am drawing here from the wording of the 1982 Scottish Liturgy of the Scottish Episcopal Church.

43 *The Documents of Vatican II*, pp. 236–7. See also E. Schillebeeckx, OP, *The Eucharist*. Trans. N. D. Smith (London: Sheed & Ward, 1968), pp. 150–1.

44 See Bouyer, *Eucharist*, pp. 448–61.

45 Schillebeeckx, *The Eucharist*, p. 150.

46 The phrase 'willing suspension of disbelief' is taken from S. T. Coleridge and his description of 'poetic faith' as he reflects upon his and Wordsworth's plan for *Lyrical Ballads*. *Biographia Literaria* (1817). Ed. James Engell and W. Jackson Bate. Collected Works, Vol. 7 (Princeton: Princeton University Press, 1983), Vol. 2, p. 6.

47 See also David Torevell, *Losing the Sacred: Ritual, Modernity and Liturgical*

Reform (London: T & T Clark, 2000), Ch. 3, 'Modernity and Disembodiment', pp. 80–115.

48 *Ibid.*, p. 115.

49 Jean Baudrillard, 'Simulacra and Simulations', in *Selected Writings*. Ed. Mark Poster (Cambridge: Polity Press, 1988), p. 167.

50 Franz Kafka, *The Trial*. Trans. Willa and Edwin Muir (Harmondsworth: Penguin, 1953), p. 243.

51 John 6.54–55.

52 See further David L. Martin, *Curious Visions of Modernity: Enchantment, Magic and the Sacred* (Cambridge, MA: The MIT Press, 2011), Ch. 2, 'Bodies', pp. 55–111.

53 *Ibid.*, p. 179.

Conclusion

1 See further, Brian Cummings, *The Literary Culture of the Reformation: Grammar and Grace* (Oxford: Oxford University Press, 2002), pp. 220–3.

2 Reprinted in David Martin and Peter Mullen, eds, *No Alternative: The Prayer Book Controversy* (Oxford: Basil Blackwell, 1981), pp. 135–8.

3 Michel Foucault, 'Truth and Power', in *Power/Knowledge: Selected Interviews and Other Writings, 1972–1977* (New York: Pantheon Books, 1980), p. 115.

4 Cummings, *Literary Culture of the Reformation*, Ch. 4, 'Erasmus *contra* Luther', pp. 144–83.

5 See, W. H. E. Sweet, 'Lydgate's Retraction and "his Resorte to his Religyoun"', in Vincent Gillespie and Kantik Ghosh, eds, *After Arundel: Religious Writing in Fifteenth-Century England* (Turnhout, Belgium: Brepols, 2011), pp. 343–59.

6 Cummings, *Literary Culture of the Reformation*, p. 198.

7 William Tyndale, *The Obedience of a Christian Man* (1528). Ed. David Daniell (Harmondsworth: Penguin, 2000), p. 15.

8 *Ibid.*, p. 19.

9 See also above, p. 77.

10 Quoted in Cummings, *Literary Culture of the Reformation*, p. 193.

11 *Ibid.*, p. 208.

12 *Ibid.*, p. 324.

13 *Ibid.*, p. 327.

14 Here I am indebted, yet again, to Brian Cummings.

15 The first known performance is in 1594.

16 Romans 6.23; John 1.8–9 (used as a sentence at the beginning of Morning Prayer, 1559).

17 Christopher Marlowe, *The Tragical History of Doctor Faustus*, Act 1, Sc. 1, lines 37–47.

18 Ian Robinson, *The Survival of English: Essays in Criticism of Language* (Cambridge: Cambridge University Press, 1973), p. 26.

19 Jacques Derrida, *Given Time: 1. Counterfeit Money*. Trans. Peggy Kamuf (Chicago: University of Chicago Press, 1992), p. 27. The reference is to Marcel Mauss, *The Gift: The Form and Reason for Exchange in Archaic Societies*. Trans. W. D. Halls (London: Routledge, 1990).

20 In Gillespie and Ghosh, *After Arundel*, pp. 523–41.

21 See, *Tyndale's New Testament*. Ed. David Daniell (New Haven: Yale University Press, 1995), p. ix; Andrew Hope, 'On the Smuggling of Prohibited Books from Antwerp to England in the 1520s and 1530s', in Paul Arblaster, Gergely Juhász and Guido Latré, eds, *Tyndale's Testament* (Turnhout, Belgium: Brepols, 2002), pp. 35–8.

22 Quoted in Powell, 'After Arundel', pp. 540–1.

23 Bainbridge, 'When Prayer goes Pop', p. 137.

24 A. D. Nuttall, *Overheard by God: Fiction and Prayer in Herbert, Milton, Dante and St. John* (London: Methuen, 1980), p. 142. See also above, Chapter 2, pp. 32–3.

Appendix: Intercessory Prayer

1 Grosvenor Essay No. 12 (Edinburgh: Scottish Episcopal Church, 2016).

2 Joseph A. Jungmann, SJ, *The Mass of the Roman Rite: Its Origins and Developments*. Trans. Francis A. Brunner. Revised Charles K. Riepe. Abridged edition (New York: Benziger Brothers Inc., 1959), p. 40.

3 In older forms of English the word 'prone' was more or less used as an equivalent to an exhortation or sermon after the reading of Scripture.

4 Diptychs were originally tablets inscribed with names of important people in the local church. George Guiver, 'Intercession', in Paul F. Bradshaw, ed., *The New Westminster Dictionary of Liturgy and Worship* (Louisville: WJK Press, 2002), p. 255.

5 W. Jardine Grisbrooke, 'Anaphora', in J. G. Davies, ed., *A New Dictionary of Liturgy and Worship* (London: SCM Press, 1986), p. 20.

6 F. E. Brightman, *The English Rite*. 2 Vols (London: Rivingtons, 1915), Vol. 1, pp. lvii–lxviii.

7 Thanks are due here to Dr John Davies of the University of Glasgow, Convenor of the Liturgy Committee of the Scottish Episcopal Church, and the clergy and people of Old St Paul's Episcopal Church, Edinburgh.

8 *An Order for Holy Communion*. Alternative Services, Second Series (Convocations of Canterbury and York, 1967), p. 3.

Index